PRAISE

To Sing with the Angels
A History of the Twin Cities Catholic Chorale

"*To Sing with the Angels* is an account of the unique Twin Cities Catholic Chorale and the splendid Latin liturgy which it sings at the Church of Saint Agnes in Saint Paul, Minnesota. Behind it all is Monsignor Richard J. Schuler, who had a consistent vision of the mandates of the Second Vatican Council maintaining the Church's magnificent treasure of sacred music; this was an unfailing guide to the liturgy, fulfilling the hermeneutic of continuity articulated by Pope Benedict XVI."

- Jeffrey Tucker
Editor, *NewLiturgicalMovement.org*
Director of Publications, Church Music Association of America

"This wonderful book is a fitting tribute to the man who kept the music alive during the darkest times of musical confusion in the Catholic Church following the Second Vatican Council. Monsignor Schuler saw the future and he knew the great music would live again, but that he had to do his part to make this happen. It's hard fully to appreciate the courage and conviction it took to do what he did. He must be remembered. This book makes that so."

- William P. Mahrt
Editor, *Sacred Music*
President, Church Music Association of America

"'Those who do not know history are doomed to repeat it,' is an aphorism known by all. However, many historical things are very worthy of replication. Dr. Schubert's remarkable history of the Twin Cities Catholic Chorale is a beautiful witness to the preservation of sacred music in the liturgy, a truly great endeavor that can and should be repeated in many parishes and dioceses throughout the world."

- Reverend Mark Moriarty
Pastor, Church of Saint Agnes, Saint Paul, Minnesota

"It is not only octogenarians who are aware that the concluding decades of the 20th century were an era of rapid world-wide changes affecting every area of human life. The Second Vatican Ecumenical Council was one of the chief agents of profound changes, and that not only in the area of religious belief. The Sacred Synod neither proclaimed any new dogma nor abrogated any defined Truth of the Faith. Yet it had an enormous impact upon the prayer and worship life of Roman rite Catholics. For instance, countless buildings, from simple chapels to parish churches and even cathedrals, suffered great damage to their interior arrangements and appointments. In too many instances, this resulted in significant cultural losses. Though the artistic heritage of Catholic sacred music was acknowledged and encouraged – also on solid theological grounds! – as a treasure of inestimable worth, *thesaurum pretii inaestimabilis*, indeed an integral part of solemn worship, five decades after the last Council the musical tradition of the universal Church has in fact been eliminated from Catholic sanctuaries and choir lofts in the course of the paradigm shift which followed the Council...except at the Church of Saint Agnes in Saint Paul, Minnesota. This books explains how and why that happened. *Vade, et tu fac similiter!* " (*Luke* 10:37).

- Reverend Robert A. Skeris
Director, Centre for Ward Method Studies
Benjamin T. Rome School of Music
The Catholic University of America, Washington, D.C.

To Sing With The Angels
A History of the Twin Cities Catholic Chorale

By
Virginia A. Schubert, PhD

SAINT CECILIA PUBLICATIONS, LLC
SAINT PAUL, MINNESOTA
© 2015

To Sing With The Angels
A History of the Twin Cities Catholic Chorale

Copyright ©2015 by Virginia A. Schubert
All Rights Reserved. Except as permitted under the U.S. Copyright Act of 1976, no part of this publication may be reproduced, distributed, or transmitted in any form or by any means, or stored in a database or retrieval system, without the prior written permission of the publisher.

Saint Cecilia Publications, LLC
2030 Stanford Avenue
St. Paul, Minnesota 55105

saintceciliapub@gmail.com

ISBN: 978-0-692-42105-5

Cover: Stained glass window in the choir loft of the Church of St. Agnes
Cover design, Dedication Page, and Color Pictures:
Christopher Foote, Modern Design, Deephaven, Minnesota
Interior Design: Rhonda Klein, Evergreen Press, White Bear Lake, Minnesota
Editor: Cindy Paslawski
Printing: Omega Press, Plymouth, Minnesota

Printed in the United States of America

To Monsignor Richard J. Schuler (1920–2007)
with admiration and gratitude.

V. A. S.

Photo: Joe Oden; used with permission.

CONTENTS

Author's Note 9

Introduction 11
A Great Tradition Remains Alive at Saint Agnes
By The Most Reverend John M. LeVoir

Preface 13
Four Decades in Frogtown
By Reverend Robert A. Skeris

PART ONE

I   Precursor – The Saint Paul Catholic Choral Society 19

II   The Twin Cities Catholic Chorale – The Early Years –
       1955/1956-1965 25

III   The Fifth International Church Music Congress – 1966
       Cantare amantis est 39

IV   The Twin Cities Catholic Chorale – 1966-1974 49

V   Europe and the Sixth International Church Music
       Congress, Salzburg, Austria – 1974 55

Commentary
The Twin Cities Catholic Chorale and the World Church 67
By Reverend Robert A. Skeris

Salzburg and the Twin Cities Catholic Chorale 75
By William Mahrt

PART TWO

VI   The Twin Cities Catholic Chorale at the Church of
       Saint Agnes – 1974-1984 83

VII   A National Broadcast and a Recording Project, 1984-1986
       with commentary by Reverend William E. Sanderson 97

Commentary
"I Must See This Place" 105
By Reverend C. Frank Phillips, CR

PART THREE

VIII   The Chorale Continues Its Program – 1986-2001 109

IX   The Team Necessary for the Latin High Mass at Saint Agnes .. 123

X   The Finances of the Twin Cities Catholic Chorale 131

Commentary
What Singing in the Chorale Means to Me 133
By Michael Eilen

Singing in the Twin Cities Catholic Chorale..135
By Mary Eilen

PART FOUR
XI   The Transition Begins – 2001-2006..139
XII   The Passing of the Baton – 2006-2013.......................................145
XIII The Fortieth Year of Residency at the Church of
       Saint Agnes – 2013-2014...155

Commentary
Memories of a Visit to the Church of Saint Agnes............................163
By Dom Alcuin Reid, OSB

"Cum Angelis Canere" Recollections of Beauty..................................167
By Reverend John Paul Erickson

PART FIVE
XIV Toward the Future – 2014 and Beyond 173
      with commentary by Dr. Robert L. Peterson
XV   Conclusion...179

Notes 183

Appendices
A. Biography of Monsignor Richard J. Schuler..............................189
    By Charles W. Nelson
B. Biography of Father Francis A. Missia 197
    By Reverend Richard J. Schuler
C. Guild of Catholic Choirmasters and Organists........................205
    By Reverend Richard J. Schuler and Virginia Schubert
D. Choir of the Church of the Nativity of Our Lord,
    Saint Paul, Minnesota – 1950-1966 209
    By Charles W. Nelson
E. The Repertoire of the Twin Cities Catholic Chorale.................215
    Compiled by Virginia A. Schubert
F. Recordings Made by the Twin Cities Catholic Chorale. 223
    Compiled by Virginia A. Schubert
G. Bibliography of Major Articles and Editorials by
    Monsignor Richard J. Schuler, published in *Sacred Music*
    from Vol. 102, No. 3, Fall 1975 through Vol. 129,
    No. 3, Fall 2002..227
    Compiled by Virginia A. Schubert

Contributors 231
Acknowledgments 237
Index 239

AUTHOR'S NOTE

The Phenomenon of the Chorale

Because 2013-14 was the fortieth year of the residency of the Twin Cities Catholic Chorale at the Church of Saint Agnes, I thought that it would be an appropriate time to organize the diverse materials in the Schuler Archives and elsewhere in order to write a narrative history of the Chorale. In point of fact, though, its history goes all the way back to its founding by Father Schuler in 1955/1956, and even further, because its origins are in the Saint Paul Catholic Choral Society, founded by Father Francis A. Missia, as Father Skeris so clearly explains in the preface to this work.

I have sung in the Chorale for all of the years of its residency at Saint Agnes and years before. I joined the high school Girls' Choir at the Church of the Nativity of Our Lord in Saint Paul, Minnesota, which the then Father Schuler directed, when I was a sophomore in high school. Therefore, I know the travails, growing pains and successes of the Chorale, and the work of its founder/director. The accomplishments of the Chorale and its founder were brought home to me especially in the three keynote addresses given in the fall of 2013 at the Church Music Association's conference presented to celebrate the fortieth year of the Chorale's residency at the Church of Saint Agnes.

My approach in this history is, first of all, to present the facts as accurately as possible without too much personal editorial comment. However, I think that it is also important to set the existence – one could even say the phenomenon – of the Twin Cities Catholic Chorale and its season of Masses with professional orchestra as an integral part of the Latin liturgy at Saint Agnes, in its context locally and also nationally and even internationally against the backdrop of Catholic church music in the United States after the Second Vatican Council.

Of course, the history of the Twin Cities Catholic Chorale is linked intrinsically to the remarkable priest who was its founder, Monsignor Richard J. Schuler. The founding and running of the Chorale would have been a significant achievement in and of itself, especially in the post-Vatican II Church, but at the same time Monsignor Schuler was pastor of the Church of Saint Agnes and superintendent of its two schools; a teacher; a mentor to seminarians who are now priests, and yes, even bishops; president of the Church Music Association of America; vice-president of the *Consociatio Internationalis Musicae Sacrae;* and editor of *Sacred Music* magazine for over twenty-two years, responsible for ninety-one issues, from fall 1975 through spring 1998.

I am sure that everyone who sang in the Twin Cities Catholic Chorale or interacted with Monsignor Schuler would have a story to enrich this book, but let this be a beginning, inadequate as it may be.

Virginia A. Schubert, PhD
President, Board of the Twin Cities Catholic Chorale
Member of the Soprano Section

INTRODUCTION

A Great Tradition Remains Alive at Saint Agnes

When I attended the College of Saint Thomas (now the University of Saint Thomas) in Saint Paul, Minnesota from 1964 through 1968, I knew of Monsignor Richard J. Schuler. He taught in both the Theology and Music departments at the College. Although I did not have Monsignor for class, he had a revered reputation among the students.

When I was discerning whether or not to enter the seminary in 1976, I went to visit Monsignor, who had become pastor at Saint Agnes Church in Saint Paul. After speaking with him, he encouraged me to apply to the seminary. I took his advice. I applied to the Saint Paul Seminary and was accepted. I attended the seminary from 1977 through 1981. It was in 1981 that I was ordained a priest for the Archdiocese of Saint Paul and Minneapolis.

As a seminarian, I wanted to learn more about sacred music and the liturgy. Since Saint Agnes celebrated Mass with both the music of the masters and Gregorian chant, there was no better place to learn about music and the liturgy than at Saint Agnes. So I joined the Twin Cities Catholic Chorale in 1977 and was a member until I was ordained a priest.

I learned a great deal from Monsignor by singing in the Chorale, which was directed by him. I never dreamt that I would be able to sing the Masses of Mozart, Haydn, Beethoven, Schubert, Gounod, and others. But the Chorale did just that, with the professional assistance of members of the Minnesota Orchestra.

Monsignor Schuler wanted above all to implement the teachings of the Second Vatican Council on the liturgy and on sacred music. He was faithful to the Council by using the organ in the liturgy, making use of Latin, and using the music of the masters for the Ordinary parts of the Mass and Gregorian chant for the Proper parts of the Mass. In addition, at each liturgy, the sanctuary had a full complement of clergy and servers to balance the power of the music.

I am grateful to Monsignor for the formation in the liturgy and in sacred music that he provided for me and for other seminarians. At the time, there was no other place in the country that provided a similar formation. Today, Saint Agnes carries on the tradition established by Monsignor Schuler. The parish is still the place to come to experience the finest in sacred music and liturgy.

The Most Reverend John M. LeVoir
Bishop of New Ulm, Minnesota

PREFACE

Four Decades in Frogtown*

Jubilee days are days of grateful remembrance and responsible reflection. In recalling the past, these days offer the jubilarians an opportunity to strengthen their own identity by recognizing the vision upon which their group was founded, and responsible reflection helps discern the legacy of that past which will shape the group's future. Vision and Legacy come together in the founder of the Twin Cities Catholic Chorale, the priest-musician who initiated the Chorale's residency at Frogtown's *Sv. Neza* (Saint Agnes in Slovenian). Richard Schuler's priest-teacher and mentor who passed on his vision to his pupil, was the Slovene immigrant Father Francis Anthony Missia (1884-1955).

It was the summer of 1903, and in response to the invitation of a frontier prelate named John Ireland, a plucky Catholic lad set out from the banks of the Mura in the old Empire of the Habsburgs on the long journey to the shores of the Mississippi. In later years, Father Missia (Latinized form of the name *Misel/Mislej* in Slovenian) proudly referred to the fact that whilst he was sailing across the Atlantic, a conclave of cardinals was meeting at the Vatican, and in fact on August 4, 1903, a successor to Leo XIII was elected. He took the name of Pius...and a few days later, on the feast of the Assumption, the 19 year-old graduate of the Jesuit *Gymnasium* at Kalksburg near Vienna arrived safely in Saint Paul, Minnesota.

Three months after Missia's arrival in Minnesota, Pope Pius X issued his *Motu proprio on Sacred Music*, calling for the revalorization of *cantus gregorianus* as *pars integralis liturgiae sollemnis.* That was to be "Missia's guiding document," his compass for the rest of his life. Even before his priestly ordination in 1908, Francis Missia took to heart these important teachings of the Pope, and he never tired of quoting them. In the liturgy, "the holy mysteries of our faith are celebrated, in which the Christian people come together to receive the grace of the Sacraments, to assist at the Holy Sacrifice of the Altar, to adore the Blessed Sacrament and to join in the public and solemn liturgical prayers of the Church...."

In order that the "true Christian spirit...be maintained by all the faithful, the first thing to which We must attend is the holiness and dignity of the churches in which Our people assemble, in order to acquire that spirit from its first and most indispensable source, by taking an active part in the sacred mysteries and in the solemn public prayers of the Church" (Introduction, *Motu proprio on Sacred Music*, Catholic Truth Society).

A great many of Missia's students (including Richard Schuler from 1940-45) never forgot how he clearly recognized the importance of what he called "definite traditions." He knew the importance of vision, and through all forty-seven years of his teaching career at the Saint Paul Seminary, his own vision was (to use one of his favorite adjectives) the "self-same" vision of Saint Pius X. And so it was on the basis of a three-year summer school course devoted to the study of the *Motu proprio,* begun at the direction of Archbishop John Gregory Murray in 1935 and taught by Father Missia, that the Saint Paul Catholic Choral Society, which was founded by him, gave its first public concert in 1938...when Richard Schuler entered the College of Saint Thomas as a freshman, aged 17 years.

The record is plain: as professor of liturgical music at the Saint Paul Seminary (1908-55) and head of Archbishop Murray's Sacred Music Commission (since 1932), Father Missia tirelessly promoted Gregorian chant and the great polyphonic music of the 16th and 17th centuries. On May 29, 1955, in a retrospective article published in the *Saint Paul Pioneer Press*, and memorializing Father Missia, music critic John Harvey recalled that "As a sort of 'showcase' for the riches of this liturgical music, Missia organized and for many years conducted the Saint Paul Catholic Choral Society whose annual concerts were revelations of authority and beauty." Even after ordination to the priesthood on August 18, 1945, Father Richard Schuler continued his collaboration in Missia's apostolate as "staff organist" of the Catholic Choral Society. In addition, the young priest-professor at Nazareth Hall, the minor seminary, and later the College of Saint Thomas, was very active as the weekend assistant and choir director at the Church of the Nativity of Our Lord in Saint Paul.

After Missia died unexpectedly on May 21, 1955, a part-time teacher at the Seminary (who was four years senior to Father Schuler) was appointed by Archbishop Murray to teach music and direct the Catholic Choral Society. That same year Father Schuler returned from his Fulbright year in Rome and was named to the faculty of the College of Saint Thomas. In 1956, upon the foundation laid by Missia in 18 years of hard work, Father Schuler founded the Twin Cities Catholic Chorale as a "metropolitan-wide choir originally composed of members of the earlier Saint Paul Catholic Choral Society as well as other younger singers attracted by the opportunity to sing Catholic church music." In September, 1969, Father Schuler succeeded his old seminary dogma professor, Monsignor Rudolph Bandas, as pastor of Saint Agnes, and five years later the Twin Cities Catholic Chorale became the resident choir of the "Frogtown Cathedral." The rest is history....

Over this long trajectory of history, the venues have changed, the membership has varied, the repertory has expanded and grown. But two elements have remained unchanged: the *vision* and the *legacy*.

The *vision* today is the "self-same" vision of Saint Pius X, confirmed at decisive points of the Liturgy Constitution of the last Council, in articles 112, 114 and 116 of chapter 6 with apposite citations which Francis Missia knew from memory. That enduring vision can be summed up in these words of Richard Schuler:

> The last ecumenical Council declared that two elements are required for music in the liturgy: it must be sacred and it must be art. Whatever is not true art is not worthy of the *servitium Dominicum,* God's service; what is not sacred does not fulfill its purpose: God's worship.

The *legacy,* valid today as it was yesterday – and not only in the Twin Cities – in the words of the Chorale's founder:

> In every way, what is done at Saint Agnes is in perfect accord with the directives of the Holy See and the reforms of the Second Vatican Council. Liturgy at Saint Agnes is not

a home-made activity. Rather it is the action of the Church, which is the Mystical Christ, and therefore the liturgy is the very action of the Redeemer Himself. Only the Church, the Mystical Christ, can determine what that is to be. It remains for the priest and the people to carry it out as the Church prescribes it with as much care, reverence, and solemnity as possible. From the beginning of the parish, this was the intention of the pastors, and nothing was spared to make the Eucharistic Sacrifice noble and beautiful, fully in agreement with the ritual of the Roman Catholic Church.

In these words lies Richard Schuler's legacy, here is his lesson for the Twin Cities Catholic Chorale and for all those who come after him, in their own circumstances. *Non jam frustra doces, Pater reverende!* (You do not now teach in vain, Reverend Father!)

Reverend Robert A. Skeris
Director, Centre for Ward Method Studies
The Benjamin T. Rome School of Music
The Catholic University of America
Washington, DC

---

*In his history of the Church of Saint Agnes, Monsignor Schuler explains the designation "Frogtown" for the neighboring area. "Origin of the designation, Frogtown, has often been misunderstood to indicate a French beginning, especially since a farmer named Lafond, after whom the present street is called, did live in the area. However, the true reason for the nickname comes from the high water table in the marshy section lying between the high ground of Calvary Cemetery and Saint Anthony Hill to the south. The meadow was alive with frogs who croaked loudly and who gave their name to the place. The Germans called it *Froschburg* and often in writing to relatives in Europe referred to their new homes in "Frogtown" (*The Church of Saint Agnes (1887-1987)*, Monsignor Richard J. Schuler, Saint Paul, Minnesota, 1987, p.17).

Part One

"Through your co-operation, the Chorale can do much to further a true cultural environment in our cities, and we can discover for ourselves…the really magnificent wealth that is the treasure of the Catholic Church."

Letter from Father Richard J. Schuler
to Chorale members, Fall, 1958

CHAPTER I
Precursor - The Saint Paul Catholic Choral Society

The Saint Paul Catholic Choral Society was established in 1936 by Father Francis A. Missia (1884-1955), professor of Sacred Music at the Saint Paul Seminary and Chairman of the Archdiocesan Commission on Liturgical Music, with the approval of Archbishop John Gregory Murray.[1] Its purpose was to exemplify Catholic church music in its threefold aspect of sacred chant, medieval polyphony, and approved modern polyphony.[2]

An article in the Sunday, January 16, 1938 *Saint Paul Pioneer Press* announces that the Saint Paul Catholic Choral Society would be "making its formal bow after months of rehearsal under the director, Father Francis A. Missia" in a concert on Wednesday, January 19, 1938, in the Saint Paul Auditorium. Miss Ruth Dindorf would be the organist.

Father Francis A. Missia, Founder and Director of the Saint Paul Catholic Choral Society (*St. Paul Pioneer Press*, August 30, 1937, used with permission). Schuler Archives.

The program began with the singing of *Ecce Sacerdos Magnus* by H. Tappert to mark the formal entrance of Archbishop John Gregory Murray in choir dress adorned with the episcopal *ferraiolo* (cape). The first part of the concert consisted of an organ recital. In the second part, the choir sang plain chant, Renaissance polyphony, and works by Isaak, Mozart, Schubert, and Grieg. This first concert received extensive notice in the *Saint Paul Pioneer Press* of January 20, 1938, even detailing the fashions worn by women patrons in attendance.

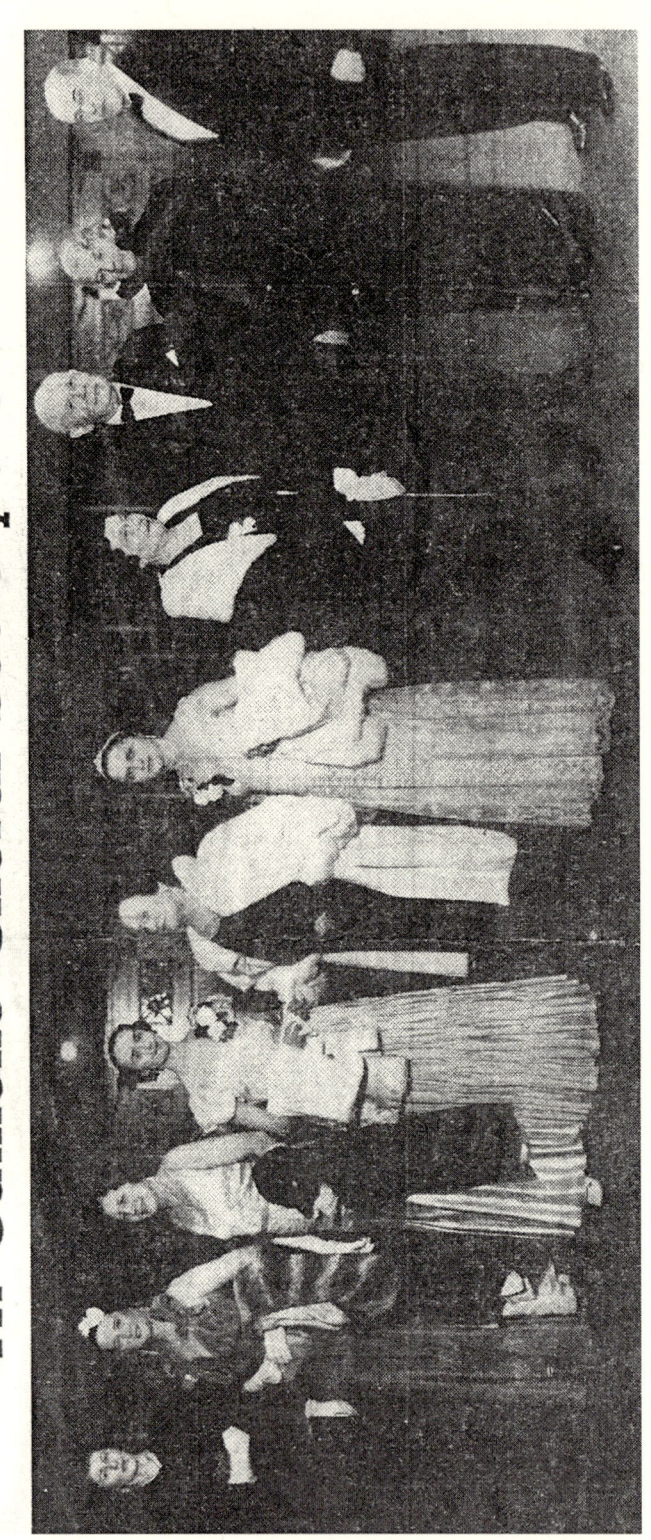

THE SAINT PAUL PIONEER PRESS, THURSDAY, JANUARY 20, 1938.

At Catholic Choral Society's Concert

Before the first concert of the Saint Paul Catholic Choral Society, January 19, 1938. From left to right, Miss Angela Bowlin, Mrs. Louis P. Branca, Mrs. J. H. Russell, Miss Rosemary McLaughlin, Mrs. C.E. McLaughlin, Miss Eugenia McLaughlin, Miss Frieda Bremer, Otto Bremer, Mrs. Paul G. Bremer and Mr. Bremer. (*Saint Paul Pioneer Press*, January 20, 1938, used with permission). Schuler Archives.

Of greater interest than the fashions, however, is the review of the concert by Frances Boardman, the music critic of the paper, which began, "An audience which filled every seat in the Auditorium theater Wednesday evening heard music that, for its own implicit beauty and for skillful interpretation, will perhaps not be surpassed in this or any other season."[3] Concerts were given annually until 1942 when they were interrupted by World War II. They followed the same format as the first concert, beginning with Tappert's *Ecce Sacerdos*. An introductory note for the program of the 1941 concert states: "In view of the forthcoming Eucharistic Congress, the major portion of the program of this evening's concert is built on the theme and melodies of the Holy Eucharist as contained in the Mass and Office of the Feast of Corpus Christi."[4]

On April 2, 1948, Archbishop Murray sent a letter to all pastors announcing that the Saint Paul Catholic Choral Society had been re-organized after the war and would resume its cultural program by giving a sacred concert at the Saint Paul Auditorium Theatre on Tuesday, May 11, and urging the pastors to attend the concert.[5] The Saint Paul Catholic Choral Society was still under the direction of Father Missia, its founder, who had at that time been head of ecclesiastical music at the Saint Paul Seminary for forty years. Father Richard J. Schuler, who was ordained in 1945, was the organist. The Archbishop re-iterated the aim of the organization as previously stated.

Concerts were given from 1948 to 1955. Each began with the *Ecce Sacerdos* by Tappert, signaling the entrance of Archbishop Murray. All except the 1949 concert included an organ prelude, the *Grand Chorus* by Dubois, played by Father Schuler. The choral programs were similar with plain chant, Renaissance polyphony, and modern polyphony. The concert given on April 13, 1950, was dedicated to Archbishop John Gregory Murray in commemoration of the fiftieth anniversary of his ordination and the thirtieth anniversary of his consecration as Auxiliary Bishop of Hartford, Connecticut. In the Modern Polyphony section were included the *Victimae Paschali* of Pietro Yon and the *Terra Tremuit* by Joseph Gruber, Easter favorites still in the repertoire of the Twin Cities Catholic Chorale. The concert given on May 12, 1953, was dedicated to the memory of Blessed Pius X on the occasion of the fiftieth anniversary of the publication of his *Motu Proprio*, governing the sacred music of the Catholic Church.

What was to be the last concert of the Choral Society under the direction of Father Missia was sung on April 21, 1955. It was reviewed by John H. Harvey for the *Pioneer Press*, who said the following: "The particular glory of these concerts is the plain chant section, for nowhere else in this area outside of the Saint Paul Seminary can one hear this ancient music, infinitely subtle and expressive, sung so well."[6] Father Schuler was not the organist for this concert because he was in Rome on a Fulbright Scholarship doing research in the Vatican Library on Giovanni Nanino. His doctoral dissertation would be a study of the composer and an edition of his works.

On May 21, 1955, Father Missia was killed tragically in a car accident as he returned from his cabin in Wisconsin. This event caused a significant change in the world of Catholic sacred music in the area. Father John A. Sweeney, former director of the Catholic Youth Center in Saint Paul, was appointed to succeed Father Missia at the Saint Paul Seminary, a position he held until 1977. When Father Schuler returned to the Archdiocese in 1955 after a year in Rome, the Archbishop sent him to teach at the College of Saint Thomas. In a biographical article in *Cum Angelis Canere*, a *festschrift* prepared in Monsignor Schuler's honor, his nephew Father Richard M. Hogan notes: "As he reflects on this assignment now, Monsignor is very pleased that the Archbishop sent him to Saint Thomas. At the time, it was rather a disappointing surprise because he had been promised a post at the seminary."[7] There is no explanation of who promised him that post.

Materials in the Schuler Archives at the Church of Saint Agnes show that for at least two years, the Saint Paul Catholic Choral Society continued under the direction of Father Sweeney. In two undated letters announcing the first year under his direction, Father Sweeney explained a change in emphasis for the group. "We are making every effort this year...to offer very practical suggestions and demonstrations, to help parish choirs, and to further the cause of congregational singing."[8]

In its first concert on May 8, 1956, the group sang the *Missa Choralis* for Mixed Choir and Congregation by Monsignor Licinio Refice (died 1954). The Saint Joseph's Academy Glee Club sang the congregation part in the Mass. This concert was announced under the patronage of Archbishop John Gregory Murray. The concert the next year on May 16, 1957 was under the patronage of the new Archbishop, The Most Reverend William O. Brady. In the second part of the 1957 concert, the Choral Society was assisted by more than 300 young people from the Catholic high schools in the city. In his review for the *Pioneer Press*, John Harvey noted that *Cantate Domino* by contemporary American composer Martin G. Dumler and three excerpts from a Mass by him "were skillfully done but in style they seemed 'safe' rather than particularly distinguished....At this juncture in its history it would appear that the Catholic Church badly needs another Palestrina."[9]

There is no further information about this group under the direction of Father Sweeney in the Schuler Archives. However, reflecting in retrospect, one can note the change in emphasis in Father Sweeney's group from that of Father Missia, a change which seems to be a foreshadowing of the changes in American church music following Vatican II.

The above choir, pictured on the steps of the Cathedral of Saint Paul, sang at the Pontifical Mass opening the National Conference of Catholic Charities in 1937. The choir was made up of 12 members of the Schola Cantorum of the Saint Paul Seminary, a mixed choir of 40 voices, and a string ensemble of six players from the Minneapolis Symphony. While this choir is not identified as the Saint Paul Catholic Choral Society, one might conclude that many of those pictured had been practicing together and would be among Choral Society members at its inaugural concert the following year. *(Saint Paul Pioneer Press,* August 30, 1937, used with permission). Schuler Archives.

CHAPTER II

The Twin Cities Catholic Chorale – The Early Years 1955/1956-1965

When was the Chorale founded? 1955 or 1956? In an article written by Father Richard M. Hogan, Monsignor Schuler's nephew, published in German in *Singende Kirche* (XXIV, No. 4, 1976-77, p.157-160), and later re-published in English in *Sacred Music* (Vol. 104, No. 4, Winter 1977), he gave the year for the founding of the Chorale as 1956. This author concludes that the date was chosen because the first concert of the Catholic Choirmasters' Chorale described below took place on December 17, 1956. However, Monsignor Schuler usually gave the year of its founding as 1955. This date probably refers to the fact that the group began rehearsing in 1955. Accepting either date means that the group had almost a 20-year history of singing concerts and Masses before beginning to sing regularly at the Church of Saint Agnes in 1974.

On his return from Rome, Father Schuler began teaching at the College of Saint Thomas and became the moderator of the Guild of Catholic Choirmasters and Organists. The first performance of a group called the Catholic Choirmasters' Chorale under the auspices of the Guild took place on December 17, 1956 at the College of Saint Catherine to honor Leopold G. Bruenner on his 65th anniversary as choirmaster and organist in Saint Paul. The program indicates that Father Richard J. Schuler was director of the group. Mrs. Myron J. Angeletti was organist. An unattributed note in the program states, "Mr. Bruenner's life-time activities as director, organist and composer have surely added lustre to the local texture of a culture too often, alas, neglected by apathy and soiled and tattered by the mediocrity of an age of mass entertainment and commercialized amusement."[10] The concert began with a section of Renaissance polyphony and continued with a second section of works by Mr. Bruenner. They included the *Mass in Honor of the Little Flower*, which the group also recorded in 1956. In his review in the *Saint Paul Pioneer Press* of December 18, 1956, John Harvey stated, "The mass, as befits the saint whom it honors, has a fresh and joyous tone...."[11]

In a letter dated September 15, 1957, Father Schuler announced the formation of the Catholic Choirmasters' Chorale, and refers to the initial concert given by the group to honor Leopold Bruenner in December of 1956. Father Schuler states, "Choral music that provides a challenge both artistically and spiritually will be the object of the Chorale's work."[12] Since many of the singers in the group were also choir directors or members of parish choirs, Father Schuler had the intention of introducing them to artistic sacred music which perhaps they could use in their parish choirs. He writes that the group will study and perform music from the Baroque era which he has on microfilm from the Vatican Library. He notes that the group will also study the *Missa Coloniensis* by Hermann Schroeder, a contemporary composer from the Rhineland, written for "a great liturgical celebration in the recently restored Cathedral of Cologne." The event referred to by Father Schuler was a Mass to celebrate the solemn re-opening of the Cologne Cathedral in 1956 after its restoration from heavy destruction during World War II. The name of the group on the roster for 1957-58 is the Twin City Catholic Choirmasters' Chorale. The membership contains many familiar names from Father Missia's Saint Paul Catholic Choral Society. Father Schuler is given as the founder and director; Mrs. Myron Angeletti, who was organist for Father Schuler's Nativity Choir, is listed as accompanist beginning in 1958. Rehearsals were held first at the Church of the Holy Childhood and then at the College of Saint Thomas, both in Saint Paul.

The first Mass sung by this group in the 1957-58 season took place at the Church of the Holy Childhood on Wednesday, February 12, 1958. Father John Buchanan, pastor, was always a great patron of this choir, which rehearsed for a time at his parish. The program for this Mass included the *Missa Coloniensis* by Hermann Schroeder, the Proper in Gregorian chant, Renaissance motets by Palestrina and Josquin des Pres, and an organ prelude and recessional, also by Schroeder.

The schedule of rehearsals for spring 1958 announces that the Chorale was scheduled to sing at three other Masses. The first, under the sponsorship of the Guild of Catholic Choirmasters and Organists and sung by the combined choirs of the parishes of the Twin Cities, was celebrated by Bishop Leonard P. Cowley on Monday, May 26, 1958. The choir sang the *Dreifaltigkeitmesse* by Guido Fassler (1913-1995). The second Mass was to have taken place at the Basilica of Saint Mary to commemorate the 50th anniversary of the laying of the cornerstone of the basilica. However, there was some misunderstanding about the participation of Archbishop William O. Brady, and the Mass at the Basilica was canceled by the pastor, Monsignor James M. Reardon, and moved to the Church of Saint Olaf. Bishop Leonard P. Cowley was the celebrant, and the Chorale repeated the *Dreifaltigkeitmesse* by Fassler rather than the previously announced *Missa Magnus et Potens* by Ernst Tittel according to an unidentified newspaper clipping. The third Mass celebrated the 25th anniversary of the ordination of Father William O'Donnell and was held in the Saint Thomas College Chapel. At this event, the Twin Cities Catholic Choirmasters' Chorale sang Hermann Schroeder's *Missa Coloniensis*.[13] The above-mentioned Masses demonstrate the pattern of the group in those years to sing music by contemporary European composers and to introduce more difficult music to parish choir members.

Father Schuler began his letter announcing the 1958-59 season of the Twin Cities Choirmasters' Chorale most enthusiastically: "It is with a great feeling of pleasure and a real sense of anticipation that I am writing to you to announce the beginning of the new season for our Twin Cities Catholic Choirmasters' Chorale." He continues by commenting on the interest nationally in their singing the *Missa Coloniensis* by Hermann Schroeder the previous year "since, as far as I know, it was the first time the Mass was sung in this country." He confirms that the choir has not yet performed the *Missa Magnus et Potens* of Ernst Tittel, but says it "should be received with equal acclaim, since it, too, is a contemporary composition of great stature." Father Schuler proposed learning the *Missa La Cristiniana* by Orazio Benevoli (1605-1672), choirmaster at Saint Peter's Basilica. Father Schuler transcribed this work for eight voices arranged in two choirs from microfilm. He also intended to continue working on contemporary composers by learning the *Te Deum* by Hermann Schroeder. He said that the choir had received several invitations to sing in parish churches. He concluded his letter with his goal for the group, a goal which still holds true today.

"Through your cooperation, the Chorale can do much to further a true cultural environment in our cities, and we can discover for ourselves and for others the really magnificent wealth of choral music that is the treasure of the Catholic Church."

The Twin Cities Catholic Choirmasters' Chorale, joined by the choir of the Church of the Nativity of Our Lord in Saint Paul where Father Schuler was choir director, marked the centennial of the apparitions of the Blessed Virgin Mary in Lourdes, France, by singing a solemn Mass on the feast of the Immaculate Conception, December 8, 1958, at the Church of the Holy Cross in Minneapolis. A clipping from the *Catholic Bulletin* of November 28, 1958, announced: "The choir of nearly 100 voices will sing the *Missa Magnus et Potens* by the contemporary Austrian composer, Ernst Tittel. The composition is scored for mixed choir, organ, a brass ensemble of two trumpets, two French horns, and two trombones."

On March 6, 1959, the group sang the *Missa La Cristiniana* by Orazio Benevoli at a Mass at the Church of the Holy Childhood. Since it was transcribed from microfilm obtained from the Vatican Library by Father Schuler for the Chorale, this is probably the first time it would have been sung in the United States. In a review in *The Wanderer* of March 12, 1959, Roger Anderson says, "The major interest of the composition consists of its excellent use of antiphonal singing between the two choirs....The performance was excellent. The spatial quality of the music was maintained by not only placing the choirs in different places, behind the altar and in the baptistery, but also by reducing the second choir to eight soloists." The reviewer also comments on the importance of performing this music in its intended setting, that is to say, the liturgy.

A program consisting of a lecture/demonstration by Father Schuler and the Twin Cities Catholic Choirmasters' Chorale was broadcast on the public television network KTCA on April 2, 1959. Polyphonic music of the Roman School including the following composers: Palestrina, Benevoli, Nanino, Soriano and Anerio, was performed.

A program from the Guild of Catholic Choirmasters and Organists' Mass on May 25, 1959, gives a more complete presentation of the kind of music sung at these annual Masses and the choirs involved. The Ordinary of the Mass was *Missa Festiva* (1956) by Marius Monnikendam, performed by the combined choirs of the Twin Cities, with organ and brass ensemble. The chant Proper was sung by the Saint Thomas College Choir. The Offertory and Communion motets and a *Magnificat* (1951) by Hermann Schroeder were sung by the Catholic Choirmasters' Chorale. It is clear that Father Schuler was trying to introduce artistically valid contemporary music as well as to continue to perform works from the treasury of Catholic sacred music (Gregorian chant, motets by Palestrina and Nanino). Thirty-nine parish choirs participated in addition to the Choirmasters' Chorale and the College of Saint Thomas Choir. This Mass was reviewed in the May 28, 1959, issue of *The Wanderer.*

A recording titled, *Twin Cities Catholic Chorale with Brass Ensemble,* was made in 1959. This recording included the *Missa Magnus et Potens,* Opus 15 by Ernst Tittel, *Ecce Sacerdos* by Strategier, *Sicut Cervus Desiderat* by Palestrina, *Diffusa est Gratia* by Nanino, *Ave Regina Coelorum* by Soriano, and *Magnificat* by Hermann Schroeder. Father Schuler was the director and Mrs. Myron J. (Agnes) Angeletti, the organist. The repertoire on this recording was diverse, representing both contemporary and Renaissance composers.

In an organizational letter announcing the 1959-60 season, Father Schuler used the new name of the group, the Twin Cities Catholic Chorale, without comment on the name change. He said that the choir would study two new Masses: Anton Bruckner's *Mass in E Minor* for double choir and wind orchestra and Franz Joseph Haydn's *Little Organ Solo Mass.* Thus, the Chorale began a custom of singing an annual concert and also occasional Masses when invited to area churches. On February 23, 1960, the Chorale sang the Bruckner *Mass in E Minor* at a Mass to close Forty Hours Devotion at the Church of the Nativity of Our Lord. The wind orchestra was replaced by the organ in this performance.

On March 28 and 29, 1960, the group of slightly over 60 singers gave two concert performances, one in Saint Paul and one in Minneapolis. The files include a letter to the Chancery office inviting the Archbishop to attend one of the concerts and asking if the concerts could be announced under his patronage. (The Archbishop at this time was The Most Reverend William O. Brady, although he was not named in the letter.) This request followed in the tradition established by Father Missia, since all of his concerts were performed under the patronage of Archbishop John Gregory Murray in his presence. However, Father Schuler received a response from the Vicar General, Monsignor

Gerald O'Keefe, stating that the Archbishop had no objections to the presentation of the concerts, but that he would prefer that they not be announced under his patronage. Both letters gave the name of the group as the Twin Cities Catholic Chorale. One concert was performed at Archbishop Murray Memorial High School in Maplewood and the other at the Prudential Auditorium in Minneapolis. The orchestra was provided through a grant from the Recording Industries Trust Fund in cooperation with Local 30 of the American Federation of Musicians. The ambitious program included a section of Renaissance motets followed by *Missa La Cristiniana* by Orazio Benevoli, Anton Bruckner's *Mass in E Minor,* and a *Magnificat* by Hermann Schroeder.

On May 3, 1960, the Chorale sang a Mass at the Church of Saint Olaf in Minneapolis to celebrate the 50th anniversary of the Dominican Sisters of the Sick Poor. Archbishop William O. Brady presided, but the announcement does not say what the group sang. The annual Mass of the Guild of Catholic Choirmasters and Organists was held on May 23, 1960, also at the Church of Saint Olaf. The combined choirs, including 27 parishes, the Chorale, and the choir of the College of Saint Thomas, sang the Bruckner *Mass in C.* The Chorale also sang at a silver tea at the Church of the Holy Childhood during the year to raise funds to buy its music.

In his 1960-61 organizational letter, Father Schuler proposed learning two contemporary works: Hermann Schroeder's *Te Deum* and *Intrada* by Hans Sabel, both for choir and brass ensemble as well as Joseph Haydn's *Little Organ Solo Mass*, and possibly Palestrina's *Missa Assumpta est Maria.* He said that he was attempting to obtain Michael Haydn's *Requiem*, which was only available in manuscript form. He would like to perform it as a tribute to Father Francis Missia because he had greatly admired Michael Haydn's liturgical music.

The 1960-61 season included several performances beginning with a Mass at the Church of the Holy Childhood on January 4, 1961 at which the Chorale sang Haydn's *Little Organ Solo Mass* with a string orchestra. A telegram in the file from the musician's union dated December 30, 1960, allowed an archival recording of the performance. A review in *The Wanderer* of January 19, 1961, called the Chorale the "foremost Catholic choir in the area."

On February 12, 1961, the Chorale represented the Catholic Church in the Brotherhood of Faiths Choral Festival which took place in Northrop Auditorium on the University of Minnesota campus. The Chorale sang Renaissance polyphony at this concert. Other choirs included those of Beth El Synagogue, Saint Mary's Russian Orthodox Church and Central Lutheran Church, all of Minneapolis.

In its 1961 concert on April 24, 1961, this time in Jeanne d'Arc Auditorium at the College of Saint Catherine, the Chorale sang, in addition to a group of motets, *Missa Ut, Re, Mi, Fa, Sol, La* or the *Hexachord Mass* by Palestrina, the *Missa Magnus et Potens* by Ernst Tittel, and *Te Deum Laudamus* by Hermann Schroeder.

The annual Mass of the Guild of Catholic Choirmasters and Organists was held on May 22, 1961 at the Church of the Nativity of Our Lord in Saint Paul, Minnesota. The Chorale, choirs of Saint Thomas and Saint Catherine's Colleges and 24 parishes sang the *Muttergottesmesse* by Ernst Tittel, a contemporary Austrian composer.

In his letter announcing the rehearsals and program of study for the 1961-62 season, Father Schuler said that the Chorale was mentioned in the program book of the Fourth International Congress of Church Music in Cologne which he had attended. He proposed that the group study two Renaissance polyphonic Masses: the *Messe super "Per Signum Crucis"* by Ludwig Senfl and the *Messe "Ich stund an einem morgen"* by Jacobus Gallus. The choir would continue working on the 16 part *Laudate Pueri* by Orazio Benevoli. Father Schuler also said that he had obtained the microfilm of the Michael Haydn *Requiem*.

On September 15, 1961, the Chorale sang Ernst Tittel's *Muttergottesmesse* for a pontifical Mass at the Church of Saint Agnes celebrated by Archbishop Pietro C. van Lierde, Vicar General of Vatican City. Archbishop van Lierde had become acquainted with Monsignor Rudolph Bandas, pastor of the Church of Saint Agnes, while the Monsignor was in Rome as an expert preparing for Vatican II.

On January 10, 1962, the Chorale sang the Schubert *Mass in G* at a Mass at the Church of the Holy Childhood. On March 4, 1962, the choir sang for Father Daniel Friberg's Mass of Thanksgiving after his ordination at the old Guardian Angels Church in Oakdale. A letter in the file from Father Friberg thanks Father Schuler and the group for making it to the church in the treacherous weather. Indeed, there was a typical March snowstorm that morning and the road to Oakdale was almost impassable. On March 17, 1962, the Chorale sang for the Ancient Order of Hibernians Mass at the Cathedral, but the material in the files does not indicate what was sung.

The 1962 concert of the Chorale was held in Jeanne d'Arc Auditorium at the College of Saint Catherine on May 10. The program included Joseph Haydn's *Missa Brevis in Honorem S. Joannis de Deo (The Little Organ Solo Mass)* and the *Mass in G* by Franz Schubert plus motets. This concert was reviewed in the *Pioneer Press* by music critic John Harvey. "Since none of the Catholic churches in this area can maintain a regularly constituted, well-equipped choir of good size to do full justice to much of this music, the Chorale performs an important service to the community." He continues: "The members of the Chorale, all mature and experienced singers, sang with full, clean tone, fine balance and response and gave the music excellent expressive shadings" (*Saint Paul Pioneer Press*, May 11, 1962).

Archbishop Binz was the celebrant of the Guild of Catholic Choirmasters and Organists annual Mass on May 21, 1962, at the Church of Saint Olaf. The massed choirs of 27 parishes, the Twin Cities Catholic Chorale, and the choirs of the Colleges of Saint Thomas and Saint Catherine sang the *Krippenmesse* by Joseph Kronsteiner. The processional was the Tappert *Ecce Sacerdos*, which had always been sung by Father Missia's Saint Paul Catholic Choral Society at its concerts and is still sung by the Twin Cities Catholic Chorale every time the group sings a Mass in the presence of a bishop.

The letter from Father Schuler announcing rehearsals for the 1962-63 year states: "For the first time in our seven years of singing we are in the black on the leger (sic) books." The works to be studied include the Michael Haydn *Requiem in C Minor* which the choir would learn and sing in memory of Father Francis Missia, and the *De Profundis* by Mozart. The choir would perfect the Senfl and Gallus Masses which they had learned the preceding year. Father Schuler obtained the Michael Haydn *Requiem in C Minor* on microfilm from Saint Peter's Abbey in Salzburg because there was no published version. On February 19, 1963, the Chorale sang the Schubert *Mass in G* at a solemn Mass as part of the Fine Arts Week at the College of Saint Thomas where Father Schuler taught.

In the organizational letter for the 1963-64 season of the Twin Cities Catholic Chorale, Father Schuler announced that the group would continue to work on the Michael Haydn *Requiem,* which had been recently been published, so it would no longer be necessary to work from the manuscript copies. Once again, he was looking for singers, especially tenors and basses.

The Chorale was to sing a High Mass at Saint Peter's Church in Delano on November 1, 1963, but there is no program in the Archives announcing what the group sang. The Chorale also sang at a Solemn Mass at the Church of the Holy Childhood in Saint Paul, Minnesota, on January 8, 1964. The program included the *Messe zu Ehren der Hl. Cacilia* by Josef von Wöss, the *Rex Pacificus* by Hermann Schroeder, and Palestrina's *Sicut Cervus*. The group was accompanied by organ, two trumpets and two trombones. The pastor, Father John Buchanan, was celebrant.

In February of 1964, Father Schuler sent a letter to potential patrons asking for contributions for a sacred concert dedicated to the memory of Father Francis A. Missia, "who for over forty years worked for the cause of sacred music." The occasion was to be the eightieth anniversary of Father Missia's birth. Father Schuler said that the Chorale would sing Michael Haydn's recently discovered *Requiem Mass in C Minor* (1771). Father Schuler said it would be the first performance in this area and possibly in the country. The concert took place on March 3, 1964, in the Nativity Auditorium in Saint Paul, the parish where Father Schuler was choir director. The program notes state that Father Missia was particularly fond of the music of Michael Haydn and never tired of pointing out how truly appropriate his works were for the liturgy. However, please note that the Michael Haydn *Requiem* was sung on this occasion in a concert, not at Mass. The program includes in an insert a reprint of an article written by Father Schuler on Father Missia and reprinted from *The Catholic Choirmaster* (Vol. XLVI, No. 4, Winter 1956 – see Appendix B). The program also includes a list of works previously studied by the Chorale. The concert was reviewed by John Harvey of the *Saint Paul Pioneer Press* (March 4, 1964). He notes the work's thoroughly liturgical spirit. He also comments on some difficulties in coordination with the orchestra, laying the cause to limited rehearsal time. Harvey does praise the choristers, saying that they were well prepared and admirably responsive.[14]

The Chorale sang at a Pontifical High Mass for the diamond jubilee of the Church of Saint Agnes on April 17, 1964. The Chorale also participated again in the annual Mass of Thanksgiving of the Guild of Catholic Choirmasters and Organists, held on May 18, 1964, at the Cathedral of Saint Paul. The combined choirs of thirty-four Twin Cities parishes sang the *Messe zu Ehren der heiligen Cacilia* by von Wöss.

In June of 1964, the Chorale made a recording, *Viennese Church Music*. It included the *Mass in G* by Franz Schubert and Mozart's *Ave Verum Corpus* on side one. The *Mass in Honor of Saint Cecilia*, Opus 32, No. 3 by Josef von Wöss and the *Ave Maria* by Anton Bruckner were on side two. Father Schuler was the conductor and John F. Vanella, the organist. Soloists were members of the Chorale. A string orchestra played. The financial ledger identifies the musicians as a student orchestra. The recording company was paid $1,250 for making the recording and producing the records.

The letter sent by Father Schuler organizing the 1964-65 season began with an announcement of the recording that the group had made the preceding spring. Father Schuler said that the price would be $4 and that he hoped they would sell many copies! There were plans to sing again in Delano, and at the mother house of the Franciscan Sisters in Rochester. The Chorale was also invited by Father John Buchanan to sing the Michael Haydn *Requiem* at the Church of the Holy Childhood on November 2, 1964. Father Schuler concluded the letter by asking once again for tenors and basses. The High Mass at the Church of Saint Peter in Delano, Minnesota, took place on December 8, 1964, the Feast of the Immaculate Conception.

The Chorale was asked once again to participate in the Brotherhood of Faiths Choral Festival at the University of Minnesota which took place on February 14, 1965. The Chorale began the program with a section of Renaissance motets. The Central Lutheran Church Senior Choir, Saint Mary's Russian Orthodox Church Choir and the Beth El Synagogue also participated as in previous years. To conclude the concert the Chorale and the Central Lutheran Church Senior Choir sang "The Lord is Lord," the world premiere of an extremely challenging work by Paul Fetler, professor of music at the University of Minnesota.

The 1965 Mass of Thanksgiving of the Guild of Catholic Choirmasters and Organists, in which the Chorale participated, was, without doubt, the most elaborate ever held. It took place on March 25 at the Cathedral of Saint Paul with Archbishop Leo Binz presiding. The celebrant was Monsignor Johannes Overath of Cologne, Germany, the first president of the *Consociatio Internationalis Musicae Sacrae* (CIMS), established by Pope Paul VI in 1963. Monsignor Overath was in the Twin Cities to plan the Fifth International Church Music Congress, organized by CIMS, which was to take place in Chicago and Milwaukee in August of 1966. The music chosen for the Mass in the Cathedral of Saint Paul reflected once again Monsignor Schuler's tendency at that time to introduce artistic contemporary music along with Gregorian chant and Renaissance polyphony. The choirs included the men's choruses of the Basilica of Saint Mary, the College of Saint Thomas, the Church of the Holy Childhood, and the University of Minnesota Men's Glee Club; the boy choirs of the parishes of Saint Gregory the Great and Holy Childhood in Saint Paul, Our Lady of Grace in Edina and Saint Mary's Cathedral in Saint Cloud; the College of Saint Thomas Liturgical Choir, the Twin Cities Catholic Chorale, plus parish choirs from 38 Twin Cities parishes. The Cathedral was full! The *Missa Salve Regina* by Jean Langlais (1907-1991) was sung by the choir and by the congregation which was made up of the massed parish choirs. Herald trumpets supported the congregational part. There were three choir directors and two organists because both the choir loft and sanctuary organs were used. It was a spectacular celebration and a real example of active participation as it was understood and promoted by CIMS, the papal church music organization.

This Mass of the Guild of Catholic Choirmasters and Organists represented a high point in the history of these Masses, both for the number of choirs participating and for the quality of the music presented. One might have concluded that, given the directives of the *Constitution on the Sacred Liturgy* of the Second Vatican Council, which Father Schuler understood as giving a new freedom to the Catholic church musician to use the great liturgical Masses of Haydn, Mozart, Schubert and Beethoven as a part of the liturgy, the period after the Council would represent a great flowering of Catholic church music that was sacred and true art. Nothing could have been further from the truth and the 1965 Mass marked the end rather than the beginning! It was those of liberal and secular thought who prevailed, those who interpreted the "spirit" of the Council as meaning a rejection of Latin, of Gregorian chant, and the great patrimony of Catholic liturgical music in favor of contemporary music in the vernacular for congregational singing (see Appendix C on the history of the Guild of Catholic Choirmasters and Organists).

On March 31, 1965 the Twin Cities Catholic Chorale sang for the consecration of Reverend James P. Shannon as Auxiliary Bishop of the Archdiocese.[15] The Chorale was joined by the Men's Chorus of the College of Saint Thomas. Bishop Shannon was president of the College of Saint Thomas at that time. For the Ordinary of the Mass, the choirs sang the *Mass in Honor of Saint Cecilia* by Josef von Wöss in English. Father Schuler set the English text to the music by von Wöss especially for the occasion. The Proper of the Mass was composed with a text in English by Father Schuler. (The Twin Cities Catholic Chorale still sings one part of that Proper, "Glorious are the Things That Are Said of Thee, O Mary" during the concert that it gives before Midnight Mass on Christmas Eve.) The processional music included Tappert's *Ecce Sacerdos* and the recessional was *Psalm 150* by César Franck.

The first Wanderer Forum, sponsored by the Wanderer Forum Foundation with the assistance of the paper of that name, was held on June 11 and 12, 1965, and the Chorale began its association with those meetings. The Chorale sang for the High Mass at the Church of the Assumption in Saint Paul, Minnesota at 9:00 am on June 12. The music included the *Mass in Honor of Saint Cecilia* by von Wöss with organ and brass ensemble.

In conclusion, during the first ten years of its existence the Chorale carried out the objectives that Father Schuler outlined in the letter he sent to singers at the beginning of the 1958-59 season: "Through your cooperation, the Chorale can do much to further a true cultural environment in our cities, and we can discover for ourselves and for others the really magnificent wealth of choral music that is the treasure of the Catholic Church."

It is interesting to note that in these early years, the Chorale sang many Masses by contemporary European composers in addition to Renaissance polyphony. The Chorale, which is known today for its classical Viennese repertoire of Masses by Haydn, Mozart, Beethoven and Schubert, only performed one Haydn Mass (*Little Organ Solo Mass*) and two Masses by Bruckner.

When Father Schuler founded the Chorale in 1955/56, he was ready to carry on the work of his mentor, Father Francis Missia, by presenting annual concerts and encouraging good choral music in parish churches. However, it should be noted that, when he asked for the patronage of Archbishop William O. Brady for concerts in 1960, which would have given his work and the Chorale an approval and prestige similar to that given by Archbishop Murray to Father Missia and his choir, it was not granted. Perhaps Archbishop Brady wanted to make clear to all that Father John A. Sweeney was officially in charge of the music for the archdiocese, implying that the Twin Cities Catholic Chorale did not have any special standing. A booklet, titled *Liturgical Music in the Archdiocese of Saint Paul* prepared by Father John A. Sweeney for the Music Commission of the Archdiocese of Saint Paul, published on September 3, 1960, with a letter from Archbishop William O. Brady, can lead one to that conclusion.

Undaunted, Father Schuler turned for support and invitations to sing Masses to his clergy friends, such as Bishop Leonard P. Cowley, who was pastor of Saint Olaf's Church in downtown Minneapolis, and Father John Buchanan, pastor of the Church of the Holy Childhood in Saint Paul. The Chorale was always recognized for the quality of its music by John Harvey, the principal classical music critic of the *Saint Paul Pioneer Press*. He did, however, note a problem of coordination with the orchestra in some of the concerts. This problem was not solved until the Chorale began singing regularly at the Church of Saint Agnes in 1974, when a cohort of talented classical musicians, mostly from the Minnesota Orchestra, were engaged to play on a weekly basis and thus guarantee a consistency of quality.

It should be noted that, then and now, the singers of the Chorale, all volunteers, practice weekly with organ accompaniment, but without the orchestra. Orchestra rehearsals are only scheduled when a new work is added to the repertoire or before a recording session. This practice is in part for budgetary reasons and in part because of the schedules of the professional musicians. However, the goal of the Chorale always is to perform the music for the Mass at the highest level possible with the talent God has given its members.

CHAPTER III

The Fifth International Church Music Congress – 1966
Cantare Amantis Est

The 1965-66 season of the Chorale places its founding director, and consequently the choir, in the midst of the controversies over various interpretations of *Sacrosanctum Concilium*, the *Constitution on the Sacred Liturgy* of the Second Vatican Council (1962-65). It should be noted, however, that for the most part, the singers in the Chorale were unaware of how crucial this moment and the upcoming Fifth Congress were in the post-conciliar Church. Father Schuler was appointed chairman of the general committee of the Fifth International Church Music Congress sponsored by the *Consociatio Internationalis Musicae Sacrae* (CIMS) and the Church Music Association of America. He was responsible for organizing the meeting of delegate-scholars in Chicago. His colleague, Father Robert Skeris, was a member of the general committee and was chairman of the activities in Milwaukee.

During the 1965-66 season, the Chorale continued to sing Masses in area churches as requested, but there is no mention of a concert. Evidently the main focus of the Chorale was preparing for the Milwaukee part of the international music congress. The program calls it "an international gathering of church musicians working with the approval of the Holy See to implement the Council decrees." To put it in context, the Council document on music and the liturgy, *Sacrosanctum Concilium,* had been promulgated by Pope Paul VI only shortly before the Congress on December 4, 1963; so the Fifth Congress was a very important opportunity to demonstrate the implementation of the document as it was understood by the papal church music society (CIMS). The theme of the Congress was a quote from Saint

Augustine, *"Cantare amantis est"* ("To sing is an expression of love.") The symbol of the Congress was "a fiery tongue of the Holy Spirit," portrayed as yellow and orange flaming tongues of fire, which were repeated against an orange background of flames on the cover of the programs for each event.

The organization of the meeting, held both in Chicago and Milwaukee, was a tremendous undertaking for Father Schuler, Father Skeris, and the large committee. Study days in Chicago, to which were invited the members of CIMS from all over the world, were followed by a weekend program (August 25 to 28, 1966) in Milwaukee where the experts were joined by choirs, organists, and speakers. In all, over 2,000 church musicians participated in concerts, lectures, special sessions, and Masses in Milwaukee. A picture taken of the congregation at one of the Masses in Milwaukee reminds us that nuns were in full habits and veils and women wore hats or chapel veils. On Sunday, selected choirs sang Masses in churches all over the city and its suburbs.

The Chorale played a central role, singing several times, first at the Saturday morning Pontifical Mass in Saint John's Cathedral. It was responsible for the Ordinary of the Mass, *Mass of the Word of God* by Daniel Pinkham, one of the Masses in English commissioned for the Congress, and it joined with the Dallas Catholic Choir in the motets.

The Fifth International Church Music Congress meetings in Chicago, August, 1966. Left to right, Fr. Richard J. Schuler, Chairman of the Congress; Monsignor Johannes Overath, President of CIMS, and Fr. Burbach. Schuler Archives.

The Pinkham Mass included a part for the congregation. The Dallas Catholic Choir sang the Proper of the Mass by Edwin Fissinger, also commissioned for the Congress. On Sunday morning, August 28, the Chorale sang the High Mass at Saint Robert's Church in Shorewood. The Ordinary of the Mass was *Missa super "Per Signum Crucis"* by Ludwig Senfl (c.1486-1542) and the Proper was in Gregorian chant. The Offertory motet was *Sicut Cervus* by Palestrina. The Chorale was also one of four choirs singing for the final Pontifical Mass in the Cathedral. The Ordinary of the Mass was Anton Bruckner's *Mass in E Minor* under the direction of Paul Salamunovich. (Salamunovich was assistant conductor of the Roger Wagner Chorale from 1953-1977 and Director of Music at Saint Charles Borromeo Church in North Hollywood from 1949-2009.) The Proper of the Mass was in Gregorian chant.

Mass at the Fifth International Church Music Congress in Milwaukee. Note Mrs. Minnie Schuler, mother of Fr. Schuler, with the white hair in the fourth row; two of Fr. Schuler's nephews are to her right. Schuler Archives.

A study of the program of this conference shows how carefully it was planned, its broad scope, and the high religious, intellectual, and cultural plane on which it was realized. The author of this history of the Chorale had the privilege of participating in some of the Chicago sessions and in all of the days in Milwaukee as a member of the Twin Cities Catholic Chorale. A group of church musicians with a liberal agenda, who disagreed with CIMS, and organized by some Americans in attendance, had come to the meetings in Chicago with a plan to derail the concluding session and the resolutions of the Congress. However, they did not succeed in this action because of some clever last-minute strategizing by the organizers of the Congress, who had been informed of what had been planned at a secret meeting the night before the final session. Nevertheless, it was evident that the minds of those opposed were already made up about the program that would take place in Milwaukee even before arriving in the city, much less experiencing the program. After the Congress there was much negative criticism of the Congress in the liberal Catholic press. To the credit of the editors of *Sacred Music*, two reviews, including a very long, negative one, were published in the Autumn 1966 issue.[16]

Here are some excerpts of the negative review by Robert J. Snow. To sum it up, nothing about either the meeting of experts in Chicago or the program in Milwaukee pleased him. With reference to the Chicago meetings, he said:

> The principal criterion for invitation it would seem was a very simple one, namely conservatism and conservatism only, and, in so far as was possible, most open-minded musicians were deliberately excluded.... The reason for such tactics was obvious. The self-assembled group of "experts" had but one goal: to present to the Holy See resolutions calling for the banning from the liturgy of all present-day experiments at making church music relevant to the various cultures and sub-cultures of the twentieth century and requesting a return to our "great heritage."...Some of these "experts" were even hoping to bring about a return to the exclusive use of Latin whenever the liturgy would be celebrated with music, i.e., as a "high" Mass! (p. 100-101).

Virginia Schubert interpreting for Dom Gajard, OSB from the Abbey of Solesmes, France, during a radio interview in Chicago. Schuler Archives.

The review continues at length in a very negative tone. One of the conclusions is the following: "The responsibility for the dismal state of liturgical and musical affairs at the Congress clearly rests on the shoulders of the general chairman and his committee members" (p. 108). The general chairman was Father Schuler.

In Appendix II of the proceedings of the Congress, *Sacred Music and Liturgy Reform after Vatican II*, [17] there is a statement discussing and refuting in detail the criticisms of the Congress along with a reproduction without comment of an anonymous and critical underground sheet distributed in Milwaukee.

Excerpts of the review by this author which arrived at very different conclusions are reprinted here:

> I was impressed first of all by the aims of the Congress, by the wide scope of its program and by the high religious, intellectual and cultural plane on which it was realized. His Holiness, Pope Paul VI, in a letter blessing the Congress, gives the following directive for the meetings: "The Fifth Congress has been rightly concentrated upon the great problems of sacred music arising from the decisions of the Council....It is only by profound meditation upon these

fundamental problems that an equitable application of the high directives of the Council can be made, thus avoiding hasty or improvised solutions which may, in the future, damage the very cause they seek to promote."

In general, I was greatly impressed by the pastoral quality of the speeches given, and by their intellectual soundness, sincerity and solid theological foundation. In particular, I would like to cite the paper of Father Colman O'Neill, a Dominican from the University of Fribourg, who in strong theological and philosophical arguments explained the meaning of *actuosa participatio populi*. He said that the first and most essential form of *actuosa participatio* (which he feels is mistranslated as "active" participation) is that participation which comes because of the character and grace of Baptism which makes us Christians and thus united mystically to Christ in the offering of the Holy Sacrifice of the Mass. Thus, even when silent, the faithful "participate" in the Mass. Lest Father O'Neill be misinterpreted, may I hasten to add that he does not advocate the "re-silencing" of the faithful, but rather he says that we must be careful not to confuse true participation with mere activity.

It was also interesting to hear the opinions of the church musicians attending the Congress and to read the proposals which were officially submitted for consideration. An example is the proposal of the French church musicians which decries the misinterpretation of the *Constitution on the Sacred Liturgy* by those who wish to eliminate the rich patrimony of sacred music in Latin, including Gregorian chant and polyphony. These musicians also object to the use in Church of music inspired by commercial ballads and jazz because it is undignified and not suitable for the liturgy. Views similar to these were among the official statements of the Congress…(p. 97-98).

As a practical application of the role of music in the liturgy there were five Pontifical High Masses. Two of these were in English, and were, in fact, Masses commissioned directly for the Congress, one by Daniel Pinkham, the *Mass of the Word of God* and the other, the *Mass in Honor of Saint Cecilia* by Hermann Schroeder. Both of these Masses included parts for the congregation and these were beautifully sung by the more than 2,000 people who jammed the Cathedral. There was one Gregorian chant Mass and the closing Mass was the Bruckner *Mass in E Minor*. I was privileged to be one of the 250 singers in the choir for that Mass and it was a religious experience that I will not soon forget. After the Mass many told me how moved they were by the Mass and how prayerfully it had been sung. This was true because I am sure that each and every one of us remembered while we were singing the exhortation of the director – that we let everyone know by the way we sing the Mass that we know and understand and firmly believe in every word that we sing. In order to include every aspect of the liturgy in the Congress, there was also a Pontifical Mass in the Ukrainian Byzantine rite, and a Scriptural service and Benediction of the Blessed Sacrament...(p. 98-99).

What touched me personally the most, however, was the intelligence, sincerity and holiness of those speaking, the high artistic, spiritual and cultural tone of the whole Congress, and the spiritual inspiration which the liturgical functions gave all of us who participated. The Congress had the effect on me of a well conducted retreat....According to Monsignor Johannes Overath, president of the *Consociatio*, "Such is the language of art, which does not turn to reason, but touches the innermost heart of man, and sets it beating faster." He continues, "Music can only be a language of love, a language created in the burning heart of an artist with faith, a language that will be understood by all men no matter what tongue they themselves happen to speak."

Here, then, is the challenge for the church musician. This is the challenge of the *Constitution on the Sacred Liturgy*. This is the challenge presented by the Fifth International Church Music Congress. The task of the creation of new music and the living preservation of the rich patrimony of sacred music is not an easy one. Let us hope and pray, however, that all those involved in church music will courageously accept the challenge given them so that music will retain in all art and dignity its rightful place in the worship of God. Let us hope that they will work so that the faithful throughout the world will in the future have the opportunity to be inspired as we were by truly artistic sacred music and not merely disedified by the monotony and mediocrity of much of what is forced upon us today (p.99).

Fifth International Church Music Congress meetings in August 1966. Left to right, Max Baumann, composer; Fr. Richard J. Schuler, and Fr. Ralph March, Director of the Dallas Catholic Choir (Photo by Frank Fusco). Schuler Archives.

Father Schuler's understanding of *Sacrosanctum Concilium* was based on his work with CIMS and also on the knowledge of the document that he received from Monsignor Rudolph Bandas, pastor of the Church of Saint Agnes, and one of the experts for the Second Vatican Council. Back in the Twin Cities after the conference, Father Schuler continued to implement the *letter* of the conciliar documents on the liturgy (not what was called the "spirit" of the Council) through the music he prepared for the High Masses that the Chorale continued to sing. He never wavered from his adherence to a strict and full interpretation of the documents of Vatican II on the liturgy, including the statement that Gregorian chant should have primacy of place in the liturgy. He also said often that *Sacrosanctum Concilium* freed the church musician to use all of the riches of the treasury of Catholic sacred music, including the orchestra Masses of Mozart, Haydn, Beethoven and Schubert, that became so central to the program at Saint Agnes.

However, the effects of the interpretation of Vatican II which came to be known as the "spirit of the Council" did affect Father Schuler's position as choir director at the Church of the Nativity of Our Lord in Saint Paul. He resigned from that position in June, 1966, a post he had held since 1950. An article in the *Saint Paul Pioneer Press,* June 10, 1966, about his departure from Nativity, bears the ominous headline "Battle Lost for Artistic Music."

Father Schuler gave as the reason for his resignation "dwindling choir participation," and "Choir music everywhere is disintegrating," he said. The article goes on to explain that, according to Father Schuler, too much emphasis has been placed on new music in the vernacular even though Vatican II called for the artistic music of the past to be preserved. This writer, a member of the Nativity Choir at that time, had not noted "dwindling choir participation" because of the loyalty of the choir to its director, but it soon became evident after Father Schuler's departure that the choir changed its focus and lost many members. To Father Schuler's credit, he never explained officially to choir members the reasons for his resignation. (See the article on the Nativity Choir in Appendix D for a more full explanation of his resignation.)

So, on the local, the national, and the international levels, the battle was joined between those who wanted a clear break from the past, with the Mass in English, congregational singing, and a liturgy with no room for Gregorian chant or artistic music in spite of what the

Council documents said, and those who were trying to interpret and implement the documents faithfully. In later years, when Monsignor Schuler was criticized for living in the past, his response always was, "I am not behind the times. I am forty years ahead of the times."

In that he was proven to be correct, which was especially evident at the CMAA conference presented in October, 2013, at the Church of Saint Agnes (Chapter 13), but it would be a steep climb and a long battle which is not yet won.

Father Schuler's prominent role in the Fifth International Church Music Congress thrust him on a national and international stage. His positions and those of his colleagues in CIMS were consistently misunderstood and he was personally vilified. However, this only served to strengthen his resolve to continue to fight for the proper implementation of the directives of the *Constitution on the Sacred Liturgy*. He did this from his platform as pastor of the Church of Saint Agnes, beginning in 1969, and from his role as editor of *Sacred Music* magazine beginning in 1975.

CHAPTER IV
The Twin Cities Catholic Chorale – 1966-1974

Neither the Schuler Archives nor the files of this author contains a program for a concert during the 1966-67 season. The Chorale did sing motets at an interfaith forum at the Fort Snelling Chapel on March 5, 1967 before a lecture by Senator Eugene J. McCarthy on religion in America. On Memorial Day, May 30, 1967, the Chorale sang the Michael Haydn *Requiem in C Minor* at a Mass in the Cathedral of the Holy Trinity in New Ulm, Minnesota. The Requiem was dedicated to the late Monsignor Walter H. Peters, a native of the parish and former professor at the College of Saint Thomas. Bishop Alphonse Schladweiler was celebrant of the Mass. Also in May the Chorale sang the same *Requiem* for Monsignor Peters and Father Albert Heer at a Mass at the Church of Saint Agnes in Saint Paul, Minnesota. The

The Chorale singing for the banquet of the Catholic Aid Association convention at the College of Saint Thomas, August, 1967; Monsignor Richard J. Schuler, conducting; John Vannella, at the piano (Photo by Glenn E. Smith). Schuler Archives.

Chorale sang twice at the third annual National Wanderer Forum in Minneapolis, June 23, 24, 25, 1967 – at the Pontifical Mass and at the awards banquet. The Chorale also sang for the annual meeting of the Catholic Aid Association at Saint Thomas College in August, 1967.

The first material in the files for the 1967-68 season includes clippings and a program from a Mass at the Church of Saint Stanislaus in Winona, Minnesota, on the Feast of Christ the King, October 29, 1967. The Chorale sang Anton Bruckner's *Mass in E Minor*. The Offertory hymn was *Sicut Cervus* by Palestrina, and at Communion the Chorale sang "Glorious Are The Things That Are Said of Thee, O Mary" by Father Schuler (written as part of the Proper of the Mass for the consecration of Bishop James P. Shannon), Mozart's *Ave Verum Corpus*, and the *Salve Regina* by Schubert. The recessional was the "Hallelujah Chorus" from Handel's *Messiah*. The program encourages the congregation to sing the processional hymn and the responses.

A letter from Father John Buchanan, pastor of the Church of the Holy Childhood, dated November 4, 1967, thanks Father Schuler and the Chorale for singing a Mass on the preceding Thursday evening. This letter leads to the conclusion that the Chorale must have sung for a Mass on All Souls' Day. An article in the *Aquin*, the student newspaper of the College of Saint Thomas, dated November 10, 1967, announces that Father Schuler had been elected first vice-president of the *Consociatio Internationalis Musicae Sacrae* (CIMS).

On Palm Sunday, April 7, 1968, the Chorale sang Antonin Dvořák's *Stabat Mater* in concert at the Church of the Assumption in Saint Paul, Minnesota. The 60 voice choir was joined by an orchestra provided by a grant from the musician's union. Mr. John Vanella was the organist, and there were four professional soloists. Archbishop Leo Binz was in attendance. The concert was reviewed in *The Wanderer* of April 25, 1968. The Chorale sang Kronsteiner's *Krippenmesse* for the Pontifical Mass on Saturday, June 22, 1968 at the fourth annual National Wanderer Forum. The Chorale also sang at the awards banquet held at the Radisson Hotel in Minneapolis. Correspondence in Father Schuler's scrapbook indicates that the Chorale must have sung for several other Masses, including a Mass for Archbishop Romolo Carboni, Apostolic Delegate to Australia and later Apostolic Nuncio to Peru and Italy, but no details are available.

In a letter in the Chorale files of this author, Father Schuler announces the 1968-69 season during which the group will begin working on *The Book with the Seven Seals*, a contemporary oratorio, written by Austrian composer Franz Schmidt and first performed in 1938. Father Schuler says that it calls for a large orchestra, pipe organ, six soloists and a large chorus that frequently splits into eight parts. This work was never performed by the Chorale. On April 2, 1969, the Chorale sang Dvořák's *Stabat Mater* at the Church of Saint Francis de Sales in Saint Paul, Minnesota. The concert was dedicated to the memory of Monsignor Walter H. Peters (1911-1967), former professor at the College of Saint Thomas.

On August 26, 1969, Father Schuler took up his duties as the eighth pastor of the Church of Saint Agnes, after the death of Monsignor Rudolph G. Bandas. This appointment brought the work of the Chorale more closely allied to that parish, an association that would be brought to fruition in the fall of 1974 when the Twin Cities Catholic Chorale began singing regularly at the 10:00 a.m. parish Latin High Mass. The press of Father Schuler's new duties perhaps explains why the pages in his Chorale scrapbook for 1970 and 1971 are blank. However, the Chorale files gathered by this author indicate that the Chorale sang the Michael Haydn *Requiem in C Minor* at a concert on November 23, 1969, as a part of the liturgical concert series organized by the Church of the Nativity of Our Lord. John Vanella was organist for the Chorale at this concert and is listed as the director of the Nativity Church Choir. The Chorale sang Dvořák's *Stabat Mater* on March 25, 1970, the Wednesday of Holy Week, at the Church of Saint Agnes. The performance was reviewed in the *Pioneer Press* by John Harvey. He commented: "The performance under Father Schuler's leadership had both reverence and tone, and fine balance was maintained among sections, soloists, and orchestra."

Some members of the Chorale flew to Dallas, Texas, in April 1970, where they sang a solemn Mass with the Dallas Catholic Choir at Saint Bernard's Church on Sunday, April 19. The Music Director of the Dallas Catholic Choir was Father Ralph S. March, O. Cist.

An article published by Jeffrey Tucker in *Crisis* magazine, August, 2013, helps put in perspective Monsignor Schuler's work from 1969 until the end of his career. Its title is self-explanatory: "The Hero of the Mighty Musical Struggle" (www.crisismagazine.com/2013/ the-hero-of-the-mighty-musical-struggle). In the article Tucker says, referring to

Monsignor Schuler:

> ...he is most known as the man who persisted in building and running the nation's most famous sacred music program following Vatican II....It was not easy for him. It's hard to imagine the scene in 1969 when he took over as pastor of Saint Agnes when he implemented his program. This was the Age of Aquarius....It took incredible conviction and courage in those days to continue singing Gregorian chant, Palestrina, William Byrd, Mozart, Haydn, and Schubert – Mass in the Roman and Viennese tradition at the same time that the world was slogging in the mud at Woodstock and the folk Mass was sweeping all before it.

It should be noted here that Monsignor Schuler inherited a parish where there had been a Latin High Mass every Sunday uninterrupted since its founding in 1887. The Latin High Mass celebrated *ad orientem* had never been replaced after Vatican II, nor had congregational singing in the vernacular been added to it although the other Masses at Saint Agnes were, and still are, said in English.

Tucker continues:

> He took the helm of the Church Music Association of America and kept publishing its journal *Sacred Music*. He trained young men in seminary. [Note: Or rather he met with seminarians at Saint Agnes in the evening, meetings that were not sanctioned by the seminary.]...He mentored musicians. He traveled to speak and teach. He would write for any publication that would print his words, and never seemed to doubt that people would someday come to their senses.

On Sunday, September 20, 1970, Father Schuler celebrated the 25th anniversary of his ordination to the priesthood at a solemn Mass at which His Excellency, Bishop Alphonse J. Schladweiler preached. The Twin Cities Catholic Chorale, joined by the Dallas Catholic Choir of Texas, formed a choir of 80 singers under the direction of Father Ralph S. March, O. Cist., director of the Dallas Catholic Choir, singing Anton Bruckner's *Mass in E Minor*. Dr. Paul Manz of Concordia College was organist. At the Mass, Bishop Schladweiler announced that Pope Paul VI had named Father Schuler an honorary prelate with the title of

Monsignor Johannes Overath, Cologne, Germany, presents the gold Orlando di Lasso medal (from the United Caecilian Societies of Germany, Austria, and Switzerland) to Monsignor Richard J. Schuler on December 27, 1973. Saint Agnes Parish Archives.

Monsignor. A special blessing was brought to Saint Paul by Monsignor Johannes Overath of Cologne, Germany, president of CIMS. The Bruckner *Mass in E Minor* was recorded live on that occasion.

The Chorale sang Beethoven's *Mass in C* for a pontifical Mass at Saint Agnes on June 19, 1971, as a part of the seventh annual National Wanderer Forum. During the 1971-72 season, members of the Chorale flew to Pueblo, Colorado, to sing a concert with the Pueblo Symphony Orchestra and Chorale under the direction of Gerhard Track.[18] The Chorale sang Guiseppi Verdi's *Quattro Pezzi Sacri (Four Sacred Pieces)* with the Pueblo Orchestra. On Sunday, April 16, the Chorale sang the *Mass in F Major* by Anton Bruckner at a Latin Mass at Sacred Heart Cathedral in Pueblo.

In October of 1972, members of the Chorale sang a High Mass at the Church of Saint Wenceslaus in New Prague, Minnesota, as part of the activities of a pilgrimage to the shrine of Our Lady of Fatima in Heidelberg, Minnesota. On November 2, 1972, the Chorale sang the Michael Haydn *Requiem* for the All Souls' Day Mass at the Church of Saint Agnes.

On December 27, 1973, the Chorale sang Joseph Haydn's *Mass in Time of War* or *Paukenmesse* at a Latin High Mass at the Church of Saint Agnes celebrating the centennial of the founding of the American Society of Saint Caecilia by Johann Singenberger and the establishment of the journal, *Caecilia. Sacred Music* magazine is a continuation of *Caecilia*, published since 1874. The Mass was offered by Monsignor Johannes Overath of Cologne, Germany, vice-president of the *Consociatio Internationalis Musicae Sacrae*, who also represented the Federated Caecilian Societies of the German-speaking countries. The Archbishop of Saint Paul and Minneapolis, The Most Reverend Leo Binz, and the Bishop of New Ulm, The Most Reverend Alphonse

J. Schladweiler, were present in the sanctuary. Father Ralph S. March, O.Cist., editor of *Sacred Music,* preached. Archbishop Binz read a congratulatory telegram from the Holy Father. The gold Lassus medal of the United Caecilian Societies of Germany, Austria and Switzerland was awarded to Monsignor Schuler, secretary of CMAA and vice-president of CIMS, for his devotion to the cause of sacred music and most particularly for his work as chairman of the Fifth International Church Music Congress in Chicago and Milwaukee in 1966.

Of note, the Society of Saint Caecilia (1874) and the Society of Saint Gregory (1913) which published *The Catholic Choirmaster* since 1915, became the Church Music Association of America in 1964. The event was described by this author in an article in *Sacred Music* (Vol.101, No.1, Spring 1974).

During the 1973-74 season, the Chorale made its preparations to travel to Europe in August of 1974, to represent the United States at the Sixth International Church Music Congress in Salzburg, Austria. There was much work to be done because the choir had to prepare its repertoire and also raise funds to lower the costs for the singers. In addition, Monsignor Schuler made several trips to Europe to set up arrangements for the Chorale. The fund raisers, the fact that a charter flight was arranged, that some of the lodging was in student residences or pilgrimage houses, and that some of the arrangements were done by Monsignor Schuler rather than a travel agent, made the pilgrimage quite affordable for the members of the Chorale.

The Twin Cities Catholic Chorale in the Saint Agnes Choir Loft, 1966. Monsignor Schuler is in the second row from the top on the right side. Mrs. Myron Angeletti, accompanist, is in the second row, second from the right (Photo by C.J. Larson, Saint Paul, Minnesota). Schuler Archives.

CHAPTER V

Europe and the Sixth International Church Music Congress Salzburg, Austria – 1974

Perhaps the best way to present the experience of this remarkable pilgrimage and participation in the Sixth International Church Music Congress in Salzburg, Austria, is to reprint several articles that were published in the Open Forum of *Sacred Music* (Vol. 101, No. 4, Winter 1974). They were written by Virginia Schubert, Monsignor Schuler, and William Pohl, and have the advantage of presenting the details from several different points of view and with an immediacy and attention to detail that cannot be re-captured. They are reprinted here with the permission of *Sacred Music*. It can be truly said that after we sang in Munich, the enthusiasm for setting up a schedule for the Chorale to sing with top flight professional musicians at the 10 a.m. Latin High Mass at the Church of Saint Agnes was spontaneous and was shared by many members of the group.

Souvenirs of an Historic Pilgrimage – Part I – By Virginia Schubert

On August 10, 1974, 180 Americans landed at the Cologne, Germany, airport to begin a truly unusual European visit. The group included some 90 singers from the Twin Cities Catholic Chorale and the Dallas Catholic Choir, their relatives, friends, and other members of CMAA who wished to join in the musical and spiritual pilgrimage which was to wend its way in four blue buses through Germany and Italy to its final destination of Salzburg, Austria, and the Sixth International Church Music Congress sponsored by CIMS.

The purpose of this article is not to give a detailed account of the whole trip, but rather to share some treasured memories with the readers of this journal. Even in the early planning stages, we called this three-week trip a pilgrimage, and in retrospect, I believe that term to be the most accurate description of our stay in Europe. Of course, the journey did include sight-seeing, shopping, parties, and relaxation (rather little of the latter, at least for the singers and organizers), but our voyage had the *raison d'être* and spiritual dimension of a true pilgrimage. Through the daily High Masses, celebrated in the Roman Rite, sung in the common tongue of Latin and in the musical styles of many periods, the singers and accompanying pilgrims came to understand what it means to belong to the universal Church. Even though we could not communicate adequately in the vernacular with the local congregations who worshipped with us, we experienced the bond of a common faith expressed in a universal liturgy. We also felt united with the historical church: with the early Christians who, like us, sang chant as they worshipped in the catacombs; with the choirs who, too, sang a Palestrina Mass in the Basilica of Saint Peter in Rome, where that composer himself had been choirmaster; and with hundreds of thousands who also have been inspired to prayer by the music of Haydn, Mozart, and Bruckner.

Our first High Mass in Europe was in the Cologne Cathedral on Sunday, August 11th. The combined Twin Cities and Dallas choirs sang Palestrina's *Hexachord Mass,* and the *Schola* chanted the Gregorian Propers as they would for Masses each day. The Most Reverend Alphonse J. Schladweiler, Bishop of New Ulm, Minnesota, who was traveling with us, celebrated the Mass and preached in the German language. We were awed by the privilege that was ours of contributing to the solemnity of the Sunday High Mass in the famous and impressive Kölner Dom. After Mass we were greeted by Cardinal Hoeffner and Monsignor Overath, chairman of the Congress, who presented us each with its official emblem, bearing the initials of the sponsoring society, CIMS.

Thus, signed with the symbol of our pilgrimage, we continued to Munich where we celebrated the feast of the Assumption in the style of Catholic Bavaria. On the eve of the feast of the Assumption, we traveled to the lovely resort town of Tegernsee, south of Munich, to sing Bruckner's *Mass in E Minor.* The Baroque church was crowded with vacationers for the early evening anticipated Mass. Later they would animate the town's open air restaurants and cafés to watch the scheduled fireworks over the lake, but during the Mass they remained in reverent, prayerful silence, neither rustling papers, nor scraping chairs, not even seeming to move. The only sound was that of the choir and the ancient organ praising God with the solemn music of Bruckner.

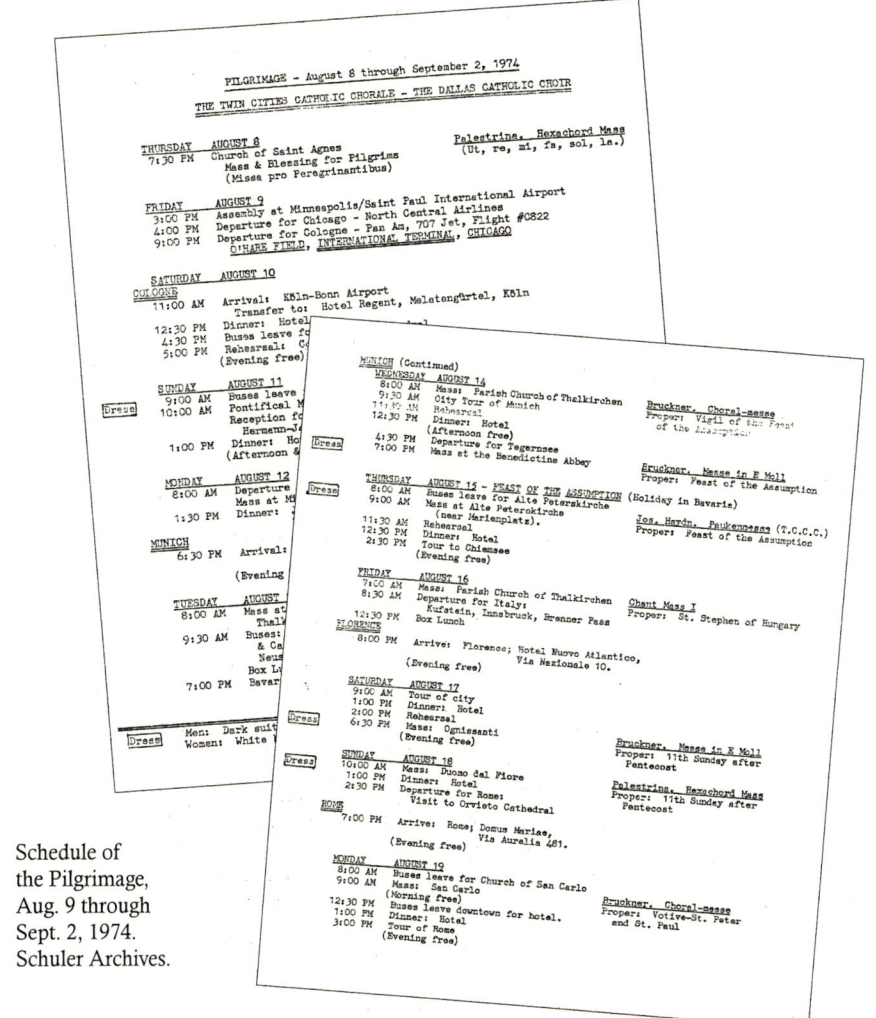

Schedule of the Pilgrimage, Aug. 9 through Sept. 2, 1974. Schuler Archives.

The next morning, August 15th, the Twin Cities Catholic Chorale sang the *Paukenmesse* of Joseph Haydn in the Alte Peterskirche in central Munich, accompanied by members of the Munich Symphony Orchestra. The beautiful Baroque interior of the Alte Peterskirche corresponded with the style of Haydn to make a glorious unity. The sanctuary was bedecked for the feast with a garland of greens hung from the ceiling, and on the altar were massive silver candlesticks, alternating with huge bouquets of gladioli. During Mass from my place in the back row of the choir I could see none of this, but only the clouds of incense mingling with the rays of the morning sun which filtered through the sanctuary windows to play on the gold decoration of the Baroque baldaquin. Although I have seen many exquisite Baroque churches during my dozen or so trips through Europe, I have never felt a fuller awareness of the appropriateness of the Baroque as an expression of religious belief than in that experience where form, space, light and sound were united to inspire worship.

The *Agnus Dei* is the part of the *Paukenmesse* that I prefer. However, sometimes the relentless beat of the tympani, as the choir sings *Dona nobis pacem*, seems to express to me a desperate cry for a peace that will be realized in this world only with difficulty, if at all. That day in Munich, as I left the Alte Peterskirche to hurry in the warm sunshine with countless others to attend another Mass (for on any Sunday or feast day in downtown Munich there is in every church a fine High Mass sung by an excellent choir, so that one has the impression that the whole city is praising God with the finest works of man's creation), the world seemed more optimistic, and I believed that God would certainly answer our entreaties, granting us both the absence of war and peace of soul.

For a Catholic, no pilgrimage to Europe is complete without Rome, a papal audience, and a visit to Saint Peter's Basilica. Italy greeted us with 104-degree heat, but with the proper siestas, the afternoon breeze from the sea and our stubborn determination, we carried on our full program for Rome which included an audience with the Holy Father at Castel Gandolfo and Mass at Saint Peter's on the feast of Saint Pius X. The new audience hall at Castel Gandolfo is airy and full of light. We arrived rather early, passed the Swiss Guard on duty and were ushered to our excellent places by the dignified papal staff dressed in formal black morning coats. We spent the time before the audience singing for the assembled pilgrims, alternating with other groups from all over the world. During an audience, the Holy Father acknowledges each group present. When we were announced, we sang the *Rex Pacificus* of Hermann Schroeder as our tribute to Paul VI.

In the afternoon of the same day, we went to Saint Peter's to sing the Palestrina *Hexachord Mass*. We marched in solemn procession, single file, down the center of the mighty nave dressed in our formal attire, women in long black skirts and white blouses, men in dark suits.

Our Mass was in the chapel of the Blessed Sacrament, with its stately interior of marble and bronze. As we sang, more and more people joined us in the chapel. Later some Americans who had also been at the audience that morning told us that they had heard our singing when they were high in the dome of the basilica and had come down immediately to attend our Mass. Although we had realized as we were singing that the chapel had very good acoustics, we thought it was quite closed off and so we were surprised to learn that the sound of our music had quite literally floated into all corners of that great basilica, up into the dome, into the side chapels and the transept and that large area behind the main altar which is in itself the size of a large church. After Mass we walked directly across the nave to the tomb of Saint Pius X where we sang several motets to mark his feast.

The last week of our pilgrimage, which was given over to the Congress, began with a pre-Congress celebration of the 150th anniversary of the birth of Anton Bruckner in his city of Linz, Austria.

Twin Cities Catholic Chorale and the Dallas Catholic Choir singing Palestrina's *Hexachord Mass* on August 25, 1974 in the Old Cathedral of Linz, Austria. Monsignor Schuler is directing (Photo from the Diocese of Linz; taken by Rudolf Mair). Schuler Archives.

The American and Polish choirs were honored by being asked to participate in the anniversary activities in recognition of the great sacrifices and difficulties involved in their respective trips. As a special tribute to Bruckner, the American choirs joined the Linzer Domchor under the direction of Monsignor Joseph Kronsteiner in singing the *E Minor Mass* in the church where Bruckner himself had been choirmaster.

The direct lineage of choir, choirmaster and place seemed to give this performance a more authentic quality than others, although I believe that it would be hard to match that of Tegernsee. After Mass we all went to the extraordinarily beautiful Baroque abbey of Saint Florian to participate in a concert in the church where Bruckner is buried. There was an organ recital on the instrument Bruckner himself had played, and the American choirs sang *Locus Iste* by Bruckner. We then all went down to the crypt to the actual site of Bruckner's tomb. There the Polish choirs sang with great emotion several Marian hymns because it was a national feast of the Blessed Virgin.

Our stay in Salzburg and our participation in the Congress were quite different from the events of the preceding two weeks. Most obvious was the fact that we settled down in one place for an extended period of time. Our four blue buses left us to return to the Rhineland, and we entered into the rhythm of life in a European city alive with tourists attending the Salzburg festival, and with the Congress participants. We sang often, presenting American music as a part of the Congress program – a new hymn in Latin by Paul Manz called *Hymnus Redemptorum* for a Eucharistic service, an Offertory verse by Paul Manz, "Praise the Lord for He is Good" for a Mass in many languages and the very impressive *Missa Internationalis* by Noel Goemanne, but we also listened to the special concerts, Masses and lectures of the Congress program. We also had time to renew friendships formed at the Fifth International Congress in Chicago-Milwaukee.

One of the most striking experiences of the week for me was the performance by the Twin Cities Catholic Chorale of the Michael Haydn *Requiem in C Minor* at the pilgrimage church of Maria Plain high on a promontory outside the city of Salzburg. The Mass was planned as a memorial to the Americans who died in the two World Wars, and the overcast sky, heavy clouds and subdued light as we climbed the hill and entered the church seemed to heighten the solemnity of the occasion. The church itself, because of its size and exquisite decoration, can only be described as a Rococo treasure. It was built to house a famous picture of the Blessed Virgin. In 1779, Mozart wrote the *Coronation Mass* to commemorate the occasion when that picture was enshrined in a silver jeweled crown. I think we were all surprised at the number of Congress participants and others who made the rather inconvenient trip by taxi, bus or private car from the city to attend this *Requiem*.

Once again Bishop Schladweiler pontificated, assisted by the priests traveling with us. The servers were also men from our pilgrimage who had formed a very dignified and experienced ceremony crew for our daily High Masses. By this time I was suffering from laryngitis, but I have decided that my malady was fortuitous because it allowed me to listen and observe. I shall never forget the moment when, at the first solemn notes of choir and orchestra coming from the second gallery, I turned around to see the procession enter the main door of the church amid clouds of incense. The ministers of the Mass wore eighteenth century Roman style vestments heavily embroidered in gold, red and a rich blue that matched the interior decoration of the church. When they reached the sanctuary, there was a striking harmony between the vestments and the huge bouquets of flowers which were in the same colors as the flowers worked into the vestments themselves. It was a most moving occasion – meditative, reverent, but not sad. As we left the church after Mass, the clouds lifted slightly, and the city of Salzburg was bathed in a pale sunset. It was a magic moment.

Part II – By Monsignor Richard J. Schuler

The Sixth International Church Music Congress in Salzburg was the third of these great international gatherings of church musicians I have attended. I was in Cologne in 1961 and in Chicago-Milwaukee in 1966. Each meeting has been quite different from the others. Cologne was tremendous with ten solid days of liturgy, concerts, lectures, new music, old music, an endless variety with all the attractions of the historical Rhineland – the Romanesque churches, the mighty Kölner Dom, Maria Laach Abbey, the Rhine itself. In Chicago-Milwaukee, I was chairman of the Congress, so the things I remember are the thousand problems that needed immediate attention, beginning with an abbot who lost his glasses, the European razors that wouldn't work on American electrical current, schedules, time factors and a thousand other matters each minute!

Salzburg was for me a total delight. It was leisurely in a truly Austrian way. While the program was filled to the brim, the compact size of the city allowed for lectures, concerts and liturgical events within easy walking distances. The variety of the offerings was astonishing. The hospitality of the Austrians was a true pleasure. The week flew by, but no one ever felt hurried.

The organizational work was extraordinarily well done. Chief credit must go to Monsignor Johannes Overath, chairman of the Congress and newly elected president of CIMS. His logical and fertile mind and imagination were responsible for the program in every aspect. Truly it was his creation, and achieving of unity amid variety is his special talent. Not one event was without purpose in the overall plan. The months of preparation, together with the obligation of finding financial resources, put a heavy burden on a man with so many other responsibilities. It can rightly be maintained that without Monsignor Overath there would have been no Congress in Salzburg. To him goes the greatest praise for a truly marvelous event that was brought off without defect. Cologne in 1961, of which he was also chairman, was greater, but Salzburg was tailored to the needs of 1974.

Mention must be made also of our vice-president of CMAA, Father Robert A. Skeris, who acted as Monsignor Overath's right hand. He spent many months in preparation for the Congress and, in particular, preparing for the American participants. His genius for organization and detail, accuracy and precision, has long been established by his part in the Milwaukee Congress in 1966. Without his endless effort, the tour of the American choirs could never have been possible. In Salzburg, Herr Joseph Bogensberger worked heroically to insure a smooth operation along with the other members of the local committee.

As I look back at the week, the events that flash before my mind take me up the mountain to the Nonnberg where the Benedictine Sisters chanted Vespers, or to the Cathedral and Mozart's *Requiem Mass* sung by the Domchor, or again to the Collegiate Church where we listened to an impeccable performance of Monteverdi's *Marian Vespers* with the Aachener Domchor standing beneath the gloriously Baroque carving of Our Lady being assumed into heaven. There was, too, the sadness that one could not help but feel for the Polish choirs who shortly had to return to their land beyond the Iron Curtain; but there was too the joy of seeing so many old friends, many of whom had been in the United States in 1966: Professor Jean-Pierre Schmit from Luxembourg, Monsignor Joseph Kronsteiner from Linz, and his brother Hermann, Joseph Lennards of Holland, Canon René Lenaerts of Louvain, Monsignor Franz Kosch of Vienna, Monsignor Wilfrid Purney of London, Father Lopez-Calo from Spain, Padre Mola from Quito, Ecuador, Abbot Urbanus of Maria Laach, and Professors

Chailley of the Sorbonne, Fellerer of Cologne, and Namura of Japan. Choirs came from all over Europe; scholars were present from every continent. Cardinals, archbishops, and other prelates represented many lands.

One afternoon during the Congress, we went to the pilgrimage church of Maria Plain on a mountain overlooking the city of Salzburg. The day was overcast and the clouds hung low giving a mysterious lighting to the churches and buildings of the city that lay at our feet. Bishop Schladweiler celebrated a Pontifical Mass of Requiem for all those who fell in World War II. We sang Michael Haydn's beautiful *Requiem* with orchestra, high up in the second balcony of that gorgeous Rococo church. The rich, brocaded vestments, the music of Haydn, the fading light of the late afternoon and the throng of people who filled the church made it a scene I shall not soon forget.

Another brief episode lingers in memory. I got up early Sunday morning, celebrated Mass at the student house where we were staying, and then caught a bus for the city center. I climbed up the Nonnberg to the convent of the Benedictines, famous from the *Sound of Music* performances, to attend a Mass celebrated in the Byzantine Rite.

The ancient church was only dimly lighted and there were few worshippers that early. I found a place and for an hour, I think I truly communed with God by means of an ancient liturgy celebrated in a language I do not know and with ritual movements I am only vaguely familiar with, adorned with a musical idiom quite foreign to my training. But these instruments of the sacred spoke to me and transcended time and place to move me toward God. Many of the convictions I have long held on Latin, chant, ritual, and participation were deepened that Sunday morning on the Nonnberg. But then I had to hasten down to the Cathedral to take part in a Mass in Various Languages. Somehow I did not find in it what I experienced on the Nonnberg.

The week brought us lectures that we should transmit to church musicians in this country. Then there were organ recitals in beautiful Rococo halls and choral concerts in Baroque and Gothic churches. There was an advisory election for the new CIMS officers who will be appointed by the Holy See. There were formal receptions and many delightful hours with friends at less formal occasions in the *weinkellerei* and restaurants. In a word, Salzburg was a Catholic congress in every sense. A Catholic spirit pervaded every facet of those days. One sensed that even with all the differences of the post-Vatican Church, the fundamentals remain the same. They remain Catholic and can be shared by men from all parts of the Church universal who see clearly.

Part III – By William F. Pohl

The 1974 European Tour of the combined Twin Cities Catholic Chorale and the Dallas Catholic Choir was not merely a concert tour; it was a genuine pilgrimage, for, in addition to our publicized performances we visited each day a number of churches and shrines. Among the important relics we venerated were the corporal of Orvieto, Saint Peter's chains, the instruments of the Passion, and the tombs of Saint Francis and Saint Clara. At each of these places we offered our private prayers, but since we formed a well-rehearsed choir with months of preparation behind us, we were able in addition to offer together a sung Mass of a high artistic level, or at least a fine motet. The focus of each day's activity was this sung Mass, on Sundays and feasts with large local congregations, but on ordinary weekdays often with only ourselves present.

At each of our Masses, the Gregorian Proper was sung in full (except on three or four occasions when it was necessary for practical reasons to omit the Gradual) by a *schola* consisting of Monsignor Richard J. Schuler, Dr. William P. Mahrt, and this writer. On ferial days, we sang votive Masses appropriate to the place, including Masses in honor of the Blessed Virgin Mary, Saint Michael the Archangel, Saint John the Baptist, the Holy Apostles Peter and Paul, and many more saints. In all, we sang sixteen distinct proper cycles, which required the preparation of more than seventy individual pieces.

To return to the story of our trip, I might mention the interest with which we explored the acoustics of the great churches of Europe, acoustics the like of which are rarely found in this country. Though three of us sang the chant, we had come to a clear understanding about the rhythm, so that we were able to sing confidently and freely and thus fill even the cathedrals of Cologne and Florence with a sufficiency of sound. In general the Gothic churches seemed best suited to the chant, their fine reverberation enhancing and emphasizing the intrinsic harmony of the melodic lines, mentioned above, without muddying it. The Baroque churches with their soft plaster interiors have acoustics more like a fine concert hall, perfect for, say, a Mozart Mass. The paintings and plaster statues of the latter churches, when considered as individual works of art, are perhaps lacking in interest. But when complemented by the proper music and ceremonial they seem almost to come alive.

In the Upper Basilica of Saint Francis in Assisi, where we sang a votive Mass of Saint Francis, our chant sounded perhaps best of all.... At the Cistercian church of Santa Croce in Rome, we sang Cistercian chant on the feast of Saint Bernard. After celebrating the feast of Saint Pius X with Mass in Saint Peter's in Rome, we went over to pray before his glass-enclosed reliquary. These are experiences I shall never forget.

- - -

There was also an article on the pilgrimage of the Twin Cities Catholic Chorale and the Dallas Catholic Choir, "American Choirs on Pilgrimage" in the English edition of *L'Osservatore Romano*, October 3, 1974.

COMMENTARY

The Twin Cities Catholic Chorale and the World Church

Every member and supporter of the Twin Cities Catholic Chorale, past and present, is well aware that the group's founder, Monsignor Richard J. Schuler (1920-2007), had before his eyes a very clear purpose which motivated his lifelong efforts as musician and priest. It was a goal set before him by his priestly mentor, Father Francis A. Missia (1884-1955), who in turn had received it from the German-Austrian Caecilian reform movement, which influenced the pastoral renewal initiated by St. Pius X in 1903. In the words of the Caecilian founder Father Franz X. Witt (1834-1888): "Our only desire is to carry out in practice the wishes of Holy Mother Church regarding music."

Since its earliest days, the Church has always had to struggle to guarantee the sacredness of its music.[1] In the sixteenth century, the decrees of the Council of Trent marked an important milestone in the progress of Catholic worship and its music. Though the passing years have brought changes, that Council's basic forms and principles remained alive into the twentieth century. Throughout the history of the Catholic Church, the central question affecting the development of church music has been the relation of music to its liturgical function. This relation has varied over time. One of the last great "generalists" of musicology (friend and mentor of this author), proposed three broad divisions of this development.

Music *of* worship denotes the growth of musical expression with and out of the liturgical forms themselves, exemplified by *cantus gregorianus*. Music *for* worship recalls the increasing independence of a musical art which went its own way in the effort to enhance the inner liturgical expression through musical means, an effort which continued approximately up to the time of the late Middle Ages (*ars antiqua* c.a.1170-1310). And music *at* worship indicates the growing influence of secular music with its subjective art of expression and an emotional creativity which perhaps reached its high point during the Baroque era in the years between the late Renaissance and early Classical periods of music history, roughly 1600-1750.[2] There followed the Enlightenment era, with its effects and consequences.

The *Motu proprio* of 1903 and subsequent papal directives concerning *musica sacra* repeated and confirmed the prescriptions of Trent. The "Tridentine" understanding of the theocentric direction of the Church's public worship continued to mature and develop. Activation of the worshipping community in the liturgy (in contrast to private devotions during public worship) became the chief concern of the liturgical movement which – already begun in the nineteenth century by Abbot Guéranger, carried forward musically by the restoration of Gregorian chant and the Caecilian societies, promoted by outstanding figures such as Pius Parsch in German-speaking countries – grew increasingly important. Various tendencies, in different directions and with contrasting views, struggled to fulfill the tasks outlined by Saint Pius X. But there remained a great continuity regarding the nature of solemn public worship and the *musica sacra*, which is one of its constituent elements, as is evident in these words of a missionary bishop on the American frontier:

> In this communion of truth and grace God is everything and man is drawn and enabled by Him to perform those inward acts of adoration, praise and thanksgiving by which God is glorified and Man sanctified. The outward form of these acts is truly sacramental, indicating as well as producing communion with God.[3]

This conviction also motivated Saint Pius X, whose basic theological principles are the basis of the sixth chapter of the Liturgy Constitution promulgated by the last Council. As one of the Fathers of that Sacred Synod put it, in terms of activity or behaviour (*quoad actionem*), *musica sacra* is *ancilla liturgiae*, a handmaiden with a ministerial role to fulfill. But in terms of its essence (*quoad naturam*), *musica sacra* is and must remain an art "which exhibits the Divine in material forms." In the words of Vatican II, as *cantus sacer qui verbis inhaeret*, (holy chant which inheres in words), sacred music is indeed *pars necessaria vel integralis liturgiae sollemnis* (a necessary or integral part of the solemn liturgy) (*SC*, n.12).[4]

Under the leadership of Monsignor Schuler, the Twin Cities Catholic Chorale played a not insignificant role in the concerted effort of Catholic church musicians to realize in practice the general statements of goals and ideals articulated by the *Vaticanum Secundum* (1962-1965) by taking an active part in the great international church music congresses at Milwaukee/Chicago in 1966 and Salzburg in 1974.

The history of the Twin Cities Catholic Chorale reminds us that the 1966 Congress convened "in the midst of the controversies over various interpretations of the Second Vatican Council,..." though many participants were not fully aware of "how crucial this moment was in the Church." This international gathering, fifth in the series of international church music congresses initiated at Rome in 1950 by the great Catalan musicologist Monsignor Higinio Anglés Pamies (1888-1969), came soon after the conclusion of the last Council, as the first and greatest "opportunity to demonstrate the implementation" of Chapter 6 of *Sacrosanctum Concilium*, the conciliar liturgy constitution. The valuable documentation contained in this history of the Chorale has a back story which clarifies the significance for the Chorale of the Fifth International Church Music Congress, in particular the public manifestations and liturgical celebrations in Milwaukee.

It is but natural that since it is the Mystical Body of Christ, the Roman Catholic Church is organized in a manner basically hierarchical, head and members participating to varying degrees in the Sacrifice of Christ the High Priest. "Hieratic or sacerdotal – this is the fundamental qualification of the office which the Church fulfills between God and man" (H. Clérissac, OP). The highest instances in this hierarchy (Supreme Pontiff, ecumenical council in solemn dogmatic definitions) normally promulgate *altiora principia*, basic general principles which form an overarching framework for belief and action. A lower instance or authority (e.g., episcopal conferences, departments of the Roman Curia) then specifies these general norms to the level of particular directives to be followed in practice. These can take different forms, as "instructions" or "directories" or "general introductions" to liturgical books, for example. All are "implementation" directives, whereby it is obvious that the lower instance cannot countermand the higher. If practical norms contradict the basic legal framework, or are not contained therein, they are invalid.

One of the consequences of the conciliar statements concerning the makeup of the Church's hierarchy and the relationship of primatial as against collegial or conciliar authority was the *Motu proprio* of Paul VI concerning the *commissiones postconciliares* (post-conciliar commissions) dated January 3, 1966.[5] By its very nature, this document is clearly and indisputably distinct from the opinions developed at the Council, thereby formally reasserting the preeminence of primatial authority over collegial or conciliar power, contrary to the hopes of progressivist or anti-Roman circles who wished to see in the last Council a return to the synodal form of governance in the Church Universal.[6] The expansions of the church hierarchy induced at Vatican II were, formally considered, four: "collegiality" of the bishops; the synod of bishops; new-style episcopal conferences; and the post-conciliar commissions.

"Collegiality" does not affect authority over the entire Church, because the decisive basis for collaboration in policy formation at that level is membership of the *hierarchia ratione jurisdictionis* (hierarchy by reason of jurisdiction), and not membership *ratione ordinis* (by reason of order), by reason of ordination alone. Hierarchical ranking and activity is founded not on the *ratio ordinis* (reason of order), but the *ratio jurisdictionis* (reason of jurisdiction), of which the highest degree is the primatial jurisdiction of the Supreme Pontiff, with his *plenitudo potestatis* (fullness or plenitude of power).

According to the progressivists' plans for change, the synod of bishops was not so much a normative limitation of papal authority as an antithesis or counterweight to one of the chief levels of church government: the (curial) cardinals. To the extent that the synod of bishops assumes the functions of the curial cardinals and the dicasteries they lead, a transition will take place from a homogeneous to a pluralistic preparation of universal directives, even though the results will always remain a compromise between local interests or needs and those of the Church Universal.

The Cardinals who lead the Congregations of the Curia are the principal instruments which the Pope uses to exercise his primacy. This is why the progressivist conciliar party opposed the Curia Romana, and the result of their opposition was the creation by Paul VI of a new structure of 12 post-conciliar offices parallel to the curial Congregations, whose competence was thereby limited to pre-conciliar directives. What might be called (with a grain of salt) the "anti-curia" received a monopoly over post-conciliar matters, excluding the Curia by and large from the interpretation and implementation of conciliar decrees. *Musica sacra* thus fell within the remit of the Commission or Council for the Implementation of the Conciliar Constitution on the Liturgy headed by Lazarist Father Hannibal Bugnini.

The tactics of this group[7] illustrate the important fact that no one can prove that the majority of post-conciliar stipulations regarding liturgy and *musica sacra* are valid conclusions which follow necessarily from the pertinent conciliar texts; for instance, article 50 of the Liturgy Constitution says that the order of Mass is to be examined with a view to facilitating the pious and active participation of the faithful, among other things. The First Implementation of 1964[8] regards this as justification for allowing joint recitation of the Lord's Prayer by priest and people (n.58G). A few years later, the Instruction *"Musicam sacram"* of 1974[9] transforms this "permission" into the rule (n.31 = *convenienter pro-fertur*, i.e., suitably or conformably brought forth). But the actual text of the Council in fact says nothing about the permissibility or the appropriateness of chanting or reciting the Lord's Prayer in common. Though such details were to be decided by experts, the opinion of the *liturgisti* on this point is far from unanimous. In other words, the party in favor of common recitation carried the day within the Bugnini Council. Had the other group prevailed, then the implementation Instruction would have contained the opposite norm. And so any assertion that community recitation of the *Pater Noster* is the will of "the Council," is, at the very least, impossible of proof.

It was precisely to prevent or at least mitigate where possible more such manipulations that during the long gestation period of the Instruction *"Musicam sacram,"* the 1966 Church Music Congress was convoked. That it achieved its goal in important areas is clear from n. 34/1-2 of the Instruction regarding polyphonic settings of the *Ordinarium Missae*.[10]

The participation of the Twin Cities Catholic Chorale in the Sixth International Church Music Congress at Salzburg in 1974 took place in a context which differed from that of the years immediately following Vatican II, though there were similarities as well. At Salzburg the motto was, *Conservare et promovere* – preserving the legacy of *musica sacra* whilst encouraging congregational singing "with every means available." The letter of greeting sent by Cardinal Villot on behalf of

Pope Paul VI to Archbishop Karl Berg of Salzburg (himself a former Cathedral choir boy), explained the purpose of the Congress in these words:

> For in accordance with the stipulations of the Second Vatican Council the liturgical celebrations are being given new forms, which accommodate the understanding and the active participation of the faithful. Congregational singing is one of the most appropriate ways of promoting this participation.... But congregational singing, which must bespeak strength, beauty and devotion, is indispensable at vernacular liturgical celebrations since this is the most widely used form of celebration for the majority of the faithful.[11]

The Twin Cities Catholic Chorale and the Dallas Catholic Choir, singly and jointly, presented a noteworthy American response to this new challenge in Salzburg when they premiered new compositions for choir and congregation in Latin and English commissioned from Paul Manz (1919-2009), *Hymnus Redemptorum* on texts from the Apocalypse, and the Offertory "Praise the Lord for He is Good" from the votive Mass for Justice and Peace, as well as Noel Goemanne (1926-2010), *Missa Internationalis*.

And so, as it marks forty years' residence at the Church of Saint Agnes, the Twin Cities Catholic Chorale can be proud indeed of its accomplishments for the cause of the praying Church and her *musica sacra*, a music worthy of the God we worship, accomplishments which have had a salutary effect far beyond the boundaries of Frogtown. May the Chorale carry on its noble apostolate by taking its pitch from God and singing together, with one voice, through Jesus Christ, *Christus Musicus*, the Divine Singer!

Reverend Robert A. Skeris
Director, Centre for Ward Method Studies
Benjamin T. Rome School of Music
The Catholic University of America, Washington, D.C.

ENDNOTES

1. J. Gelineau (tr. C. Howell), *Voices and Instruments in Catholic Worship*, (Collegeville 1964) 47/52.

2. K.G.Fellerer (tr. F. Brunner), *History of Catholic Church Music*, (Baltimore 1961).

3. See J. Singenberger, *Guide in Catholic Church Music* (Milwaukee: H. Zahn & Co., 1891) *Caput XIII de cantu sacra*, p. vi, citing Martin Marty, OSB, Bishop of Dakota.

4. The distinction is that of Dom Jaime de Barros Camara (1894-1971), Cardinal Archbishop of Sao Sebastiao de Rio de Janeiro 1943/71. On November 12, 1962, he explained in the aula of St Peter's that it is imprecise to speak of *musica sacra* solely as "handmaiden of the liturgy." He pointed out that church music is the *ancilla liturgiae quoad actionem* but not *quoad naturam*. Cited by J. Overath in R. Skeris (ed. and tr.), "Crux et Cithara" *MuSaMel 2*," (Altötting 1983) 73/84, here 75.

5. Text in *AAS* 58 (1966) 37/40.

6. For a detailed analysis of this situation as described here, see H. Barion, *Das Zweite Vatikanische Konzil*, Kanonistischer Bericht : Der Staat 5 (1966), 341/52, now H. Barion (ed. W. Bockenforde), Kirche und Kirchenrecht (Paderborn 1984) 538/49, here 544/8.

7. On this see the canonistic analysis of Gg. May, "Remarks on Ecclesiastical Legislation after the Second Vatican Council with Special Attention to Liturgy and Church Music," in R. Skeris (ed. and tr.), "Crux et Cithara" (FN 4) 129/55, here 131/2.

8. Text in *AAS* 56 (1964) 877/900.

9. Text in *AAS* 59 (1967) 300/20.

10. Thus H. Flatten, On the Legal Situation of *Musica Sacra* after the Second Vatican Council: "Crux et Cithara" (FN 6) 108/21, here 119/20.

11. On the papal letter and the three chief themes of the Congress aimed at carrying out the Pontiff's wishes, see J. Overath (ed.), *Conservare et Promovere*, Proceedings Congress Salzburg 1974, (Roma: CIMS, 1974) 7/9, 18/20 tr. R. Skeris.

COMMENTARY
Salzburg and the Twin Cities Catholic Chorale

The fortieth anniversary of the residence of the Twin Cities Catholic Chorale at Saint Agnes Church is the occasion of reflections on this history. The most evident fact is that this project is the extremely successful project of Monsignor Richard Schuler. Not only did he establish and cultivate it for decades, but he also provided for its continuation after himself. It thrives today as one of the most noted institutions of the liturgical employment of concerted Masses in our country, indeed, in the world.

Monsignor Schuler was a triple-threat as a pastor. He was an accomplished musician, having completed a PhD dissertation in musicology on Giovanni Maria Nanino and having taught music at the college level. He was a noted practical liturgist, in the sense that he understood the integration of all of the elements of the liturgy – music, architecture, ceremony, vestments, preaching – in the Solemn High Mass of the tradition and in the Mass in the new rite "celebrated solemnly in song, with the assistance of sacred ministers and the active participation of the people" (*Constitution on the Sacred Liturgy*, n.113). And he was an accomplished pastoral theologian, especially in sermons that approached every aspect of Catholic life deeply and pointedly.

Schuler was known for his patronage of seminarians, and over the years there was often a first Mass celebrated at Saint Agnes by a newly ordained priest who had been fostered by the Monsignor. One such seminarian was Alexander Sample, who has recently been appointed Archbishop of Portland, and whose compelling address to the recent Colloquium of the Church Music Association of America was a sensation; one sees the line of sound liturgical theology from Missia through Schuler to Sample.

I came to know Monsignor Schuler through William Pohl. Pohl was professor in the department of mathematics at Stanford University and founded the Gregorian chant choir at Saint Ann Chapel, the Newman Center for Stanford. As a new graduate student at Stanford and by a providential set of circumstances, I was present at the first rehearsal of this choir. After a year, Pohl was appointed to the mathematics department at the University of Minnesota and left me to direct the choir; I am still directing it after fifty years.

After Monsignor Schuler was appointed pastor at Saint Agnes, Bill Pohl soon discovered this kindred spirit and eventually came to assist with the liturgy at Saint Agnes, singing and directing chant Propers for the High Mass. During the feasts following Christmas, I and a few other singers would gather each year to sing Mass, Vespers, and Compline at Saint Agnes. One year I joined them for the entire Holy Week as well. Sometimes I would stay with Pohl, but other times, another singer would be staying with him, and I would be housed in the rectory at Saint Agnes; this meant, above all else, breakfast with Monsignor Schuler. This was not an occasion for idle chit-chat, but rather for the most intense discussion of topics of mutual interest, particularly those touching on music and liturgy.

Schuler's views on these subjects were comprehensive, trenchant, and logical. He saw the intimate link between beauty and the sacred in the liturgy. He had been on the American bishops' committee on music, when, in an ill-fated meeting in the '60s, this committee voted to approve the use of "folk music," which was just beginning to be employed in the liturgy. His own bishop was on the committee and voted for the proposition. Schuler reported that the bishop later admitted that this had been a mistake. The issue was the sacred; folk music had essentially secular connotations. This was different from times past, when secular idioms were incorporated into music that retained its basically sacred style. Indeed, the crux of the link between beauty and the sacred in the liturgy was music. The musical liturgy had the force to assist the worshipper as a member of the Body of Christ actively to participate in the transcendent action of offering sacrifice to the Father, something so crucially more important than the popular notion of "active participation."

In 1973, Monsignor Johannes Overath joined the Christmas-week festivities. He was chairman of the organizing committee of the upcoming international congress on sacred music, and he had come to discuss the participation of the American contingent. Father Ralph March, O.Cist., whose choir would participate, was also present. This was a group which shared deep and fundamental views, and the preparations for the congress were intermixed with discussions of the principles of music and liturgy, as well as with much jovial conviviality.

So in August, 1974, the Twin Cities Catholic Chorale led by Monsignor Schuler and the Dallas Catholic Choir led by Father March, went on pilgrimage to Salzburg and the International Congress of Sacred Music there. (We flew from Detroit to Cologne, and I will never forget hearing the announcement in the Detroit airport that President Nixon had just resigned.) The pilgrimage began at Cologne and progressed through Munich, Rome, Florence, Assisi, and then to Salzburg, singing a High Mass in a famous church each day. The Chorales would sing a polyphonic or concerted Ordinary and Bill Pohl and I would sing the Propers in Gregorian chant. The German part of the pilgrimage was accompanied by Bishop Alphonse Schladweiler, former pastor of Saint Agnes and retired bishop of New Ulm. The presence of a bishop with us opened doors that we would not have otherwise had. I remember at a Benedictine Abbey in Germany, a monk eagerly running to find the crosier which they kept just for such an occasion. Bishop Schladweiler was of German extraction, and so for the Sunday High Mass at Cologne Cathedral, he preached in German. Monsignor Overath saw to it that they rang all the bells that morning, something otherwise reserved for major feast days. The Chorale sang the Palestrina *Mass Ut, Re, Mi, Fa, Sol, La*, a work in six voice parts. The acoustics of Cologne Cathedral are complex; there is a great length and height with side aisles through which the sound echoes back and forth. This provided the Gregorian chant with its own kind of polyphony, with the melodies attractively returning upon themselves; but it was too much for the Palestrina – six parts returning upon themselves made for quite a mélange.

When we got to Rome, we sang in Saint Peter's Basilica. Our Mass was in the Blessed Sacrament Chapel, a large room of Renaissance proportions, and there the same Palestrina Mass sounded perfectly. Saint Peter's was accustomed to many such pilgrimages, and did not go out of its way to provide for them. Monsignor complained that there were better vestments to be had at Saint Peter's after the sack of Rome.

The culmination of the trip was for the whole troupe to attend the Church Music Congress and sing for Masses there. Monsignor Overath wanted to feature an American, so I was asked to give the keynote address. I had misunderstood how long it was to be, and was asked to cut it down; I tried to keep some of my best ideas by reading faster, but the translators who were making simultaneous translation could not keep up, so in the midst of their translation, they said "tell him to slow down." Afterward, I was introduced to Professor Karl Gustav Fellerer of Cologne, perhaps the most distinguished German Scholar of Catholic Church music. He said of my talk, *"er hat 'was gesagt."*

The congress was the occasion of addresses, performances, and perhaps most important of all, solemn liturgies, especially in the Salzburg Cathedral. The first Mass was at the Linz Cathedral, as a commemoration of the hundred and fiftieth birthday of Anton Bruckner, and our choirs joined the Linz Cathedral choir singing Bruckner's *Mass in E Minor*. The highlight of that commemoration, however, was a visit to the tomb of Bruckner in the crypt of the Abbey of Saint Florian, where we sang Bruckner's *Locus Iste,* "This place is made by God.*"*

The Congress included solemn Masses each day; the American choirs were featured for three of these, singing Palestrina's *Missa Ut, Re, Mi, Fa, Sol, La,* Michael Haydn's *Requiem in C Minor*, and the *Missa Internationalis* of Noel Goemanne. European choirs sang Masses of Josquin, Leopolita, de Monte, Mozart, and Frank Martin, as well as works of contemporary composers, including some composed for the occasion; Masses with Gregorian Ordinaries were also sung. I think these Masses inspired the singers of the Chorale more than anything else. This, of course, was Monsignor Schuler's plan, that the experience of singing the treasures of the tradition of sacred music in great and historic churches and worshipping with an international community in a common liturgical language would infuse the group with an enthusiasm for and commitment to upcoming projects at home.

I had experienced a similar enlightenment in the sixties. I had been conducting the Gregorian chant choir at Saint Ann Chapel for a couple of years, when I went on a fellowship to Munich, Germany. While there, I attended as many liturgies as I could and heard Gregorian chant Propers, Masses in classical polyphony, Masses with orchestra by Haydn and Mozart, and occasionally Masses by modern composers. Outstanding were the Masses celebrated by the Capella Antiqua; this group had made a name for itself by recording chant and Medieval and Renaissance polyphony; they met one weekend a month to work on recordings. But being devout Bavarians, they also sang for a Mass on that weekend. I was able to experience as a worshipper Masses by Machaut, Ciconia, Dunstable, Dufay, Josquin, Senfl, Lasso, and others, all performed to perfection. When I came home, my pastor was ready to ask me to change our music into English, and I shocked him by saying that on the basis of my experience in Europe, I thought, rather, that we should expand the repertory of Latin polyphonic Masses with full Gregorian Propers, which we have done ever since.

So when the Twin Cities Catholic Chorale returned from its pilgrimage, they were ready to take their place among the great choirs dedicated to the noble task of the cultivation of the "Treasury of Sacred Music," in the words of the Second Vatican Council. Monsignor Schuler, therefore, invited them to be the resident choir for the High Mass at Saint Agnes, and the rest is history.

William Mahrt, PhD
President, Church Music Association of America
Editor, *Sacred Music*
Professor of Music, Stanford University

Part Two

*"The sung High Mass **is** the liturgy, from the first prayers to the final benediction. Sacred music is that which is set aside for the worship to the glory of God. It is for the edification of the worshipers, to inspire and make them more purposeful Christians."*

Monsignor Richard J. Schuler, quoted by Gareth Hiebert
Saint Paul Dispatch, Sept. 19, 1983

CHAPTER VI

The Twin Cities Catholic Chorale at the Church of Saint Agnes – 1974-1984

In the autumn of 1974, a letter was sent to the Friends of the Chorale by the Funding Committee. The letter was signed by Gareth D. Hiebert (columnist for the *Saint Paul Dispatch* under the pseudonym of Oliver Towne) and Michael F. Ettel, President of the Catholic Aid Association. It gave some of the highlights of the August pilgrimage and then announced plans for a series of Masses to be sung by the Chorale at the Church of Saint Agnes. This would be the Chorale's first season of residency at Saint Agnes. While the letter was signed by the Funding Committee, it was written by Monsignor Schuler. It said:

> The experiences of the pilgrimage encouraged the Chorale in its belief that such opportunities for divine worship should exist here in the Twin Cities and not just abroad. It has, therefore, decided to increase its activities substantially. The proposed program for this autumn and early winter is enclosed. In general, the Chorale intends to sing a High Mass, frequently with orchestra, on the third Sunday of each month at the Church of Saint Agnes in Saint Paul, and also for special feast days as outlined. In addition, it will be available to sing elsewhere on invitation. In order to help the Chorale implement its program, which will involve the engaging of professional musicians for orchestral accompaniment, we have undertaken to form a committee to raise a projected sum of $8,000 for the 1974-75 season.

It is important to explain what Monsignor Schuler meant when he wrote that it would be necessary to engage professional musicians. Previously, the Chorale had also used "professional" musicians for concerts, most often through a grant from the musicians' union, and not always with great success. In a review in the *Saint Paul Pioneer Press* (March 4, 1964), John Harvey, the principal classical music critic, noted problems of coordination between the choir and the orchestra, laying the cause to limited rehearsal time. Monsignor Schuler knew that for this new project to be a success, he would need the best classical musicians available in the Twin Cities because it would be impossible to arrange and pay for rehearsal time on a continuing basis. Therefore, he began working with a violinist from the Minnesota Orchestra, who became the contractor for the orchestra for the Chorale. He arranged for a group of musicians to play for the Chorale on the designated Sundays, most of whom were regular members of the Minnesota Orchestra. In fact, four of the original musicians were still playing with the Chorale in 2014-2015, the 41st season.[19] In the beginning, Monsignor Schuler chose the soloists from among the members of the Chorale, who were all volunteers. This system had worked well when the Chorale only sang occasional Masses and one concert a year. However, Monsignor Schuler soon learned that it put too much strain on the Chorale to take soloists from the sections. He eventually concluded that it was also necessary to hire professional soloists.

The donors would be called "Friends of the Chorale." This solicitation of donations to support the activities of the Chorale was not new, because programs of concerts back to the first concert in 1956 list names of patrons of the concerts. However, it is evident that in announcing a season of only six Masses, of which one was in Renaissance polyphony without orchestra, Monsignor Schuler was not at all sure how successful the fund raising would be. In addition, he probably did not want to displace entirely the existing parish choir. For that reason, the Chorale was only scheduled to sing once a month.

The season began with Mozart's *Coronation Mass* on October 20, 1974. The program continued with the Michael Haydn *Requiem solemne in C Minor* on the evening of All Souls' Day, November 2. The other Masses were: Anton Bruckner's *Mass in E Minor* on November 17; Joseph Haydn's *Mass in Time of War (Paukenmesse)* on November 24; Palestrina's *Missa Ut, Re, Mi, Fa, Sol, La* on December 15, and a repeat of Haydn's *Mass in Time of War* for midnight Mass on Christmas. Unless indicated, all of the Masses were sung for the 10:00 a.m. Sunday Latin High Mass.

Evidently, enough money came in to continue the season until Corpus Christi. A second schedule was sent out announcing 15 more Masses, of which 12 were with orchestra. They began on January 5, 1975, with the *Coronation Mass* by Mozart on the Feast of the Epiphany and included Haydn's *Mass in Time of War*, Schubert's *Mass in G*, Beethoven's *Mass in C*, Haydn's *Little Organ Solo Mass*, Bruckner's *Mass in E Minor*, Haydn's *Mariazellermesse* and *Heiligmesse*. Two Masses by Palestrina were also sung, *Missa Dies Sanctificatus* and *Missa Ut, Re, Mi, Fa, Sol, La*, and Orazio Benevoli's *Missa La Cristiniana* in 8 parts.

A letter dated May 15, 1975, reminded the Friends of the Chorale of the end of the regular season on Pentecost Sunday, but also announced three special Masses. On the Solemnity of Corpus Christi Bishop Alphonse J. Schladweiler of New Ulm and former pastor of Saint Agnes, would celebrate the Mass for which the Chorale would sing Schubert's *Mass in G*. The Chorale would also sing two Masses for the National Wanderer Forum on June 28 and 29. Included with the letter was a list of 21 Patrons ($100), 23 Sponsors ($50) and 69 Donors ($25). A more complete analysis of the financing of the Chorale will be found in a separate chapter.

In addition to completing its season at Saint Agnes, some members of the Chorale flew once again to Pueblo, Colorado, to participate in the national convention of the Church Music Association of America from January 31 to February 2, 1975. The Chorale joined the Dallas Catholic Choir and the Chamber Choir of the College of Saint Benedict and Saint John's University in Minnesota, to sing Beethoven's *Mass in C* at a sacred concert which was part of the annual Mozart Festival. Gerhard Track conducted the Pueblo Symphony Orchestra. He had previously directed the Vienna Boys Choir and the choir at Saint John's University in Collegeville, Minnesota. The Chorale also sang Anton Bruckner's *Choralmesse* for a Mass at the Church of Saint Joseph in Red Wing, Minnesota, on May 3, 1975.

In a Fall,1975, letter to donors signed by the Funding Committee, Monsignor Schuler announced the second season of Chorale Masses at Saint Agnes, saying, "The generosity of more than one hundred fifteen 'Friends of the Chorale' permitted a most successful first year during which the Chorale sang twenty-five times, accompanied by professional orchestra musicians." Note: 25 Masses include 4 that were not part of the regular schedule. The letter continues, "We are proud of our program which stands as a beacon and a model in the nation, because it carries out on a regular basis the new Latin liturgy as envisioned by the Second Vatican Council."

In an undated clipping from the *Saint Paul Dispatch,* Gareth Hiebert, who wrote a popular column under the pseudonym "Oliver Towne" and was a member of the Funding Committee, also announced the season with great fanfare and not a little hyperbole about the numbers in attendance at some of the Masses and the number of donors. However, one could say that there was no exaggeration when he stated, "The Chorale added a new dimension to civilization in the Twin Cities...."

The program enclosed with the letter was only for the first half of the year, perhaps indicating that Monsignor Schuler was still tentative about the funding from the Friends of the Chorale. It announced thirteen Masses, from Sepember 4, 1975, to January 18, 1976. One of the Masses, during Advent, was a polyphonic Mass by Palestrina without orchestra in keeping with the penitential season. The program for the second half of the season listed eleven additional Masses, concluding on June 20, 1976, with Mozart's *Coronation Mass* on the Solemnity of Corpus Christi. The Masses were presented more or less every other week. Once again, the Chorale sang a Palestrina Mass during the penitential season of Lent. The Chorale sang an additional Mass at Saint Agnes on June 19 for the National Wanderer Forum.

In the program book of the Minnesota Orchestra, *Showcase,* Vol. VII, No. 8, March 21, 1976, the program notes for Anton Bruckner's *Mass No. 2 in E Minor,* mention the Chorale's repertoire at Saint Agnes, "Though this marks the debut of this work at these concerts, it has been repeatedly used for worship at the Church of Saint Agnes in Saint Paul, where, under the leadership of musicologist Monsignor Richard J. Schuler, great masses are presented in repertory at services." The Director and members of the Chorale greatly appreciated the recognition.

Monsignor Schuler became editor of *Sacred Music* magazine with the fall issue of 1975 (Vol. 102, No. 3) and held that position until 1998 (Vol. 125, No. 1). This author assisted him with the magazine and knows from experience that he not only wrote a major part of the journal, but also entered it all into the computer to send to the printer. His work with *Sacred Music* gave him an important platform for teaching and analyzing the state of Catholic church music in the United States. His very important articles like the seven-part "Chronicle of the Reform" published in *Sacred Music*, Vol. 109, No. 1,2,3,4; Vol. 110, No. 1, 2, 3, presented a definitive explanation and interpretation of the period from the *Motu proprio* of Saint Pius X through the encyclical *Musicae sacra disciplina* of Pope Pius XII and the *Constitution on the Sacred Liturgy* of the Second Vatican Council and the documents that followed upon it. These articles, which are still highly regarded, are available on the Church Music Association of America website *musicasacra.org*. A bibliography of some of the most pertinent articles from *Sacred Music* may be found in Appendix G.

A letter from the Funding Committee dated September 7, 1976, announces the third season, and adds, "This program, which solemnifies the new Latin liturgy of the Second Vatican Council with music of the great classical composers, is unique in the United States." The first program sent out announced nineteen Masses from October 3, 1976 through May 8, 1977, including two Masses by Palestrina sung without orchestra during the penitential seasons of Advent and Lent. The Mozart *Requiem* was sung for the first time for the Feast of All Souls. A second program was sent out, beginning with December 7, 1976, and extending the season to June 12, 1977, a total of twenty-two Masses (twenty with orchestra). It should be noted that at this time, the programs were in a very simple format. A half sheet enclosure announced the original three giving options: Patron, $100; Sponsor, $50; and Donor, $25. Patrons were offered a complimentary subscription to *Sacred Music* magazine, for which Monsignor Schuler had become editor in 1975. The second mailing included a list of Friends of the Chorale. A third letter was sent out in June, reminding Friends of the Mass for the Solemnity of Corpus Christi.

Showcase magazine, the program book of the Minnesota Orchestra, featured an article about the Chorale by Monsignor Schuler in its October 13 to 29, 1976, issue (Vol. IX, No.2). A schedule of Masses through January was also included. In the Sunday *Saint Paul Pioneer Press* on November 7, 1976, Gareth Hiebert, writing as "Oliver Towne," announced that David Bevan, a young organist formerly from Westminster Catholic Cathedral in London, had joined the staff at Saint Agnes. Mr. Bevan earned his degree from Queen's College, Oxford, at 18 and was organist and assistant director of music at Westminster Cathedral. The contact was made with him by Harold

Hughesdon, parishioner and later permanent deacon at Saint Agnes. When Mr. Hughesdon was a boy, he himself had been a student at the Westminster Cathedral Choir School, not as a chorister, but as a server. The original plan was for Mr. Bevan to stay for three months, but he stayed for several years. During his tenure at Saint Agnes, David Bevan also directed the *Schola Cantorum* and thus was responsible for the Gregorian chant sung at the Latin High Masses.

The 1976-77 season included an interesting development because KSJN-FM, the Minnesota Public Radio station, which was founded at Saint John's University and located there at that time, broadcast the Latin High Masses from Saint Agnes for a short period of time. The live broadcasts began with Midnight Mass on Christmas, 1976, and included the following Sundays: January 2, 9, February 6, March 6, April 10, 17, and May 8, 1977.[20] There is no written record of why these broadcasts did not continue, but there was a supposition that by mistake the Mass from Saint Agnes had been broadcast in greater Minnesota, thus pre-empting the Mass from the abbey church at Saint John's, the founder and sponsor of the FM station.

In the Spring 1976 issue of *Sacred Music*, Monsignor Schuler wrote an article, "How Can You Have a Latin Mass?" (Vol. 103, no. 1) which began with an amusing anecdote. He wrote:

> Some time ago I was at dinner in a clerical gathering after Confirmation in a parish church. About ten priests were present at table with the bishop. One pastor called down to me to inquire how well the Latin High Mass in my parish was attended. Before I could reply, a young priest sitting next to me interjected, "How can you have a Latin Mass?" I did not have time to answer either question, because the bishop spoke up and said to the young priest, "Father, not only does Monsignor not need to explain how he has a Latin Mass, but rather those who do not have one should explain why they do not." After that, as the Scriptures put it, "They asked him no further questions."

This story is a good example of Monsignor Schuler's wit. It also illustrates the prevailing understanding, even among the clergy, that Masses in Latin were not allowed. Unfortunately, it did not put the subject to rest.

Before the beginning of the 1977-78 season, the Chorale sang a special Mass during the visit of Reverend Jean-Pierre Schmit, professor of music and president of the Conservatory of Music in Luxembourg. Monsignor Schuler and Father Schmit had met at a church music conference in Europe and became good friends. During World War II, Father Schmit was imprisoned in a Nazi concentration camp because he had helped young men from Luxembourg escape from being conscripted into the German army. At the time he had been composing a Mass for a shrine to Saint Oranna in the German town of Berus. When he was dragged away by the Nazis, all of his belongings were dispersed. However, the uncompleted manuscript of the Mass was rescued by a German officer who saw that it got to the shrine of Saint Oranna. After the war, the manuscript of the Mass was returned to Father Schmit by the pastor of the shrine. Father Schmit finished the Mass and more than thirty years later, *The Mass in Honor of Saint Oranna* was premiered in the United States by the Twin Cities Catholic Chorale at the Church of Saint Agnes. It was a magnificent and moving occasion, well publicized in the local press, and attended by the many people in the area with origins in Luxembourg.

The letter announcing the fourth season of the Chorale Masses at Saint Agnes is the first that is signed by Monsignor Schuler and does not include the names of the funding committee on the letterhead. The letter makes three important points:

1) The number of Masses will be increased to twenty-nine.
2) A new giving group called Benefactor is being established at $500.
3) The parish of Saint Agnes offers the Chorale its beautiful church, but no financial support is given to the project by the parish.

This last point is very important, for no matter how often it is repeated, some still believe to this day that the Chorale receives its financial support from the parish.

The season began on September 25, 1977, and concluded on May 28, 1978. This is the first year that the Chorale sang **every** Sunday except during Advent and Lent when it sang Palestrina Masses on one Sunday only. The Chorale sang twenty-seven times with orchestra. The Chorale added two Masses by Haydn to its repertoire: the *Theresienmesse* and the *Schöpfungmesse*. In the letter traditionally sent during Lent asking for funding, Monsignor Schuler repeats the statement that the parish does not fund the Chorale. An article written by Father Richard M. Hogan on the Chorale, which had been published in an Austrian church music magazine in German and reprinted in English in *Sacred Music,* was enclosed in the mailing.[21] In a June 20, 1978, letter thanking donors, Monsignor Schuler announced two Masses with orchestra that would be sung at Saint Agnes in July for the National Wanderer Forum. The Chorale also sang the Mozart *Coronation Mass* for the 100th anniversary of the Catholic Aid Association in August. The Catholic Aid Association, now Catholic United Financial, remains a faithful supporter of the Chorale. The list of contributors for 1977-1978 included ten Benefactors, fifty-two Patrons, seventy Sponsors and one hundred forty-seven Donors.

During the 1977-78 season, the new organist David Bevan gave two recitals, one at Macalester College and the other at Saint Agnes. In February of 1978, David Hawley wrote an article on the Chorale Masses at Saint Agnes which was widely disseminated by the Associated Press. It begins:

> Nearest the aisle a woman in a dust-colored scarf and thread-bare dress knelt, silently reciting her rosary. Beside her sat a pair of obvious "tourists" gazing in silent appreciation at the stained glass windows....They had expected a concert. They were surprised when it turned out to be High Mass.

The article concludes with the words of Monsignor Schuler:

> It is not a concert; it is not entertainment. It is part of the worship of God.

The fifth season (1978-79) began on October 15, 1978 with Haydn's *Mariazellermesse* and concluded on June 17, 1979, with Mozart's *Coronation Mass.* The season was composed of a total of 30 Masses with orchestra. In addition, the Chorale sang the Mozart *Requiem* twice: on the occasion of the death of Pope Paul VI and the unexpected death soon after of the newly elected Pope, John Paul I. The Chorale added Haydn's *Nelson Mass* and Schubert's *Mass in C* to its repertoire.

In his Lenten letter, Monsignor Schuler announced that Gerhard Track, director of the Pueblo, Colorado Symphony and president of the Church Music Association of America, would conduct the Chorale in Haydn's *Theresienmesse* on Laetare Sunday. Monsignor Schuler also announced that a sacred concert would be presented in the church on Palm Sunday by the soloists, a string quartet of the musicians who regularly play for the Sunday Masses, and David Bevan, the organist from London. The concert was a thank you to the Friends of the Chorale, but also at the same time, a fund raiser. The Lenten letter states again that Saint Agnes gives a home to the Chorale, but the parish does not underwrite the project.

An article by Clark Morphew, religion writer for the Saint Paul newspapers, appeared in the *Dispatch* on May 5, 1979. Morphew says, "The 10 a.m. Mass at Saint Agnes is proper in every respect. It is appropriate praise to the Lord of the church who gave His best to us. It is also a reminder to the church in America that our liturgy and ritual ought to reflect the magnitude of our devotion." He notes that Saint Agnes is perhaps the only place in America where Masses composed by the masters can be totally experienced.

In July of 1979, Monsignor Schuler, as pastor of Saint Agnes, appointed Paul W. LeVoir as cantor and conductor of the *Schola Cantorum*, a position he still holds today. Paul had joined the Chorale several years before and became part of the *Schola* the year before he took it over, succeeding David Bevan. On the first Sunday in his new position, Paul remembers Monsignor Schuler saying, "I'll sing the Mass and you sing the chant." With the support of Monsignor Schuler and Deacon Harold Hughesdon, a strong program of chant was developed and exists today. Gregorian chant plays a vital role in the Latin High Mass at Saint Agnes, which always must be a prayer, not a concert. The role of the *Schola Cantorum* is discussed more fully in the chapter on the team necessary for the Latin High Mass.

Mary Elizabeth Gormley (now LeVoir)[22] was appointed parish organist and organist/accompanist for the Chorale in the summer of 1980. Today it is hard to imagine the Chorale continuing without this accomplished organist and liturgist. Her role is also discussed in the chapter on the team necessary for the Latin High Mass.

Monsignor Schuler announced the 1979-80 season, the sixth year of singing Masses with orchestra at Saint Agnes. He emphasized the fact that these Masses in Latin with Propers in Gregorian chant are fully in accord with the reforms instituted by Vatican II, something that could not be repeated often enough because Saint Agnes was constantly criticized as being a pre-Vatican II parish since the High

Mass was in Latin, and the common misconception was that Latin had been banished by Vatican II. The season began on October 14, 1979, with Haydn's *Schöpfungmesse* and finished on June 8, 1980, on the Solemnity of Corpus Christi. The Chorale sang twenty-nine times with orchestra. The new Mass added this year was Mozart's *Mass in C*, K 337.

The Chorale Masses at Saint Agnes were featured prominently in two articles in the Saint Paul papers. An article by John Camp in the *Pioneer Press* (April 21, 1980) makes some interesting points. The Mass at Saint Agnes is not trendy, but it is a powerful religious experience. Monsignor Schuler has organized what might be the most serious program of sacred music in the nation. He concludes, "So if you want to hear the best in classical sacred music, try Saint Agnes at any 10 a.m. Sunday High Mass by June 8." He even makes a pitch for contributions to help meet the $30,000 budget for that year.[23]

The second article was written by the faithful friend of the Chorale, Gareth Hiebert. Appearing in the *Saint Paul Dispatch* (April 16, 1980) as part of his "Oliver Towne" column, it was a general discussion of the program, emphasizing the unique experience available at Saint Agnes. Hiebert traveled often to Europe so he was well aware of where such Masses were performed in Munich and Vienna. He said, "There is perhaps, only one higher level (not even Saint Peter's in Rome) where one can hear such music. 'And that might be heaven,' says the sly-humored Monsignor, who is architect of his Chorale's Viennese-style Mass." The other emphasis in the article was the difficulty of fund raising which is a perennial problem to this day.

The 1980-81 season, the Chorale's seventh at Saint Agnes, began on October 19, 1980 with Mozart's *Coronation Mass* and finished on June 21, 1981 with the same Mass. As was and still is the custom, the Chorale always finishes its season on the Solemnity of Corpus Christi. There were twenty-nine orchestra Masses sung that year. The Chorale added Haydn's *Harmoniemesse* to its repertoire.

The *Catholic Bulletin*, the diocesan paper, published a full page spread on the Latin Masses sung by the Chorale at Saint Agnes (January 9, 1981). The lead paragraph said that Saint Agnes is the only parish in the archdiocese to offer a regular Latin Mass. Monsignor Schuler made the point in the article that Saint Agnes has had a Latin Mass continuously since the parish was founded in 1887. The feature included several pictures. One shows Monsignor Schuler conducting members of the orchestra. Another shows some of the members of the Chorale while they are singing. In another, one sees the procession of fourteen altar boys, and the priest, deacon, and subdeacon wearing birettas. Another depicts Father Michael Ince distributing Communion in the traditional manner: on the tongue to kneeling communicants. Another shows a young woman in a traditional chapel veil. How pre-Vatican II it must have appeared to the readers! Yet every Chorale schedule included on the last page a statement of the conformity of the Latin High Mass at Saint Agnes to the directives of Vatican II.

The 1981-82 season began on September 27, 1981 with Haydn's *Heiligmesse* and ended on June 13, 1982, the Solemnity of Corpus Christi, with Mozart's *Coronation Mass*. The Chorale sang thirty-two Masses with orchestra. Mozart's *Piccolomini Mass* and Gounod's *Saint Cecilia Mass* were added to the repertoire. The Gounod *Saint Cecilia Mass* was sung on the traditional feast of Saint Cecilia which was replaced that year by the feast of Christ the King because it fell on the Sunday before Advent. The first performance of the Gounod *Saint Cecilia Mass* was sponsored by a Saint Paul family for whom the famous melody from the *Sanctus* had a special meaning. The father of the family had been a church musician who had the habit of whistling that melody to call his children home from playing to eat dinner! The Gounod Mass has become a great favorite of the worshippers at Saint Agnes. A long list of Friends of the Chorale for the previous year was sent with the program in the fall. Included was a list of gifts to the Sustaining Fund from December 31, 1979 to August 31, 1982. The Sustaining Fund was an attempt to put the budget of the Chorale on a firmer ground so there would not be the constant worry about making expenses every year. This effort met with some success, but the concern about raising enough money to meet expenses persists to this day.

In a letter dated September 1, 1982, Monsignor Schuler announced the ninth year of Viennese classical Masses at Saint Agnes. The season began on October 3, 1982 and finished on June 5, 1983. Thirty Masses with orchestra were announced. The Chorale sang Mozart's *Waisenhaus Mass* for the first time. As usual the list of donors from the previous year was included in the mailing. There were six Benefactors ($500 and up), sixty-six Patrons ($100 and up), seventy-five Sponsors ($50 and up) and a myriad of Donors.

The 1983-84 season marked the tenth anniversary of the project.

Monsignor Schuler announced that the anniversary year would begin on October 2, 1983 with the Beethoven *Mass in C*, followed by a reception. As Monsignor Schuler said, "It is our 10th birthday party!" The season of thirty-one Masses concluded on June 24, 1984, the Solemnity of Corpus Christi, with Schubert's *Mass in B Flat*. Potential contributors were informed that fees for the instrumentalists and the cost of musical scores had increased. In the Lenten letter, Monsignor Schuler reminded donors that Saint Agnes Parish does not fund the Chorale.

A major feature article by Patrick Marx appeared in the Sunday *Pioneer Press* on September 18, 1983. Then, as now, the Chorale was pleased to receive any notice in the secular press, even if the article could be interpreted to have a rather negative slant. The headline announces the tone of the beginning of the article, "Pastor-choir leader holds vigil to preserve tradition." In the opening paragraph, Marx calls Saint Agnes Church a "haven for Catholics who miss the pomp, circumstance and majesty of traditional church worship, faded rituals perhaps best epitomized by the Latin High Mass and Gregorian chant." In paragraph two the author says that Monsignor Schuler "pays homage to the old ways," including "the arcane vestments that have all but disappeared after two decades of church reform and turmoil." Paragraph three comes to the crux of the matter: "It's his personal mission to preserve the richness of the sacred liturgies, which he believes one day will again be part of Catholic worship."

As the article continues and the author begins to quote Monsignor Schuler extensively, those of us who knew him can almost hear his voice stating: "Music in a church has to be prayer." And again "(Church) music must not only be sacred, it must be art....Out of step? No, I'm 40 years ahead of the times....People always tell me they hope the church will go back to what it was, but I say I hope the church will catch up to what it really said it was doing." In fact, as the section of this book on the CMAA Conference in October 2013 will show, the three keynote speakers all recognized how Monsignor Schuler's revolutionary vision is influencing the revival of the Latin liturgy and Gregorian chant in the United States today.

In his "Oliver Towne" column on September 19, 1983, Gareth Hiebert also announced this tenth season in a column in the *Saint Paul Dispatch*. A fan of the Chorale since the beginning and a member of the original funding committee, he wrote with his usual enthusiasm.

He quotes Monsignor Schuler thus, "What we have done is take the beautiful, inspiring musical Masses out of the concert hall and the theaters and bring it back where it belongs, as part of the Catholic liturgy....There are those who suggest that the singing of a great Mass is a concert, an appendage to the Mass itself....They couldn't be more wrong. The High Masses written by the famed composers are just what they imply – they *are* the Masses, not something tacked on or filled into the liturgy. The sung High Mass *is* the liturgy, from the first prayers to the final benediction. Sacred music is that which is set aside for the worship to the glory of God. It is for the edification of the worshipers, to inspire and make them more purposeful Christians."

And so the Chorale finished its first ten years of residency at Saint Agnes. During that time the number of Masses sung each year increased; the repertory grew. The program became more solidly established, but then as today, it received just enough in contributions to pay its expenses and relied heavily on volunteers for the work that was needed. The program received some publicity, especially in the Saint Paul newspapers. However, it had to struggle to make itself understood by the broader Catholic community who believed that Latin Masses had been forbidden by Vatican II and thus believed that Saint Agnes and the Chorale represented a dissident group who had rejected the directives of Vatican II. Nothing was further from the truth. Most Catholics thought it was wrong to sing in Latin. They were used to the new and mostly mediocre music written for congregational singing. As Jeffrey Tucker, the former managing editor of *Sacred Music* magazine and current Director of Publications for CMAA, said in a previously quoted article "The Hero of the Mighty Musical Struggle" (*Crisis Magazine,* August 29, 2013), commenting on the work of Monsignor Schuler, "Let us remember and appreciate, and never take for granted, the gifts our generation has been given. Sacred music lives today because we are blessed by brilliant workers in the vineyard that have come before."

CHAPTER VII

A National Broadcast and a Recording Project 1984-1986

Monsignor Schuler announced the eleventh season of the orchestra Masses at Saint Agnes with the news that on October 14, 1984, the Chicago public radio station WFMT would record the Beethoven *Mass in C* live for later broadcast on a National Public Radio program called "Lincoln's Music in America." Unfortunately, the documentation on the making of this program and also on the later recordings is not in the materials in the Schuler Archives and was probably disposed of with some of Monsignor's personal files. The recording engineer for the WFMT program and for the recording project which took place at a later date, was Evans Mirageas. To give more detail about both of these events, the author of this history asked Father William E. Sanderson, who sang with the Chorale for the October 14 Mass and was the celebrant for the Masses recorded in 1986, to write of both of these projects based on correspondence that he had with Monsignor Schuler during those years. Father Sanderson is a graduate of the Saint Paul Seminary and is now a pastor in Omaha, Nebraska. His comments follow:

> One of the most memorable experiences of my life as a priest was being invited by Monsignor Schuler to be the principal celebrant for the recordings of three complete Masses at Saint Agnes sponsored by the Leaflet Missal Company. As a seminarian I spent a great deal of time at Saint Agnes where Monsignor became familiar with my vocal talents and aware of my devotion to the *Novus Ordo* Latin Masses there.
> Two years before the triple Mass project, I was invited to sing with the Chorale at Saint Agnes on Sunday, October 14,

1984, when the Beethoven *Mass in C* was to be featured in an hour-long program on National Public Radio called "Lincoln's Music in America." The program was engineered and hosted by Evans Mirageas. According to his website, Mirageas is currently the Harry T. Wilks Artistic Director of the Cincinnati Opera, the Vice-President for Artistic Planning for the Atlanta Symphony, and an independent artistic advisor to symphony orchestras, opera companies, festivals, and individual classical music artists throughout the world. In 1984 he was employed by WFMT Radio in Chicago. "Music in America" featured the work of various musicians, choirs, and ensembles around the country. Each program contained interviews and brief musical selections to tell the particular story. The first national broadcast (of the Mass from Saint Agnes) during the week of October 22-28 was not carried by KSJN-FM of Minnesota Public Radio. They received scores of calls and letters. It was, however, carried by WCAL-FM of Saint Olaf College in Northfield, Minnesota, on December 9, 1984.

Mirageas sent copies of the program to Monsignor with the following comments in a letter dated October 19, 1984. "Here are finished tapes of the 'Music in America' program on Saint Agnes. I hope that we have done justice to your efforts. I was mightily impressed with the dedication and spirit of your performers, both in the choir and the soloists. And to have the Minnesota Orchestra as instrumentalists was a real pleasure....I cannot thank you and the other Fathers enough for the assistance and cooperation you extended before and during last Sunday. It was a pleasure to be able to carry your musical message to our audience....Your parishioners are very lucky to have you, Father."

The program was re-released during the week of October 14-20, 1985. In a letter to Monsignor Schuler, Mirageas wrote, "This program has received more letters and calls than any other in the three seasons of 'Music in America.'" A year later MPR still did not carry the program.

This program might have been the genesis of the 1986 triple Mass project. In a letter dated April 19, 1986, Monsignor issued his invitation that I be the principal celebrant. The services of Evans Mirageas of WFMT had already been secured for the recording sessions scheduled for June 2 and 3, 1986. Interestingly, the recordings were made utilizing a VHS tape rather than another kind of recording material.

The recording sessions were divided into various segments to make them time-efficient and cost-efficient (as paid musicians were involved for the orchestra). The first and perhaps longest session involved the orchestra and the Chorale. The Ordinaries (*Kyrie*, *Gloria*, *Credo*, *Sanctus*, *Benedictus* and *Agnus Dei*) of the three Masses were done in succession in the church in the late afternoon and early evening when external traffic noise had died down. The choir and orchestra were assembled in the loft at Saint Agnes as usual. I sat in the pews below. Mirageas, also seated in the loft, followed each score wearing headphones. Frequently he would stop the music and ask that the musicians return to a specific measure. There must have been dozens, perhaps hundreds of "re-takes," but the end product was a seamless whole.

One session was held specifically for the chant choir led by Paul W. LeVoir; another session focused specifically on the solo organ pieces with Mary Gormley (now Mary E. LeVoir). The morning session on June 3 involved the parts proper to the principal celebrant. The orations and prefaces were chanted for each Mass in succession; the Roman Canon was chanted once and used for all three Masses. Members of the Chorale were present to sing the congregational responses. Since the church was empty, and sounded so to the recording engineer initially, the microphones were re-positioned to create a fuller, rather than a hollow sound. Initially, the microphones were set up facing the choir members. To affect the change, the booms were put out over the choir loft rail, angled down and then pointed toward the front doors of the church rather than the sanctuary. This helped diminish the empty church sound. The dialogues between priest and "congregation" were sung once. The homilies were recorded during this session as well. I gave the one for Christmas. (Author's note: Monsignor Schuler gave the homily for Easter and Deacon Harold Hughesdon for Pentecost.)

Monsignor Schuler wanted to make certain the recordings were complete to the last detail, including the ringing of the Saint

Agnes Church bells (which were turned off during the actual recording session). In order to capture the sound authentically (rather than substitute a recording of someone else's bells) a few of us went to the yard behind Saint Agnes rectory. We used card tables as baffles to direct the sound more carefully into the recording microphone. The neighbors were probably perplexed as to why the bells were ringing so erratically that afternoon.

The last written communication I had with Monsignor Schuler about the Mass recordings came in a letter to me dated June 28, 1986 in which he wrote: "I spent Thursday with you in Chicago, even though you weren't there!! Evans Mirageas and I edited the tapes of the Masses, and during the day we heard you singing. It was all very fine. You did a wonderful piece of work. The editing is now done, and the tapes will be sent back to Saint Paul for reproducing. We hope to have them ready by August 1. I will let you know."

This concludes Father Sanderson's reminiscences of the two projects. Monsignor Schuler conceived the recording project as a way to demonstrate the *Novus Ordo* in Latin as published by His Holiness, Pope Paul VI in 1969, thus dispelling the commonly held view that the Mass after Vatican II could not be in Latin and had to be celebrated in the vernacular, when quite the opposite was true. These three recordings of the Masses for Christmas, Easter, and Pentecost were originally made as recordings of the entire Mass. Monsignor Schuler insisted that these recordings would be an aid to devotion, allowing shut-ins to listen to a reverent Mass. The recordings were paid for by the Leaflet Missal Company, whose owners, Peter and Diane Welvang, were also members of Saint Agnes parish. They were originally sold as cassette recordings: the three Masses in a sturdy case for a price of $29.95. The Mass for Christmas was Charles Gounod's *St. Cecilia Mass;* for Easter, Haydn's *Paukenmesse;* and for Pentecost, Beethoven's *Mass in C*. Sections of the original pamphlet giving more detail about the recordings and used to advertise the Masses are reproduced here.

Several of the current members of the Chorale sang in this recording project. We remember showing up at the designated time for the recording and being very nervous about the challenge. Beyond that, Monsignor Schuler bore all the responsibility for the planning, conducting, and editing of the tapes. Since his death, as the new conductor and the Board of the Chorale take more responsibility for projects, we realize what a monumental task this was. Not the least of the challenges were the negotiations with the musicians' union about the union fees for recording. As this author remembers the project, Monsignor Schuler negotiated for special fees for limited distribution. The original cassette tapes, which included the full Masses, were later edited and made into CDs and are still sold by the Leaflet Missal Company.[24]

Brochure advertising sale of cassettes of recorded Masses. Schuler Archives.

Here is a recapitulation in chronological order of the activities of the Chorale in 1984-85 and 1985-86. In addition to the WFMT recording of the Beethoven *Mass in C* on October 14, 1984, during the 1984-85 season, the Chorale sang the *Fourth Mass in C* by Luigi Cherubini for the first time. The 1984-85 season began on October 7, 1984 with Haydn's *Paukenmesse* and finished on June 9, 1985, the Solemnity of Corpus Christi, with Schubert's *Mass in C*. It consisted of 30 orchestra Masses.

The 1985-86 season began on October 5, 1985, with Haydn's *Nelson Mass* and terminated on the Solemnity of Corpus Christi, June 1, 1986, with Mozart's *Coronation Mass*. The Chorale sang twenty-nine Masses. The recording sessions of the three Masses were made on June 2 and 3, 1986. In his letter announcing the season Monsignor Schuler again reminds potential donors that the parish does not fund the program. He also states that the program at Saint Agnes is unique in the United States.

Jim Klobuchar, a very popular columnist for the *Minneapolis Star Tribune*, published a column on December 25, 1985, discussing what distinguishes Saint Paul from Minneapolis and sets the city apart. He gave as an example, not the Ice Palace of the Winter Carnival, but Latin High Mass at Saint Agnes! Here is a bit of that column:

James Klobuchar

Nobody is going to hustle a church in its tourist propaganda and it would unhinge you if they did, but the man wanted to know some of the things I found captivating about Saint Paul. I told him to find the way to Saint Agnes' Church. I don't know any place on earth where I could have heard and seen what I did a few Sundays ago. This is the church where the Masses of the great composers are sung and played as part of the living celebration of a traditional Latin Mass. There are times when religion should be relevant and times when it should simply soar and galvanize, bridging the centuries both with ritual and witness. The service began, and in a few moments, the choir and orchestra poured out on the congregation the transcending genius of Wolfgang Amadeus

Mozart in the Kyrie of his *Coronation Mass*. It ignited the blood. The sound of the choir's voices, filling this auditorium of worship with Mozart's music, blended in an incomparable way the highest expression of human art with the benediction of the word. It was history and yearning and beauty; it somehow made God and humanity one, and it was all here in a church in Saint Paul.

Gareth Hiebert, in the *Saint Paul Dispatch* on June 6, 1986, wrote a column about the difficulty of financing the program of the Chorale. Monsignor Schuler announced a new strategy, finding sponsors for the music at a certain Mass. This is an idea that had never been implemented fully until the Fund Raising Committee put together a plan for the 40th anniversary season in 2013-14 to develop it. Hiebert's column announces the recording project previously discussed. It also quotes a listener of public radio from New England, who, after having heard the "Lincoln's Music in America" program, called Monsignor Schuler, saying, "I surely envy the people of Minnesota who can attend."

COMMENTARY

"I Must See This Place"

One of my best friends from St. Louis, Missouri told me about a program he heard on the radio about a parish in Saint Paul, Minnesota, which does "orchestral Masses AT Mass." Years earlier, I was in Munich and attended the High Mass in Saint Michael's where they were singing a Schubert *Mass in C*. The Mass was in German and facing the congregation, but the music was the chant and the Schubert. I was totally amazed. So needless to say, when I heard of Saint Agnes and was able to hear the broadcast myself, I said to myself: "I must see this place."

What impressed me during my listening to the interview was Monsignor Schuler's explanation of sacred music in that Vatican II did not desire the loss of our musical heritage. I also liked his description of his liturgy team. "I am the liturgy team," quipped Monsignor.

I made a phone call and began with all the basic questions of the how's and why's of the misunderstanding of *Sacrosanctum Concilium*, and then Monsignor invited me to offer the High Mass for the Solemnity of Corpus Christi. The Chorale would sing the Mozart *Coronation Mass*.

Walking into Saint Agnes, meeting Monsignor, listening to the Chorale rehearse, I felt that I had "come home." Offering the Mass *ad orientem*, with deacons and all the proper ceremonies, I felt as if I had entered the Beatific Vision. Over the years I knew that I could count on Monsignor for advice and guidance, which I did, until Monsignor entered eternity.

To me, Monsignor was like the lone voice crying out in the wilderness, trying to make straight the abuses of liturgical reforms which plagued one too many parishes. It is only now that we are beginning to see the fruits of his labors and dedication to the sacred liturgy. For many years, his parish brought forth young men wishing to follow Christ to the altar. If I understand it correctly, there was at least one vocation from Saint Agnes each year. These men are now ordained and carry with them the flame, the spirit of what Monsignor taught them.

As for me, I cherish the knowledge he imparted to me about the sacred liturgy and what Vatican II really taught about the liturgy. I have been able, for the past twenty-six years as pastor of Saint John Cantius, to implement what not only Monsignor Schuler did at Saint Agnes, but also what Monsignor Martin Hellriegel taught me during my stay with him at Holy Cross Church in Saint Louis, Missouri. Both men were spiritual giants and their love of the liturgy continues to this day with each priest, deacon and lay person that these two influenced.

Reverend C. Frank Phillips, CR
Pastor of Saint John Cantius
Chicago, Illinois

Portrait of Monsignor Richard J. Schuler in the Church of Saint Agnes by Christopher Foote. Photo: Christopher Foote; used with permission.

The Twin Cities Catholic Chorale on the steps of Saint Peter's Basilica in Rome in August 1974 after having sung a Mass in the Basilica. Photo: Schuler Archives.

The Basilica of Maria Plain just outside of Salzburg, Austria, August 1974, where the Twin Cities Catholic Chorale sang Michael Haydn's *Requiem in C Minor*. **Top:** The Most Reverend Alphonse J. Schladweiler, participating clergy and servers on the lawn of Maria Plain before Mass. **Middle:** View of the interior of the Basilica with the painting of the Virgin and Child, venerated at this pilgrimage site, for which W.A. Mozart wrote the Coronation Mass, K 317. **Bottom:** View of Salzburg and the surrounding mountains from the Basilica. Photos: VAS.

Exterior of the Church of Saint Agnes in Saint Paul, Minnesota, circa 2000.
Photo: Church of Saint Agnes Advancement Office; used with permission.

Monsignor Richard J. Schuler directing the Twin Cities Catholic Chorale, Feast of Saint Agnes, 2004. Photo: Caecilia Lee; used with permission.

Monsignor Richard J. Schuler celebrating Mass on Palm Sunday with permanent deacons Bernard Pedersen and John Mangan, both of whom sang in the Twin Cities Catholic Chorale. Photo: Joe Oden; used with permission.

Permanent Deacon Harold Hughesdon praying at the High Mass in the sanctuary of the Church of Saint Agnes. Photo: Joe Oden; used with permission.

Monsignor Richard J. Schuler directing the Twin Cities Catholic Chorale. Photo: Joe Oden; used with permission.

Monsignor Richard J. Schuler directing the Twin Cities Catholic Chorale, 2000. Photo: Joe Oden; used with permission.

Monsignor Richard J. Schuler standing next to the "Richard Bell" on the day of its blessing, August 15, 1990. It was given to the Church of Saint Agnes as a tribute to Monsignor Schuler on the 45th anniversary of his ordination. Photo: VAS.

Mass celebrated by His Excellency Alexander K. Sample, Archbishop of Portland, Oregon, at the Church of Saint Agnes on the Feast of the Ascension, June 1, 2014. Father Mark Moriarry, pastor of Saint Agnes, is to the left of Archbishop Sample. Photo: Richard Graner; used with permission.

Interior of the Church of Saint Agnes from the choir loft, November 2, 2014. Photo: Richard Graner; used with permission.

The Twin Cities Catholic Chorale and orchestra in the choir loft, November 2, 2014.
Photos: Richard Graner; used with permission.

Photo of the Chorale and orchestra as it appeared in the May/June, 2014 issue of *Our Catholic Journey* magazine. Photo: Joe Oden; used with permission.

Top: The Saint Agnes Schola Cantorum under the direction of Paul W. LeVoir singing the Proper of the Mass in Gregorian chant. **Bottom:** Mary Elizabeth LeVoir, organist at the Church of Saint Agnes and Chorale accompanist, November 2, 2014.
Photos: Richard Graner; used with permission.

Music Director Dr. Robert L. Peterson conducting the Twin Cities Catholic Chorale in the choir loft of the Church of Saint Agnes, Fall, 2013. Photo: Joe Oden; used with permission.

Part Three

"It is through art that man comes to God....Jesus Christ is the supreme art of the Father. Our art must be a reflection of Him in whose image we are all made. Such liturgy is the aim of Saint Agnes, Sunday mornings."

"Saint Agnes, Sunday Morning"
by Monsignor Richard J. Schuler
Sacred Music (Vol. 114, No. 3)

CHAPTER VIII

The Chorale Continues Its Program – 1986-2001

The fifteen years from 1986 to 2001 were years of growth and consolidation of the repertoire for the Chorale. From 1974 to 1985-86, the Chorale added fifteen new Masses to its repertoire in addition to keeping active the Masses that were sung before its residency at Saint Agnes. From 1986-87 to 2000-2001 seven Masses and Mozart's *Vesperae solemnes de confessore*, K 339, that is to say eight major works, were added. In addition, the Chorale made a recording of Christmas music.

It is difficult to convey in writing the beauty, reverence and spiritual quality of the Latin High Masses at Saint Agnes, celebrated as they were and still are with great solemnity of ceremony and music as befitting the Holy Sacrifice of the Mass. The reputation of the Masses, with the classical music of the great masters, spread to attract worshippers and singers alike.

For example, Neil Dexter, who sang bass in the Chorale until his death in 2012, wrote about how and why he joined the Chorale in a book of memories published after the death of Monsignor Schuler.[25] He began:

> In the fall of 1986 I was at a crossroads. I had sung in Catholic church choirs for twenty years and was burned out. I had watched as once-numerous good Catholic choirs bit the dust in a steady decline since Vatican II. I was told by a priest that Vatican II had outlawed the singing of Latin. When I asked why they could still sing Latin in Rome, he told me that Latin was allowed only in special places like Rome and that I should get over it.

Neil continued by listing music aberrations prevalent in churches at the time.

> The wonderful Masses we used to sing were replaced by guitars, polka Masses, and by utility music where Mass names started with the word "Peoples."

Then he remembered having heard the Twin Cities Catholic Chorale sing a Mass at Saint Agnes for a Wanderer Forum. He wondered if they were still in business since Latin was not allowed. When he called Monsignor Schuler, he was told that the choir season was about to start and all Neil had to do was be there for practice. Neil continued, "It soon became apparent that I had found far more than a choir; I had found a home. Monsignor Schuler was a pastor who understood that his job was to get his flock to Heaven and I wanted to be part of his flock. As a pastor, he gently pushed every aspect of Saint Agnes parish to be its best."

Near the end of his life, Neil Dexter made his own contribution to the Latin High Mass at Saint Agnes by creating a beautiful and instructive guide, *High Mass at The Church of Saint Agnes*.[26] In the preface, he explained, "I love the Mass and appreciate the way it is celebrated at the Church of Saint Agnes....The Church of Saint Agnes has many visitors, many of whom are non-Catholic, and I wanted to write something that would welcome them and explain what we do at Mass."

He included two anecdotes. On the feast of Corpus Christi, probably in the 1980s, an Archbishop who was celebrating the Mass remarked to Deacon Harold Hughesdon that Saint Agnes was an "island." Deacon Hughesdon replied, "No, Your Excellency, not an island – an island is a desert surrounded by water; Saint Agnes is an oasis – water surrounded by desert." Another anecdote recounted the visit of a Las Vegas businessman who came to hear the Mass when the Chorale sang the Mozart *Requiem* for the Feast of All Souls. He was so impressed that he came to Chorale rehearsal the next evening to tell the singers, "I came to Saint Agnes expecting a concert – and a Mass broke out, and it was the most beautiful Mass I have ever attended." Neil Dexter came to the Chorale as many singers have done, drawn by the beauty of the music and the sacred solemnity of the liturgy. His contribution was exceptional.

The Chorale began the 1986-87 season (its thirteenth) on October 6 with Mozart's *Coronation Mass* and finished the season on June 21, 1987, the Solemnity of Corpus Christi, with Mozart's *Piccolomini Mass*. The Chorale sang thirty-one Masses with orchestra. The annual program advertised for the first time the cassettes of the Masses recorded the previous year.

In the spring of 1987, in preparation for the celebration of the centennial of the founding of the parish in 1887, the church interior was filled with scaffolding for an extensive redecoration, a project that took the whole summer. The church had not been painted for thirty years. Monsignor Schuler always said that because of lack of funds when the church was built, it was never really decorated in the true style of the Baroque churches of Austria and Bavaria. The Conrad Schmidt Studios of New Berlin, Wisconsin, undertook the project which, according to the *The Church of Saint Agnes (1887-1987)*, written by Monsignor Schuler, cost in excess of half a million dollars. Decorative gilt plaster work was added; the mural of Saint Agnes in the dome was recreated; a sunburst was added over the main altar; marble and *faux marbre* were added to the pillars: all in all, the interior became as elaborate as the exterior. Three newly ordained priests offered their Masses of Thanksgiving that spring for which the Chorale sang. The events were festive in spite of the scaffolding.

Scaffolding in the Church of Saint Agnes during the restoration of the church for the centennial of the parish in 1987. Saint Agnes Parish Archives.

The Corpus Christi procession passes through the church filled with scaffolding during the restoration. Saint Agnes Parish Archives.

Fall mailing, 1987. Schuler Archives.

The program for the 1987-88 season was in a new format and was announced under the title "Saint Agnes, Sunday Morning." The first Mass of the season was the Haydn *Heiligmesse* sung on October 4, 1987, and the last Mass was on the Solemnity of Corpus Christi when the Chorale sang the Mozart *Coronation Mass*. The Chorale sang thirty-one

Masses with orchestra. The pamphlet sent with the annual program was a triple fold. The cover said, "For the past 200 years, people have been finding inspiration in the same old bars." On the inside, illustrated with bars of music, was the invitation, "Come hear the Masses of Mozart, Haydn, Schubert and Beethoven at Saint Agnes, Sunday morning." Much information is given about the Chorale along with quotations about the experience of attending a Chorale Mass. There was the usual request for a donation.

On Sunday, October 11, 1987, the Chorale sang the Mass of Thanksgiving for the opening of the parish centennial year at 4:00 p.m. The Chorale and orchestra presented Beethoven's *Mass in C*. Bishop J. Richard Ham, auxiliary bishop of the Archdiocese, was the celebrant, and Bishop Alphonse J. Schladweiler, retired bishop of New Ulm and former pastor of Saint Agnes, was the homilist.

YOUR PRESENCE AT THIS EVENT WILL HELP SET THE CHURCH BACK 200 YEARS.

Back to the magnificent masses of Mozart, Haydn, Schubert and Beethoven.

Saint Agnes celebrates over thirty orchestral Masses each year with the accompaniment of the Twin Cities Catholic Chorale and members of the Minnesota Orchestra.

The Chorale performs complete Masses by the great Viennese composers the way they were meant to be performed, within the Latin Liturgy of the Roman Catholic Church.

This classicism is carried throughout the architecture of Saint Agnes itself. Built by immigrants from the old Austro-Hungarian Empire nearly a century ago, Saint Agnes stands as a reminder of the elaborate Baroque churches of their homeland.

Their sense of tradition and inspiration is kept alive today, right here in Saint Paul, at Saint Agnes, Sunday Morning.

There's nothing else like it this side of the Atlantic. Says Sean Cassedy of Middletown, Rhode Island, "...one of the most beautiful and moving experiences of our lives in witnessing Schubert's Mass in C major...Listening to this music brought tears to my eyes."

Invitation to a Mass and reception on October 22, 1987. Schuler Archives.

On October 22, 1987, the Friends of the Chorale were invited to a Mass and reception by Monsignor Schuler and a number of co-hosts whose names were well-known in the Twin Cities, including Mr. and Mrs. Stanislaw Skrowaczeski. He was music director of the Minnesota Orchestra. The guest of honor was Ronald M. Bosrock, Honorary Consul General of the Republic of Austria. The invitation was very clever. On the front it said: "Your presence at this event will help set the church back 200 years," and, on the inside, it said: "Back to the magnificent Masses of Mozart, Haydn, Schubert and Beethoven." The Chorale and orchestra presented Mozart's *Coronation Mass* with the Proper of the Mass in Gregorian chant. Following the tradition at Saint Agnes when a bishop is present, a tradition that dates back to the concerts of the Saint Paul Catholic Choral Society under the direction of Father Missia, the processional hymn was the *Ecce Sacerdos* by Tappert.

In the Fall 1987 issue of *Sacred Music* (Vol. 114, No. 3), Monsignor Schuler wrote an article with the title "Saint Agnes, Sunday Morning." It began: "The Second Vatican Council gave us great liberty. In the field of church music this was particularly true." He continued by saying that the reforms of Pope Pius X with his *motu proprio* had, in the first half of the 20th century, cleaned out much of the objectionable profane repertory, but had also thrown out the baby with the bath water. "But the Council established clearly that music is an integral part (*pars integrans*) of liturgy; it *is* liturgy. Two requirements, not new to the Council because Pius X had reiterated them, were demanded; music for the liturgy must be *sacred* and it must be *art*. All the musical styles developed through the long history of Christianity that fulfill the requirements may be used if they are found to be fitting. Thus today, in the light of the conciliar decrees, Mozart, Haydn, Beethoven, Schubert and many others are once again legitimized, since they have indeed produced compositions for the Church that are both sacred and true art."

He then continued by describing the program at Saint Agnes and the importance of the ceremonies which must also be carried out with solemnity. His conclusion was:

> It is through art that man comes to God. Music, architecture, painting, sculpture – indeed flowers, candles, incense, vestments and ceremony – all can be the means of grace and prayer, provided that they are worthy of the Creator of all art and holy

as He is. Jesus Christ is the supreme art of the Father. Our art must be a reflection of Him in whose image we are all made. Such liturgy is the aim of Saint Agnes, Sunday mornings.

This is Monsignor Schuler's very clear explanation and oft-repeated rationale for the musical program for the Latin High Masses at Saint Agnes.

The program for the 1988-89 season carried the headline: "Come hear the Masses of Mozart, Haydn and Beethoven at Saint Agnes, Sunday Morning." The season began on October 2, 1988, with Haydn's very festive *Nelson Mass*. Easter fell on March 26 that year, so the season ended early, on the Solemnity of Corpus Christi, May 28, with the *Coronation Mass*. The *Mass in D* by Antonin Dvořák was added to the repertoire. It was sung on the Feast of Saint Agnes and has become a favorite. The Gounod *Saint Cecilia Mass* was sung for the celebration of the Anniversary of the Dedication of the Church. The Chorale sang twenty-seven Masses with orchestra. In June 1989, Monsignor Schuler traveled to Rome and presented the cassette recordings made by the Chorale to His Holiness, Pope Saint John Paul II. A photograph of this occasion is featured on the program for the 1989-90 season.

The 1989-90 season began on October 1, 1989, with the *Paukenmesse* by Haydn and finished on June 17, 1990, with Mozart's *Mass in C*, K 337. The Chorale sang thirty-two Masses and added Mozart's *Missa Longa* to its repertoire. On August 15, 1990, Bishop Alphonse J. Schladweiler of New Ulm blessed the three bells, which were reconditioned for the occasion, and a new bell presented to the parish in honor of the 45th anniversary of Monsignor Schuler's ordination to the priesthood. The new bell, weighing 5,665 pounds and sounding B, was baptized Richard. The other bells are John, weighing 1,683 pounds and sounding F sharp; Agnes, weighing 2,331 pounds and sounding E, and Anthony, weighing 3,330 pounds and sounding D. Monsignor Schuler published an article on church bells in *Sacred Music* (Vol. 116, No. 3, Fall 1989, p. 25) at this time.

The 1990-91 season began with the Beethoven *Mass in C* on October 7, 1990, and ended on the feast of Corpus Christi, June 2, 1991 with Mozart's *Coronation Mass*. The *Mass No. 1 in G* by Carl M. von Weber was added to the repertoire and was sung for the first time on Trinity Sunday, May 26. The Chorale sang twenty-nine Masses with orchestra.

The eighteenth season of orchestral Masses began on October 6, 1991, with Haydn's *Nelson Mass* and finished on the Solemnity of Corpus Christi, June 21, 1992, with the *Mass in B Flat* by Franz Schubert. The Chorale sang thirty-two Masses with orchestra and added no new Masses to its repertoire. The program for 1991-92 also announces the availability of Christmas music recorded on both cassette tape and CD which can be purchased through the Leaflet Missal Company.[27] The recording, *Christmas at Saint Agnes,* includes music sung traditionally by the Chorale during the concert preceding Midnight Mass. Featured are German and Austrian carols, Mozart's *Exsultate, Jubilate* and Schubert's *Ave Maria*. It opens with a Mozart organ sonata and concludes, as the concert always concludes, with Schnabel's *Transeamus usque Bethlehem,* sung as the statue of the Infant Jesus is carried in the solemn procession of clergy and altar servers, one of whom is dressed in the brown robe of a Franciscan, to the crib, and placed in the manger.

The 1992-93 season of the Chorale, its nineteenth, began on October 4, 1992, with the *Paukenmesse* by Haydn and finished on the Solemnity of Corpus Christi, June 13, 1993, with Haydn's *Heiligmesse*. After the Mass on Corpus Christi traditionally there is an outdoor procession with Benediction at several altars before returning to the church for the final Benediction. The Chorale leads the congregational singing for this procession. The Chorale added Carl M. von Weber's *Mass No. 2 in E Flat* to its repertoire and sang thirty-one times.

The Chorale began its twentieth season (1993-94) on September 26, 1993, with Haydn's *Paukenmesse*. This Mass has been a favorite of the Chorale ever since it was sung on the feast of the Assumption, 1974, in Munich, the event which was the inspiration for the Chorale orchestral Masses at Saint Agnes. The final Mass of the season was on the Solemnity of Corpus Christi, June 5, 1994, when the Mozart *Trinitatismesse* was sung. Thirty Masses with orchestra were sung. No new Masses were added to the repertoire.

Lest these paragraphs recounting the yearly activity of the Chorale in brief begin to sound mundane, it should be remembered that each year entails maintaining and perfecting an ever-growing repertoire and sometimes adding to it; recruiting new singers and integrating them into the existing choir; and the not insignificant task of raising the money to fund the program.

The 1994-95 season began on October 2, 1994, with the *Paukenmesse* by Haydn. The season ended with Haydn's *Heiligmesse* on the Solemnity of Corpus Christi on June 18, 1995. The Chorale sang thirty times with orchestra. No new Masses were added.

The 1995-96 season began on October 1, 1995, with the Mozart *Coronation Mass*. The last Mass was on the Solemnity of Corpus Christi, June 9, 1996, when the Chorale sang the Mozart *Piccolomini Mass*. The Chorale sang thirty Masses with orchestra.

On December 10, 1995, Mary Elizabeth LeVoir played an organ recital on the newly restored Wicks organ at Saint Agnes. The organ had been purchased in 1957 when Bishop Alphonse J. Schladweiler was pastor with the advice of Father Schuler and was renovated in 1995. Mary LeVoir's recital included *Praeludium* by Vincent Lübeck; *Seven Pastels from the Lake of Constance* by Sigfried Karg-Elert; *Trio Sonata V in C Major,* BWV 529 by J.S. Bach; *The Embrace of Fire* by Naji Hakim; and *Pièces de Fantaisie, Improptu,* Op. 54 and *Toccata,* Op. 53 by Louis Vierne.

The 1996-97 program was the first to list, not only the music of the Chorale, but also the schedule of the Chamber Choir, and a listing of the chant Masses sung by the *Schola Cantorum*. The Chorale season began on September 29, 1996, with the Mozart *Coronation Mass* and concluded on June 1, 1997, with Haydn's *Paukenmesse* on the Solemnity of Corpus Christi. The Chorale sang twenty-nine Masses and added Josef Rheinberger's *Mass in C,* Op. 169 to its repertoire. The *Mass in C* by Rheinberger has become a very popular addition to the repertoire.

In the Summer 1997 issue of *Sacred Music* (Vol. 124, No. 2), Monsignor Schuler published an important article entitled, "The Sacred." In it he says that the disintegration of the Roman Catholic liturgy, and, in general, of the practice of the religion, is because the concept of the "sacred" has been eliminated from Catholic life and practice. What must we do to counter this trend? His answer is that "everyone must take part in finding again the path to God by means of the sacred"(p.15). He says that to come to God and to holiness we need beauty of place. The churches must not be mere meeting halls; the art must be accessible, but it must not be kitsch. (A member of the Chorale used to say that one should not be able to turn a church building into a supermarket in fifteen minutes!) To continue with Monsignor Schuler's ideas, there must be a beauty of movement. "Dignity, reverence, order and purpose must mark the sacred action" (p.16). The third point is that there must be beauty of sound. Here he states that the iconoclasm after the Council which banned the Latin language succeeded in banning the great art of the music from the past. He also says that liturgical music *is* liturgy and that listening *is* active participation. "Very often it is the one who can listen who is moved to the highest degree of prayer, because he does not have to turn his attention to the demands of performance" (p.16). "The liturgy of earth is but a faint reflection of the liturgy of heaven, carried out by the choirs of angels and the Saints of every class....The sacred art we employ is only a sensitive, prophetic anticipation of that glory which will one day outshine and overwhelm all human art and make it superfluous" (p.16). This article on the sacred is a very good description of the Church of Saint Agnes and its liturgies. This is why the faithful sought out and continue to seek out Saint Agnes, sometimes driving many miles and many hours to participate in the Masses, and why singers join the Chorale. An example of the reach of the Masses at Saint Agnes and the Twin Cities Catholic Chorale is that there are currently 296 zip codes represented on the Chorale's data base. Registered parishioners at Saint Agnes come from miles around and from 145 zip codes.

The Chorale began its twenty-fourth season (1997-98) on September 28, 1997, with Haydn's *Theresienmesse* and finished on June 14, 1998, with the *Piccolomini Mass* by Mozart. It sang thirty Masses with orchestra and added no new Masses to its repertoire. This program listed the whole schedule of the Chorale and the Chamber Choir, and, for the first time, the availability of CDs as well as cassettes of the three Masses recorded by the Chorale in 1986. The CDs represent edited versions of the cassette tapes, eliminating the prayers of the Mass by the celebrant and the homilies. They include the Masses by Gounod, Haydn and Beethoven with the chant for the feasts sung by the *Schola Cantorum* and organ preludes and recessionals played by Mary Elizabeth LeVoir.[28]

An article in the Fall 1997 issue of *Sacred Music* (Vol. 124, No. 3, pp 5-6) with the title, "A Visit to a Vatican II Church," written by Lyle Settle, describes his visit to Saint Agnes on the Solemnity of Corpus Christi for the sixth national convention of the Latin Liturgy Association. It happened also to be the First Mass of Father Michael Creagan. The author comments that the phrase "Reconversion to

Catholicism" was buzzing around in his head. Monsignor Schuler suggested that perhaps this is because Saint Agnes steers clear of home-grown liturgies and rather tries earnestly to follow the mandates of the Council. The article contains a detailed description of the High Mass and Corpus Christi procession. The author also mentions that prayers for vocations said at the Sunday Masses every week for thirty-five years are being answered because there have been seventeen First Masses celebrated at Saint Agnes in the past fifteen years. When the article was written there were ten young men from the parish studying in the archdiocesan program of priestly training, both in the college seminary and the major seminary. The author concludes, "The liturgy at Saint Agnes manifests the transcendent art of the Catholic Church, and showed no trace of the distracting influence of modern liturgists or the influence of the entertainment industry. Even though many elements have been retained that in other places have long ago been replaced, the quality of popular participation at Saint Agnes is ideal, and attentiveness to sacred devotion is exemplary" (p.6).

The twenty-fifth season of the Chorale's residency at Saint Agnes (1998-99) began on Sunday, October 4, 1998, with Haydn's *Theresienmesse* and ended on June 6, 1999, the Solemnity of Corpus Christi, with Mozart's *Piccolomini Mass.* The Chorale sang twenty-nine times.

The 1999-2000 season began on October 3, 1999, with Haydn's *Nelsonmesse* and terminated on June 25, 2000, the Solemnity of Corpus Christi, with the Mozart *Mass in C*, K 337. It is interesting to note that in spite of the fact that the schedule went late into June, which meant that the choir loft risked being very hot because the church is not air conditioned, the last Masses on the program used large forces of choir and orchestra. They included the very demanding Schubert *Mass in A Flat*, which was added to the repertoire and sung for the first time by the Chorale on May 28. The Chorale sang an unusually long schedule of 32 Masses. In addition, the Chorale learned the *Vesperae solennes de confessore*, K 339 by Mozart, which it sang at a special Vespers ceremony on Tuesday evening, May 9, 2000 at 8:00 p.m. At this ceremony, the new monumental wood carvings of Saints Peter and Paul, which were to be mounted in the sanctuary of the church, were blessed. After the ceremony in the church, everyone went out to the parking lot for an official first view of the lighting of the tower and onion dome steeple.

The Honorable Norman Coleman, Mayor of Saint Paul, threw the switch. A reception followed.

The printed program for the 2000-01 season took a slightly different format and included for the first time the organ preludes and postludes played by the very accomplished organist for the Chorale Masses, Mary Elizabeth LeVoir. The year began with great festivity on October 1, 2000, with Haydn's *Nelsonmesse* followed by Schubert's *Mass in A Flat*, which had only been added to the repertoire the preceding year. The Chorale sang thirty-one times, concluding as usual on the Solemnity of Corpus Christi, June 17, 2001.

Perhaps this is a good place to include several amusing anecdotes about Monsignor Schuler as a director. He sometimes lost his grip on what he was holding in his hand, flipping it over the choir loft railing into the congregation. For a description of such an event when he directed the choir at the Church of the Nativity of Our Lord, please see that section in Appendix D. At the Church of Saint Agnes, it was his baton that flew out of his hand and went down into the congregation. If memory serves, both times the objects landed in the aisle, or at least, they did not hit anyone on the head! Francis Thevenin, violinist, who has played with the Chorale orchestra since 1974, remembers another incident which was more frightening for all. He wrote in the *View Behind the Painting*, "One Sunday morning, he was very demonstrative with an upbeat and as he brought the baton across, the tip of it pierced the back of his left hand, went under the skin and emerged about two inches further. As he pulled the baton out, continuing to conduct, I got up and gave him a handkerchief, which he clutched around his hand until the end of the movement. When he removed the handkerchief it was amazingly not bleeding. After Mass I told him he should seek medical attention. He replied stoically, 'Oh it will be all right'." This author and some other singers also repeated the advice to go to the emergency room. He simply said that he did not know how he was going to explain the injury when he got there!

A memory in *View Behind the Painting*[29] from two flutists in the orchestra, Elaine and David Eagle, expresses well the feelings of the orchestra for this great founder-director of the Chorale.

"The infamous day that we lost Monsignor Richard Schuler gave us all reason to grieve. He was the kind of true Renaissance man of which the world needs more, but finds irreplaceable.

"A high-ranking ecclesiastic who was also a respected musicologist was not easy to find, especially one with a loveable personality who did what he considered right, even in the face of powerful opposition. What he gave to Saint Paul in particular, and Minnesota in general, was a reputation for authoritative performances of 18th and 19th century Masses (mostly Viennese) that the rest of the world's churches have chosen to ignore.

"Father Schuler was a rarity – a conductor who was loved by his orchestra and his vocal soloists....He had his human side too which added to his charm and occasionally caused a chuckle in the balcony."

Monsignor Schuler presents Mass recordings of the Chorale to Pope John Paul II (now Saint John Paul) in June, 1989. He was accompanied by his nephew, Reverend Richard M. Hogan, to his left in the photo. (Photograph by Arturo Mari, copyright Servizio Fotografico, *L'Osservatore Romano*. Used with permission)

CHAPTER IX

The Team Necessary for the Latin High Mass at Saint Agnes

This is a good place to discuss what is necessary for a "Chorale Mass" at the Church of Saint Agnes.

From the very beginning of the residency of the Chorale at Saint Agnes forty-two years ago in the fall of 1974, Monsignor Schuler made it very clear that the music of the orchestra Masses was an integral part of the celebration of the High Mass in Latin in what we now call the Ordinary Form as allowed by the Second Vatican Council in *Sacrosanctum Concilium*. The music was in no way to be considered a concert.

The beautiful Masses by Haydn, Mozart, Beethoven, Schubert, and other composers, sung by the members of the Chorale with orchestra, were meant to be a prayer to God and an inspiration to the faithful. Monsignor Schuler believed that *Sacrosanctum Concilium, The Constitution on the Liturgy,* freed the Catholic church musician to choose from the great treasury of music which included the orchestra Masses of the eighteenth and nineteenth centuries.

Latin High Mass had been sung at Saint Agnes since the founding of the parish in 1887. Fortunately, there was a rich tradition of ceremonies for the Latin High Mass with a celebrant, deacon and sub-deacon and a contingent of altar servers who had been well-trained by Mr. Harold Hughesdon, who himself had been schooled as an altar server at Westminster Catholic Cathedral in London. Mr. Hughesdon was ordained as a permanent deacon on September 26, 1981, and continued to be in charge of the ceremonies at Saint Agnes until his death in 2012.

The Pastor and Clergy

It has been possible to continue the tradition of Latin High Mass with reverent ceremonies at Saint Agnes because each of the pastors who followed Monsignor Schuler embraced the tradition for which the parish was well known. Although currently the pastor is the only priest assigned to Saint Agnes, and two of our permanent deacons are recently deceased, it has been possible to continue with the Latin High Masses with the generous aid of the several priests in residence at the rectory, one permanent deacon, several lay lectors, and a contingent of well-trained and very reverent altar boys.

The Music Director of the Chorale

The founding director of the Chorale, Monsignor Richard J. Schuler, was uniquely prepared for the complexities of his position. He not only held a doctorate in musicology from the University of Minnesota, and before that, a Master of Arts from Eastman School of Music, but he knew well and loved the tradition of orchestra Masses so beloved in Munich, Salzburg, and Vienna. He was active in the Church Music Association of America, was its president, and became editor of *Sacred Music* magazine in 1975, a position he held for over twenty years. He was also active in the papal church music association, the *Consociatio Internationalis Musicae Sacrae*. He knew very well the *Constitution on the Sacred Liturgy* of the Second Vatican Council. He believed in and advocated the "letter of the Council," rather than the "spirit of the Council," which he considered to be a misinterpretation. When he became pastor of Saint Agnes, he was in a position to implement the Council fully. As editor of *Sacred Music*, he had a forum from which he could teach. Those who knew him, as singers in the Chorale did, knew he was demanding, but kind, and had a warm wit. He could not stand self-appointed "visiting artists," but bestowed the title with affection on some of the older singers who felt the need to retire from the Chorale. He also could not abide "foot tapping." He was the director and he set the tempo. He was known to walk over to a singer and gently put his foot on top of the tapping one in front of him. Those who knew him in other circumstances knew him to be fearless and stubborn in doing what he believed to be right. Without his knowledge, strength of character, and devotion to the reverent celebration of the Holy Sacrifice of the Mass, the program he established at the Church of Saint Agnes would have been impossible.

Before he had to give up directing the Chorale because of advanced age and ill health, he chose and prepared his successor, Dr. Robert L. Peterson. This transition is discussed in the chronological history of the Chorale. Dr. Peterson had had a brilliant career in high school and college choral music. He was well prepared for the very demanding task of directing a choir of volunteers, professional soloists and orchestra every Sunday for about 30 weeks of the year with a large repertoire of Masses and inadequate rehearsal time. And thus, in 2015, the program Monsignor Schuler set in place is being continued.

Chorale Members

The Chorale is currently composed of about sixty-five singers. All are volunteers, ranging in age from high school students to retirees. They come from all corners of the greater metropolitan area of the Twin Cities. Most are Roman Catholics, but some, although not Catholic, have been attracted by the repertory of the choir and the reverence of the liturgy. Because of the richness of the musical program (in 2014-15 the Chorale sang 27 times with orchestra and only repeated two Masses), the newer members realize what a challenge it is to join the Chorale, and thus the organization is attracting more experienced singers, or at least those who are committed to attending rehearsals, and willing to work outside of rehearsals to learn the repertoire.

Singing in the Chorale is often a family event. The Eilen family is an example. Michael Eilen, the father of the family, is in the tenor section. His wife Kathleen and his daughter, Mary, both sing alto. Michael's brother, Allen, now a priest, sang in the choir before he went to the seminary, and as time allowed, during his seminary years. Kathleen's father, Richard Byrne, was a professor of music at the University of Minnesota and director of the choir at the Saint Paul Cathedral as well as substitute director for Monsignor Schuler on occasions when Monsignor Schuler was the celebrant of a Mass at which the Chorale sang.

The Pedersen family is another example. Deacon Bernard Pedersen, lately deceased, was drawn to the Church of Saint Agnes by the liturgy and the music of the Chorale. He was a member of the Anglican communion at the time, but converted to Roman Catholicism through Monsignor Schuler's influence. He joined the Chorale in the mid-eighties and remained an active singer until his ordination to the diaconate when he took his place in the sanctuary. Currently, his widow, Judy Pedersen, sings alto, and his daughter, Ruth Anne Pedersen Halverson, sings soprano. Deacon Pedersen's son, Father Bryan Pedersen, sang in the Chorale until his ordination to the priesthood; another son, Karl, and another daughter, Ellen Pedersen Martinez, also used to sing in the choir.

Vocations to the priesthood have always been very important to the parish where the sacred liturgy is central. In *The Church of Saint Agnes (1887-1987)*, Monsignor Schuler notes: "For thirty years the parish has been praying for religious vocations." (p. 168) Beginning in the late 1970s, Monsignor Schuler began working actively with seminarians who came to him for spiritual counseling. He urged that all aspiring seminarians sing with the Chorale. For a number of years, beginning in 1981, there was at least one, and often two, and once in a while, three Masses of Thanksgiving offered by newly ordained priests every year at Saint Agnes. Many of these priests are now pastors of parishes in this archdiocese and have developed reverent sacred music programs for the liturgies in their churches. Three of the priests mentored by Monsignor Schuler have been named bishops: The Most Reverend John M. LeVoir, Bishop of New Ulm, Minnesota; The Most Reverend Paul D. Sirba, Bishop of Duluth, Minnesota; and The Most Reverend Alexander K. Sample, Archbishop of Portland, Oregon.[30] The author of this work hesitates to name all of the priests mentored by Monsignor Schuler for fear of omitting one.

A community of Sisters, the Sisters in Jesus the Lord, was formed in the convent at Saint Agnes in 2003. The first postulant for the order was Kelly Whittier, now Sister Maria Stella. When she came to Saint Agnes, she was already an accomplished musician. In *The View Behind the Painting*, she said:

> Seeing the music and liturgy focus at Saint Agnes helped me in my decision to come, as I realized that even if the hope of becoming a missionary sister for Russia did not come to fruition, being at Saint Agnes would be the much needed "internship" I could not find in graduate school. I had not yet

been able to incorporate more traditional music in my parish music and liturgy work, as I had never seen it done on a regular basis at any parish in America (p.23).

After several years of formation and rigorous preparation, Sister Maria Stella is currently part of a team of sisters from that small community working in the city of Vladivostock in Far Eastern Russia. Two American priests stationed there have restored the Roman Catholic Cathedral where classical liturgical music concerts play a central role in attracting worshippers.

Three of the current members of the Chorale have sung in the Chorale for over 40 years. They are Cornelia Bieza, alto; Bernadette Lamb, soprano; and Virginia Schubert, soprano. For the vitality of the choir, the Music Director works constantly and diligently to attract new and younger singers.

The Organist

Mary Elizabeth LeVoir has been the organist and accompanist for the Chorale and also the parish organist since 1980 when she was hired by Monsignor Schuler. She graduated with a Bachelor of Music degree from the Oberlin Conservatory and holds a Doctor of Musical Arts from the University of Minnesota. Although she modestly says that she is only the parish organist, she is well-recognized for her organ preludes and postludes. In addition, as an accompanist, she fills in the orchestra parts as needed at rehearsal. She has an excellent sense of *tempi* and both she and her husband Paul serve as liturgy advisers to the Music Director.

The Orchestra and Soloists

When the Chorale began its residency at Saint Agnes in 1974, Monsignor Schuler decided that it was necessary not only to hire professional classical union musicians, but that it was essential to engage musicians of great expertise who were used to playing the repertoire of the Chorale. He therefore began working with a violinist who was a member of the Minnesota Orchestra to serve as contractor in order to engage a stable group of musicians to form the orchestra. Monsignor Schuler knew that rehearsal time with the orchestra would be very limited, both because of the added cost for rehearsals and because of the time involvement for the players, the singers, and the director.

Thus, the contractor hired the orchestra, depending on the requirements of the score, mostly from members of the Minnesota Orchestra. Currently, four instrumentalists have been playing for the orchestra Masses since the beginning of the residency in 1974. Many others have been with the Chorale for many years and are very loyal to its mission. There is more information about the costs of the orchestra in the chapter on finances.

The Chorale has engaged four soloists almost since the beginning of its residency. Initially, the soloists were drawn from the Chorale, but it became too difficult both for the choir and the individuals who were to sing the solos. The choir suffered from the absence of what one could call a section leader and the choir members/soloists felt the difficulty of having different solo parts ready each week for the Mass that was scheduled. As it is with the orchestra, the current professional soloists are faithful members of the team.

The *Schola Cantorum*

As was requested by Vatican II, Gregorian chant is given pride of place in the liturgy at Saint Agnes. The *Schola Cantorum*, directed by Paul W. LeVoir since 1979, sings the chant Propers at all of the Chorale Masses and is responsible for all of the music when the Chorale does not sing, for example during Advent, Lent, and the summer months. Members of the *Schola* sing a Latin High Mass in chant on Saturday mornings. The *Schola* also sings Latin High Mass during the octave of Christmas and is responsible for the Holy Week liturgy as well as *Tenebrae*. Vespers in Latin are sung every Sunday at Saint Agnes.

The Architectural Space

No analysis of the Latin Masses at Saint Agnes with Chorale and orchestra is complete without some comments on the architectural space. The Baroque style of the church is modeled after a monastery church in Upper Austria, Kloster Schlägl, near the town of Aigen in Mühlviertel. The Church of Saint Agnes is physically a beautiful space, and its acoustic corresponds perfectly to the Viennese Masses sung there. In addition, there is probably no choir loft in a church in the archdiocese that would accommodate the size of the choir and orchestra necessary for some of the Masses which can include 65 or 70 singers and as many as 30 instrumentalists.

Conclusion

Without this team of very talented people in leadership positions and the volunteer members of the Chorale, all of whom are committed to this mission in this beautiful church, these Masses would be impossible. It is the opinion of this author that if it ever ceased, it would be impossible to start up again.

CHAPTER X

The Finances of the Twin Cities Catholic Chorale

Since its founding in 1955/1956, the Twin Cities Catholic Chorale has always had to raise the funds needed to finance its program. It has also depended on the frugality of those who made the decisions, in the beginning, Father Richard J. Schuler, and on the generosity of donors and volunteers. The first year for which there is financial information in a ledger is 1957-58. The finances, as recorded by Father Schuler, were simple and direct. The expenses were $221.74, including $21.75 for copies of the *Missa Coloniensis* by Hermann Schroeder and two scores and seventy-five voice parts of Tittel's *Missa Magnus et Potens*, which cost $33. As for income, gifts from members of the group are listed as $37. The books were balanced with a donation from Father Schuler of $76.52.

In 1958-59, nine brass players (students) were paid $100 for a recording. Expenses were $325.22; income $213, and the deficit $112.22. In 1959-60, the choir purchased 65 choir robes for $992.81. These were worn for the first time in the two concerts given by the group in the spring of 1960. Expenses were $1,974.94. Income came from donations from members of the choir, a fund raising silver tea, and the income from the two concerts. The total income was $1,781.71. There was a deficit of $210.03, owed to Father Schuler.

The letter sent by Father Schuler in the fall of 1962 to organize the 1962-63 season said that, for the first time, the Chorale was in the black with a balance of $26.82. This did not last long because, at the end of 1964, the Chorale owed Father Schuler $564.01, probably because of the fees paid to the recording company for the recording and production of the record, *Viennese Church Music.* Record sales in 1964-65 brought in $636. By the close of the 1964-65 season, the bank balance was $27.90.

In August of 1969, Father Schuler became pastor of the Church of Saint Agnes in Saint Paul. It is important at this point to emphasize that the Chorale was not then and never has been funded by the Church of Saint Agnes. In fact, after the Chorale began to sing regularly at Saint Agnes in 1974, Monsignor Schuler's letters announcing the season at Saint Agnes and asking for contributions for the Chorale stated that fact very clearly, emphatically and repeatedly. For example, in his letter of September 12, 1977, Monsignor Schuler says, "The Parish of Saint Agnes offers the Chorale its beautiful church, but no financial support is given to the project by the parish."

The expenses of the Chorale changed dramatically when the choir began to sing regularly at Saint Agnes because of the fees paid to the union musicians on a regular basis. Monsignor Schuler kept detailed records of the fees for each Mass. The first was Mozart's *Coronation Mass* on October 20, 1974. Each of the sixteen players, who were members of the Minnesota Orchestra or with equivalent qualifications, was paid the union scale of $30 for the performance and $16 each for a rehearsal. The total cost for that Mass was $794. The orchestra fees for that first year amounted to $10,892.82. During all the years that Monsignor Schuler directed the Chorale, he was not paid for his professional services.

To compare that first year with 2013-14, the last year for which we have complete records, the annual report gives the expenses for musicians and music as $98,862. The Chorale sang thirty Masses with orchestra. The average cost of a Mass is now $3,500. Union scale is now $100 per musician. In addition, the director is now paid. The choir members are, and always have been, volunteers. In addition, many other volunteers donate countless hours of their time to manage, promote, and raise funds for this program. The Chorale would not be able to fulfill its mission without the strong support of the pastor of the parish who invites the Chorale to provide the music for the Latin High Mass on Sunday. In addition, the Church of Saint Agnes supports the Chorale by offering rehearsal space and a room for the Schuler Archives. It is customary that the parish also sponsors the music for one Mass each year.

COMMENTARY

What Singing in the Chorale Means To Me

My journey to the Twin Cities Catholic Chorale began in 1993 when my father-in-law, Dr. Richard Byrne, retired from his position, after sixteen years, as choral director at the Cathedral of Saint Paul in Saint Paul, Minnesota. I remember asking him, a most effective choir director and teacher, what I should do now that he was retiring. And at the same time, I began to ponder what it meant to me to sing as a tenor in the Cathedral choir from the time I met my wife Kathleen (his daughter) in February of 1987. Dick mentioned to me that I might like to join the Chorale at the Church of Saint Agnes in Saint Paul. I remember saying to him: "Isn't that the church where they say the Mass in Latin." He said, "Yes, and I think you might enjoy singing the Viennese Masses of Mozart, Haydn, and Schubert, along with the Minnesota Orchestra." Inasmuch as I had been an altar server in the 1960s and a seminarian at Saint John Vianney College Seminary in the 1970s, I thought the Latin would come back to me; so after prayerful consideration, I decided to give it a try.

I recall meeting, for the first time that fall Tuesday, experienced tenors such as Deacon John Mangan, John Alvarez, Dr. Jim Kromhout, Hal Williamson, and Omar Connor. Each one of these men became mentors to me and started me down the road on a journey of fulfillment – what I would now describe as a most profound kind of "prayerful music." Monsignor Richard J. Schuler, our founder and choral director, was fond of saying that the music we sing here at Saint Agnes is not meant to be a concert, but must be thought of as an integral part of our worship of Almighty God, done within the context of the Holy Sacrifice of the Mass. In other words, it is to be considered a prayer for God's glory – not a concert! I have never forgotten this, and what began on that first Tuesday in October of 1993, has blossomed in my heart into a great appreciation and love not only for the Catholic Church, but also for the great Viennese masters of the Church's music such as Mozart, Haydn, and Schubert.

When I joined the Chorale, I had no formal training in music, only a natural gift and love for singing. However, under Monsignor Schuler's guidance, not only has my knowledge of music grown, but I have come to regard my time in the Chorale as not just volunteer, but as a sincere call from Almighty God to give back to Him what He has given to me in the form of talent, energy, and dedication. Furthermore, my wife Kathleen and our six children have also been "giving back" by joining the Chorale and singing in other parish choirs at Saint Agnes.

Ultimately, I have come to regard the other members of the Chorale as part of my extended family; and having sung in the Chorale now for twenty-one years, I can honestly say that my participation in the Chorale makes me feel each Sunday as though I have at the same time one foot on earth and one foot in heaven.

Michael Eilen, Tenor

COMMENTARY

Singing in the Twin Cities Catholic Chorale

(Note: The daughter of Michael Eilen, Mary joined the Chorale in 2012-13 after her graduation from the University of Saint Thomas. She teaches third grade at Saint Agnes Grade School.)

The Twin Cities Catholic Chorale is an organization unknown to many in this city, state, and country. However, those who experience its beauty and the enormity of its tasks, find that it is an organization of great importance. This organization finds a way to fill people with awe when they experience the wonder of its works. The people who help to keep the Chorale afloat are not those who can take full credit for its beauty. It is by allowing the Almighty to work through its members that this organization continues to grow and provide music which moves its listeners.

The Twin Cities Catholic Chorale has always been a part of my life. It was not something that I experienced entirely on my own. If it were not for the influence of my grandfather and my parents, I may have never come in contact with the Chorale. My parents have both been in church choirs since before I was born. They were members of my grandfather's choir at the Cathedral of Saint Paul many years ago. When my grandfather retired from directing the choir, he suggested to my parents that they come to Saint Agnes and become members of the Twin Cities Catholic Chorale. Each Sunday as a little girl, my parents brought me to the 10:00 a.m. High Mass at Saint Agnes Church. I became used to the beauty of the church and to the music that I heard, almost taking it for granted. Each and every Sunday included a large orchestra with 50 to 60 choir members. My father joined the choir when our family became parishioners of Saint Agnes, while my mother spent time taking care of my brothers and me. I remember feeling proud of my father for working hard to practice and sing faithfully in the tenor section each week. I always felt that I could hear him singing his heart out to God, even from the pew. He practiced so faithfully that I had the privilege of hearing the Masses at home as well as at the church. It was such a large part of my childhood that I can hardly imagine growing up without it.

What is special about the Chorale? Why does it mean so much to me? There are a variety of answers to these questions. One is that it played a role in how I was brought up as a Roman Catholic. It is a part of my family. It is one of the many influences that allow me to claim music as a very important aspect of my life. I love to sing, play the piano, listen to music, etc. As my father would describe it, there is drama in the Masses that we sing. Hearing and singing orchestral Masses is something a person can only experience in a very few places in this world. You can listen to the music in a concert hall. Even then, it is moving. Yet, within the Mass, the Holy Sacrifice, there is added drama, added emotion, a greater aspect of spirituality. The music of these Masses helps one to enter into the Holy Sacrifice of the Mass (Jesus' sacrifice on the cross for our sins) with a deeper faith, truly meaning what we say when we sing *Kyrie Eleison* (Lord Have Mercy), or *Agnus Dei* (Lamb of God). The music is classical; it is romantic; it is beautiful; it is challenging; it reminds us that life is complex, sacrificial, and will hopefully lead us to eternal happiness.

Having grown up listening to the particular beauty of this choir, I know what a gift the Chorale is to the world. This is music for the Lord. It is music that continues because of Our Lord. I have since joined this choir because I want to be a part of singing for the Lord and making this extraordinary music last for as long as Our Lord wills it.

Mary Eilen, Alto

Part Four

"Every age must stand squarely on the shoulders of those who have gone before.... Musical styles develop with their roots in the past; eliminate the past and one finds that the wellsprings of musical inspiration and composition dry up too."

"Church Music after Vatican II"
by Monsignor Richard J. Schuler
Sacred Music (Vol. 103, No. 4)

CHAPTER XI

The Transition Begins – 2001-2006

Monsignor Schuler had long been looking for an assistant director and possible successor. He had tried out several candidates, but, for one reason or another, they had not worked out. In the spring of 2000, this author, who was a professor of French at Macalester College in Saint Paul, Minnesota, introduced Dr. Robert L. Peterson, Acting Chair of the Macalester Music Department and Visiting Professor, to Monsignor Schuler. Bob Peterson had retired from a distinguished career in choral music at Edina Senior High School, before coming to Macalester. Here is a quote from a letter this author wrote in 2008: "Bob and Monsignor Schuler immediately formed a personal bond. Bob immediately joined the choir in order to learn more about our complex repertoire. Bit by bit, Monsignor asked Bob to help him with directing. Bob also had another connection to Monsignor Schuler because he was a close friend of Father Michael Creagan and his parents. Father Creagan had been mentored by Monsignor Schuler when he was in the Saint Paul Seminary and had celebrated his Mass of Thanksgiving at the Church of Saint Agnes in 1997."

Bob Peterson writes about his first experience with the Chorale:

> In the fall of 2000 I began my prep work to conduct three Masses....In the fall of 2001 Monsignor assigned nine Masses to me, including the Mozart *Requiem* in November. That fall we discussed the *Mass in E,* Opus 87, by Heinrich von Herzogenberg. He wanted me to have the experience of purchasing a new work, and taking over all aspects of rehearsals leading to the first performance (including the rehearsal with orchestra and soloists). We performed that work the following season.

Herzogenberg's Mass had been lost and only recently rediscovered, published, sung, and recorded in Germany. Bob Peterson met the German publisher at a national conference that summer, ordered the scores from Germany, and negotiated with the publisher to buy, not rent, the orchestra parts. (Because the Chorale sings its Masses in repertoire, Monsignor Schuler decided from the beginning that the Chorale must own the orchestra parts, not rent them from the publisher, so they would be readily available.)

On June 30, 2001, Monsignor Schuler ended his tenure as pastor of the Church of Saint Agnes which had begun on August 26, 1969. He continued to reside in the rectory as pastor emeritus until 2006. He was succeeded by Father George Welzbacher, the ninth pastor of Saint Agnes from 2001 to 2006. As pastor, Father Welzbacher was always very supportive of the program of the Chorale and its residency at Saint Agnes. Monsignor Schuler continued to make decisions for the Chorale as well as to conduct most of the Masses so there was little change in the functioning of the Chorale. In 2001-02, the Chorale sang twenty-nine times, beginning on September 30, 2001, with Haydn's *Nelsonmesse* and concluding on June 2, 2002, with Mozart's *Mass in C,* K 337. The cover of the program for this season is a picture of the sanctuary of the church with the new statues installed.

The program of the twenty-ninth season, (2002-03) is the first that lists Dr. Robert L. Peterson as associate director. In addition to directing other works and taking rehearsals, he prepared the choir to sing Heinrich von Herzogenberg's *Messe in E minor,* Opus 87, and directed its first performance. This work was and continues to be very demanding for the singers because its style is more modern than the Chorale had been used to. It also uses a very large orchestra so the choir has to be at full strength. The Mass was believed to have been lost or destroyed during World War II. It was discovered in archival holdings sometime between 1994 and 1996. Herzogenberg (1843-1900) was a student and friend of Brahms and dedicated this Mass to the memory of his life-long friend and Bach scholar, Phillip Spitta, who died in 1894. What the Chorale believes to be the North American premiere of the Herzogenberg Mass was sung on June 8, 2003, the Solemnity of Pentecost. It should be noted here that, when a new Mass is added to the repertoire, there is always only one orchestra rehearsal. For Bob Peterson, whose background was in high school and college teaching, this was a new and challenging experience as was the general lack of rehearsal time with the choir. However, it was clear that Bob Peterson could handle the challenge superbly. The Chorale season began on October 6, 2002, with Haydn's *Theresienmesse* and ended on June 22, 2003, with Mozart's *Mass in C*, K 337. The Chorale sang 30 Masses with orchestra.

The thirtieth season of the Chorale (2003-04) began on September 28, 2003, with Haydn's *Theresienmesse* and concluded on June 13, 2004, with Mozart's *Coronation Mass*. The Chorale sang thirty times. Because of his failing health, Monsignor Schuler asked Bob Peterson to conduct all but five of the Masses that year.

The thirty-first season of the Chorale's residency at the Church of Saint Agnes (2004-05) began on October 3, 2004, with Haydn's *Nelsonmesse* and ended on May 29, 2005 with Schubert's *Mass in G*. In its regular season, the Chorale sang twenty-eight Masses with orchestra. In addition, the group sang the Mozart *Requiem* with orchestra at 7:30 p.m. on April 12, 2005, at a Mass in memory of His Holiness, Pope John Paul II, who had died on April 2, 2005. The Church of Saint Agnes was full of worshippers for that occasion.

The thirty-second season of the Chorale (2005-06) began on October 16, 2005, with Haydn's *Heiligmesse* and concluded on June 18, 2006, the Solemnity of Corpus Christi, with Schubert's *Mass in G*. On Sunday, October 30, 2005, Saint Agnes parish celebrated the sixtieth anniversary of Monsignor Schuler's ordination to the priesthood. For that occasion, the Chorale sang Haydn's *Paukenmesse*, the Mass that the Chorale had sung in the Alte Peterskirche in Munich on the Feast of the Assumption in 1974. The Chorale considered this Mass in Munich performed with a first rate orchestra as the inspiration for its program of Masses at Saint Agnes, and therefore it was especially fitting for this magnificent occasion. Father Richard M. Hogan, Monsignor Schuler's nephew, was the celebrant and homilist at the Mass. He spoke on the priesthood. The Mass was followed by a large and festive reception in Bandas Hall of the school at which Monsignor Schuler was presented with an endowment for the Chorale which had been established in his honor with the Catholic Aid Association (now Catholic United Financial). A great crowd of parishioners, present and former Chorale members, Friends of the Chorale, and many of Monsignor Schuler's former students from Saint Thomas College (now the University of

Saint Thomas) were in attendance. There were twenty-eight Masses scheduled for the regular season of the Chorale that year.

Several articles about Monsignor Schuler and the Chorale were published in 2005-2006, in part because of the 60th anniversary of Monsignor Schuler's ordination. The article in *The Wanderer,* October 20, 2005, by Father John Zuhlsdorf bearing the title, "The Mended Net and the Well-Tuned String" is about Monsignor Schuler on his sixtieth anniversary. In his conclusion, the author said, "In his service as a priest, Monsignor Schuler has been both a noted Church musician as well as an exceptionally successful 'fisher of men.' In his effort to promote true sacred music in the Church, he always tries to adhere to the Church's legislation about the same, always understanding that sacred music is not just an 'add on' to the liturgy, but rather it is *pars integrans,* an integral part of the liturgy itself." Father Zuhlsdorf had been attracted to sing with the Chorale when he was a student of Classics at the University of Minnesota. He became a Catholic after instruction by Monsignor Schuler and was ordained in Rome by His Holiness, Pope Saint John Paul II, in 1991. There was also an article in *AD 2000* (November 2005), which is published in Sydney, Australia, and another in *Sacred Music* (Winter 2005, Vol. 132, No. 4).

Two important events happened before the end of the 2005-2006 season. In May 2006, Monsignor Schuler asked a lawyer to prepare articles of incorporation and bylaws to incorporate the Twin Cities Catholic Chorale as a nonprofit corporation in the state of Minnesota. Up to this point, the Chorale had the status of an unincorporated nonprofit organization. Since 1974, it had been recognized by the Internal Revenue Service as a nonprofit so that contributors were allowed to deduct their donations from their income tax. It is clear, in retrospect, that Monsignor Schuler was preparing to leave the organization in good order for those who succeeded him. He met with the lawyer and this author on May 27, 2006, to go over the drafted articles of incorporation and bylaws and signed them several days later. (The Secretary of State issued the certificate of incorporation on June 5, 2006.) On Saturday, May 27, another "son of Saint Agnes," Father Sean Magnuson, was ordained to the priesthood at the Cathedral of Saint Paul and celebrated his Mass of Thanksgiving at Saint Agnes on Sunday, May 28, the Solemnity of the Ascension. The Chorale sang Haydn's *Harmoniemesse.*

On Memorial Day, May 29, 2006, Monsignor Schuler left the rectory to have dinner with friends and family and never was able to return there. He probably had a small stroke while at dinner. His last months were spent in an assisted living facility and several nursing homes. Little did we imagine when we began the 2005-2006 season the tremendous change that would happen at its end.

CHAPTER XII

The Passing of the Baton – 2006-2013

    The letter that Monsignor Schuler sent to the Friends of the Chorale with the program for the 2006-07 season contained the sad news that his health would not allow him to continue conducting the Chorale, but that "the music will be under the capable direction of Dr. Robert Peterson, Director of Choral Activities at Macalester College, who has worked with me for the past several years." Happily, Bob Peterson was well prepared to take over because he had been working with Monsignor Schuler and the Chorale since 2000, singing in the bass section when he was not conducting. He was thus very familiar with the repertoire and the functioning of the Chorale.

    Equally important, the members of the Chorale were used to working with him, and liked and respected him as a musician and as a human being. The transition from one director to another is not an insignificant thing for a choir, especially for a volunteer choir like the Chorale in which each and every member felt a personal loyalty to its founder, Monsignor Schuler. Monsignor Schuler continued his letter by asking the Friends of the Chorale to attend the 10:00 a.m. High Masses often and to continue to contribute to the Chorale "which is supported exclusively by the Friends of the Chorale." Joined to this letter was a statement from the new pastor, Father John L. Ubel, giving his support to the Chorale and asking for the continued support of the Friends of the Chorale. Bob Peterson also sent a message asking for the continued support of the Friends for "this unique program."

    In the annual program, Monsignor Schuler is still listed as the Director and Dr. Robert Peterson as the associate director. However, in point of fact, from the beginning of this season, Bob Peterson became the only director of the Chorale. The season began on October

22, 2006, with Haydn's *Paukenmesse* and ended on June 10, 2007, the Solemnity of Corpus Christi, with Schubert's *Mass in G*. The Chorale sang twenty-seven times in its announced schedule. The committee that planned the schedule considered cutting it to twenty-one Masses because it was uncertain whether the Friends of the Chorale would continue to contribute as generously if Monsignor Schuler were no longer in charge. However, the decision to go ahead with twenty-seven announced Masses proved to be a prudent one because enough money was contributed to complete the schedule. This was an important transitional season because the Chorale sang its full schedule for the first time under a new director. In addition, the new pastor, Father John Ubel, had begun his tenure on July 1, 2006.

The 2006-07 season proved to be a very difficult one for several reasons. The officers and board members of the new corporation took over making decisions that had previously been made exclusively by the founding director of the Chorale, Monsignor Schuler. Arriving at a trust level and a working relationship is never easy when such a significant change in organization is made. However, the most difficult situation was Monsignor Schuler's deteriorating health. Monsignor Schuler died on April 20, 2007. His funeral Mass, for which, at his request, the Chorale sang the Mozart *Requiem* with orchestra, took place at 7:00 p.m. on April 24, 2007. Bob Peterson warned the choir not to cry, because if we did, he would too. The Chorale sang with great emotion, but also with self-control. Approximately 100 priests concelebrated the Mass. The church was full to capacity. Father Richard M. Hogan, Monsignor's nephew, preached the homily. A letter from His Holiness, Pope Benedict XVI, was read at the funeral. Monsignor Schuler knew personally both Cardinal Ratzinger and his brother, Father Georg Ratzinger, longtime director of the Cathedral Choir of Regensburg.

In August 2007, Bob Peterson sent out the organizational letter to current singers, asking them for their continuing commitment to the Chorale. He said: "Everyone who has worshipped with us at Saint Agnes for years under Monsignor Schuler will be watching to observe how we survive. It is our job to perform the music for Mass at the highest level possible with the talent God has given us as individuals." In reviewing this letter and the minutes of the Board meetings, it is evident that all were feeling their way in this new situation, while working as hard as possible to ensure the continuing success of the Chorale. Bob's letter also announced the new logo and format for the annual schedule which had been conceptualized by the Marketing Committee with the approval of Monsignor Schuler before his death and completed *pro bono* by a talented professional graphic artist. This is perhaps the place to emphasize the fact that *everything* necessary for the organization and management of the Chorale was and continues to be done by talented volunteers, who generously give their time and talents because they believe in the mission of the Chorale. The Chorale has no paid management staff.

3339 MASSACHUSETTS AVENUE, N.W.
WASHINGTON, D.C. 20008-3687

APOSTOLIC NUNCIATURE
UNITED STATES OF AMERICA

Prot. No. - 5548   24 April 2007

Your Excellency:

The Secretariat of State of His Holiness Pope Benedict XVI has instructed me to convey the following message:

THE MOST REVEREND HARRY J. FLYNN
ARCHBISHOP OF SAINT PAUL AND MINNEAPOLIS

THE HOLY FATHER WAS SADDENED TO LEARN OF THE DEATH OF MONSIGNOR RICHARD J.SCHULER, PASTOR EMERITUS OF SAINT AGNES CHURCH. RECALLING WITH GRATITUDE MONSIGNOR SCHULER'S COMMITMENT TO THE CHURCH'S RICH MUSICAL HERITAGE AND HIS LONG YEARS OF PRIESTLY MINISTRY IN THE ARCHDIOCESE, HIS HOLINESS OFFERS FERVENT PRAYERS FOR HIS ETERNAL REST. TO ALL PRESENT AT THE MASS OF CHRISTIAN BURIAL HE CORDIALLY IMPARTS HIS APOSTOLIC BLESSING AS A PLEDGE OF CONSOLATION AND STRENGTH IN THE LORD.

CARDINAL TARCISIO BERTONE
SECRETARY OF STATE

With sentiments of esteem, I remain

Fraternally yours in Christ,

Archbishop Pietro Sambi
Apostolic Nuncio

Most Rev. Harry J. Flynn
Archbishop of St. Paul and Minneapolis
226 Summit Avenue
St. Paul, Minnesota 55102-2197

Letter of condolence from His Holiness, Pope Benedict XVI, transmitted by Cardinal Bertone, Secretary of State of the Vatican, on the occasion of the death of Monsignor Richard J. Schuler. Schuler Archives.

The fall mailing for the 2007-08 season used, for the first time, the new format for the annual program and a new letterhead. It featured a stained glass window from the choir loft representing musician angels. The letterhead used that logo with the phrase "Classical Music in a Heavenly Setting." It listed Monsignor Richard J. Schuler as Founding Director of the Chorale and Robert L. Peterson as Music Director. It also gave the names of the newly-elected officers and board: Deacon John Mangan, president; Michael Eilen, vice-president; Virginia Schubert, Executive Director and Secretary; Richard Ellsworth, Treasurer. Board members included: Kathleen Bedor, Kathleen Eilen, Diane Foote, Roger Huss, James Kromhout, M.D., Jeanne Mayer, Sarah Murray and Father John L. Ubel. The mailing announced the sale of a memory book, *View Behind the Painting: Memories of Monsignor Richard J. Schuler.* This book was assembled by several members of the Chorale and included reminiscences of current and former choir and orchestra members. Its publication helped the Chorale grieve, and it provides invaluable memories, especially of the Saint Agnes years. Bob Peterson's letter stated that the Chorale would add a new Mass to its repertoire: Mozart's *Missa Brevis in D*, K 194, and that the Mozart *Requiem* would be sung twice, on November 2 for the Feast of All Souls, and on April 22, 2008 in memory of the first anniversary of Monsignor Schuler's death. The Chorale sang twenty-five times with orchestra.

Minutes of the February 11, 2008 board meeting include the fact that Father William Sanderson, who studied at the Saint Paul Seminary, sang in the Chorale, was the celebrant on the cassette tape versions of the recordings of Masses, and currently a pastor in Omaha, Nebraska, would be the celebrant and homilist for the memorial Mass for Monsignor Schuler.

On October 19, 2008, the Chorale began its 35th season in residence at the Church of Saint Agnes with Schubert's *Mass in C.* The Mass on October 26, 2008, was offered for the intention of the Friends of the Chorale and was followed by a reception. The Chorale sang H. von Herzogenberg's *Messe*, Op. 87 for that occasion. At the request of the pastor, Father Ubel, the Chorale sang the *Requiem in D Minor* by Gabriel Fauré rather than the Mozart *Requiem* for the Feast of All Souls on November 2, 2008. The Chorale sang twenty-seven times with orchestra. Articles appeared in several publications celebrating the

35th season of the Chorale's residency at Saint Agnes. They include *The Catholic Spirit,* October 16, 2008; *The Wanderer,* October 16, 2008, and *The Catholic Servant,* September, 2008.

The Chorale began its 2009-10 season on October 18, 2009, by singing the Mozart *Missa Brevis in F,* K 192 for the first time. Father Ubel, pastor of Saint Agnes, decided to alternate the Ordinary and Extraordinary Forms of the Mass at the 10:00 a.m. Latin High Mass. This decision influenced the programming of the Masses because the Extraordinary Form of the Mass (1962 *Missale Romanum*) is a little longer so the Chorale had to be careful to schedule "shorter" Masses on those Sundays (1st, 3rd and 5th). The several *Missa Brevis* of Mozart were perfect because they met the stringent time constraints imposed by the Prince Archbishop of Salzburg, Hieronoymus Colloredo. The Chorale sang the Mozart *Requiem* again for the Mass on November 2 by popular request. The Chorale sang 27 times with orchestra, finishing its season, as usual, on the Solemnity of Corpus Christi, which fell that year on June 6, 2010.

Advertisement announcing the Masses of the Twin Cities Catholic Chorale placed in program books of major classical music organizations. Schuler Archives.

In his September letter, Bob Peterson reminded the Friends of the Chorale in a paragraph in bold face that the Chorale is entirely dependent on the financial and spiritual support of the Friends. In the Lenten letter jointly signed by Bob Peterson and Father Ubel, it was announced that professional live recordings of two of the High Masses sung by the Chorale had been made by Minnesota Public Radio for possible future broadcast. Nothing has come of that initiative to this point. It was also announced that photos of the Mass on January 24, 2010, the celebration of the patronal feast of Saint Agnes, appeared in the online newsletter NewLiturgicalMovement.org on January 26, 2010. In addition, there was an article about the Chorale in *Twin Cities Metro*, Dec. 2009, titled "Believe It or Not, This Choir Rocks: Whereby the Author Skeptically Visits Saint Paul's Church of Saint Agnes, Only to Fall Under the Spell of The Twin Cities Catholic Chorale." *Twin Cities Metro*, which only existed for a short time, appealed to a younger demographic. This article was a result of the work of the chairman of the Marketing Committee, who made a concerted effort to increase the visibility of the Chorale in the secular media. The minutes of the March 8, 2010 Board Meeting announced the approval of a series of secular advertisements that would be run in the program books of the Minnesota Orchestra, the Saint Paul Chamber Orchestra, the Minnesota Opera, and the Schubert Club during the 2010-11 season.

After the death of Monsignor Schuler, the work of the Officers and Board of the newly incorporated organization became essential to the integrity and continuation of the Twin Cities Catholic Chorale. The letter sent from the music director, Bob Peterson, and the pastor of Saint Agnes, Father John L. Ubel, announced not only the 2010-11 season, but also several initiatives. A small matching fund grant had been set up to enlarge the donor base and to encourage current donors to increase their contributions. The letter also informed the Friends of the Chorale of the full color advertisements that would be placed in the fall program books of the Minnesota Orchestra, the Saint Paul Chamber Orchestra, the Schubert Club, and the Minnesota Opera as an effort to increase the Chorale's visibility in the arts community of the Twin Cities. These ads were paid for by a special gift from a generous donor. For the first time, the fall mailing also included an annual report. The season began on October 17, 2010, with Mozart's *Missa Brevis in F*, K 192 and finished on June 12, 2011, which was Pentecost Sunday. This

culture / **not pop** by jamie thomas

BELIEVE IT OR NOT, THIS CHOIR ROCKS
WHEREBY THE AUTHOR SKEPTICALLY VISITS ST. PAUL'S CHURCH OF ST. AGNES, ONLY TO FALL UNDER THE SPELL OF THE TWIN CITIES CATHOLIC CHORALE.

Until recently, I'd never thought of church as a venue for great classical music. Even as a kid at church with my parents, I could tell the music was not exactly worthy of Orchestra Hall. Sitting obediently through the hour of piano-accompanied soccer moms belting out hymns usually earned me a donut afterward. So as I steered my Subaru down I-94 on a recent Sunday morning, bound for Catholic mass and a morning full of music of worship, I promised myself a stack of pancakes for whatever I was about to endure. I was on my way to see the Twin Cities Catholic Chorale, a group that has been singing classical hymns during mass at the Church of St. Agnes in St. Paul since the mid '70s.

As I took my pew at St. Agnes, I decided that the interior of the church alone was worth the trip, great music or not. If you're accustomed to polite brick and mortar churches with whitewashed walls and slender crosses, St. Agnes will pretty well blow your mind. Columns of blush-colored marble, gilded moldings and saints dressed in sapphire blue and salmon pink decorate the church. Austro-Hungarian laborers built this Baroque-style beauty exactly 100 years ago—the cornerstone was laid in St. Paul in 1909. With its German stained-glass windows and Italian marble altar, St. Agnes is a little bit of Europe smack-dab in the middle of Frogtown.

I twisted around in my back-row pew, looking in vain for a choir. Suddenly an organ swelled and a cascade of voices flowed down from a loft hidden at the back of the church. Not only were the acoustics impressive, the Chorale's position in the loft gave one the sense that a choir of angels was preparing to descend upon the pews. The hour flew by on the melodic wings of organ and vocals and before I knew it, the postlude played and mass was over.

Afterward, I ventured up to the choir loft to speak with Chorale Director Bob Peterson, a former Macalester music professor who has led the group since 2004. He explained that the Latin High Mass, in which the service and hymns are recited in Latin, was commonplace in the Catholic Church until the mid-1960s, when a widespread movement to make services more accessible to all meant churches in the U.S. began saying mass in English. St. Agnes is somewhat of a time capsule, where Latin mass and the classical music that goes with it were preserved by the efforts of former pastor and music lover Richard Schuler, who passed away in 2007. Schuler has achieved hero status among the St. Agnes community for his dedication to the music. There's even a bell in the church tower named in his honor.

Today the Chorale, which consists of 70 volunteer singers and a handful of professional musicians and soloists, has a repertoire of about 50 masses. Most are by Mozart, Beethoven, Haydn and Schubert—the heavy hitters of the Viennese school. Mozart's *Missa Brevis in F* was performed the Sunday I visited. To my uninitiated ears, the piece seemed impossibly intricate, with repetition of words and melodies that seemed to double back on themselves, creating a rich, reverberating sound.

Peterson likes to point out how modern church music lacks this intricacy. He says that it increasingly channels pop music, with "praise bands" and simple music shown on retractable screens that allow parishioners to "follow the bouncing ball." He couldn't be more proud that the Chorale represents an opposite style. In order to raise support for the non-profit group, Peterson gives presentations around town, inviting all those with a passion for music, regardless of religious affiliation, to come experience the Chorale at St. Agnes.

As I tipped syrup onto my short stack at Perkins afterward, I thought about how I'd always taken church music for granted. But the classical music at St. Agnes represents more than the worship of God or the church—it represents true devotion to beautiful music, something increasingly rare in this day and age. And any lover of music, religious or not, will likely lose themselves in the sounds and sights of this unique experience, tucked away in an enchanting church in the heart of St. Paul. +

✝

LATIN HIGH MASS
Sundays, 10 a.m.
The Chorale will perform a three-hour Christmas Eve service, featuring Austrian carols and Mozart's Coronation Mass, 12/24 at 11 p.m.

CHURCH OF ST. AGNES
548 Lafond Ave., St. Paul
651.925.8800; stagnes.net

The Twin Cities Catholic Chorale performs each week with a full orchestra at the Church of St. Agnes in St. Paul.

is the first time that the Chorale did not conclude its season on the Solemnity of Corpus Christi. However, the *Schola Cantorum* and men from the Chorale sang the *Messe Cum Jubilo* by Maurice Duruflé with organ for Corpus Christi.

At the final meeting of the Board that June, the Constitution and Bylaws of the Chorale were revised. Little was done with the Constitution, but the Bylaws were modified rather substantially to give the organization a clearer working structure. The fiscal year was changed to end on July 31, instead of August 31, in order to allow enough time to compile a list of donors to be included in the fall mailing.

There were two articles about the Chorale in the secular press, thanks to the fine work of the chair of the Marketing Committee. One was in the November, 2010, issue of *Minnesota Monthly*, the magazine of Minnesota Public Radio. The other was written by Katherine Kersten, a columnist for the Minneapolis *Star Tribune*, and was published in the December 24, 2010 edition of that paper. Its title, "Music That Offers a Glimpse of Heaven," conveys the tone. Kersten says, "Worshippers and visitors will have to pinch themselves to remember they're in Minnesota and not in a cathedral in Vienna or Munich." It is interesting to note that this column picked up the same theme as an article by Jim Klobuchar in the December 25, 1985 edition of the *Star Tribune*.

The 2011-12 season began on October 16, 2011, with Haydn's *Heiligmesse*. However, the official season was preceded by the performance of the Duruflé *Messe Cum Jubilo* with organ by the *Schola Cantorum* and the men from the Chorale. On Sunday, October 23, members of the Mozart Society of America, who were in the Twin Cities for their biennial conference, attended the 10:00 a.m. Sunday High Mass at which the Chorale sang Mozart's *Missa Longa in C*, K 262. The Chorale introduced Johann Nepomuk Hummel's *Mass in B Flat* to its repertoire during this season. This Mass by Hummel has become a favorite of the singers and the congregation. The season concluded on June 10, 2012, the Solemnity of Corpus Christi, with Mozart's *Mass in C*, K 337. The Chorale sang 28 times with orchestra.

This season, for the first time, a letter from the president of the Board accompanied the letter signed by Bob Peterson, the music director, and Father John L. Ubel, pastor. The annual report announced the good news that there was a balance of $8,868 on hand at the beginning of the new fiscal year. Advertisements for the Chorale appeared again in the program books of the major music organizations, but the Marketing Committee recommended that they not continue for another year because it was not possible to measure their effectiveness. A clever full color brochure was sent as the Lenten mailing. It posed the question: "What heavenly thing does **The Church of Saint Agnes** in Saint Paul have that even Saint Peter's in Rome, Notre Dame in Paris and Saint Patrick's in New York do not have?" And the answer: "**The Twin Cities Catholic Chorale** and orchestra."

At the end of the year, the Board gave the officers permission to withdraw funds from the endowment, if it were deemed necessary to balance the budget, but fortunately it was not. Father Ubel was made Rector of the Cathedral of Saint Paul, and Saint Agnes received a new pastor, Father Mark Moriarty. Father Moriarty grew up attending the 10:00 a.m. High Mass with his family and offered the Mass of Thanksgiving after his ordination at Saint Agnes. Thus he was well acquainted with the mission and history of the Chorale at Saint Agnes and most of the repertoire.

The 2012-13 season was the 39th in the Chorale's residency at Saint Agnes. The year began on October 14, 2012, with the *Paukenmesse* by Haydn and finished on June 2, 2013, the Solemnity of Corpus Christi, with Mozart's *Mass in C*, K 337. The Chorale sang 27 Masses with orchestra. As a postlude, the *Schola Cantorum* and the men of the Chorale sang Duruflé's *Messe Cum Jubilo* on the following Sunday.

The fall mailing included a letter from the President of the Board and the Annual Report which announced a deficit of $74 in the operating budget of the previous year. Three new Board members were elected to replace three veterans who left the Board. The focus of the work of the Board for the year would be twofold: to reorganize the Fund Raising Committee and develop new fund raising activities, and to begin to lay plans for the celebration of the Chorale's 40th year in residence at Saint Agnes. A very successful fund raiser intended to attract new donors was held in a beautiful home in Sunfish Lake, a suburb of Saint Paul. The owners very generously opened their home and garden for the event. A quintet composed of musicians from our orchestra volunteered their time and talents to provide a concert in the garden on an idyllic September day.

CHAPTER XIII

The Fortieth Year of Residency at the Church of Saint Agnes – 2013-2014

The fortieth year of the Chorale's residency at the Church of Saint Agnes began on October 13, 2013, with Haydn's *Paukenmesse,* an appropriate choice because it was the Mass sung in Munich on August 15, 1974, on the occasion which launched this whole project. The letter from the president announced a season of 30 Masses with orchestra, including Haydn's *Nicolaimesse*, which would be added to the Chorale's repertoire. The fund raising event at Sunfish Lake would be repeated. A goal was set to increase the music sponsorships for Masses from four to ten. The Chorale would sell Christmas cards as a fund raiser. Plans were also announced to prepare and publish a history of the Chorale.

The Church Music Association of America Conference
October 13-15, 2013
Church of Saint Agnes and the Cathedral of Saint Paul

In response to a request by this author, CMAA agreed to sponsor a conference in honor of the 40th anniversary of the residency of the Chorale at Saint Agnes to honor the work of Monsignor Richard J. Schuler in the area of church music. The theme selected was "The Renewal of Sacred Music and the Liturgy in the Catholic Church: Movements Old and New." Dr. Jennifer Donelson, former Academic Liaison of CMAA and now Managing Editor of *Sacred Music* magazine, was appointed by CMAA to chair the conference. She worked with a committee from the local sponsoring organizations: the Church of Saint Agnes, the Cathedral of Saint Paul, the Archdiocese of Saint Paul and Minneapolis, and the Twin Cities Catholic Chorale. Some ninety participants came from all over the United States and Canada for the three-day conference. Two days were held at Saint Agnes and one day at the Cathedral of Saint Paul. All three keynote lectures honored the heroic work of Monsignor Schuler during the very difficult years after the Second Vatican Council. Here is a brief summary of each keynote lecture.

"Chant as Free Culture:
The Legacy of Monsignor Schuler's Revolutionary Resistance"
Jeffrey Tucker, formerly Managing Editor of *Sacred Music* **and now Director of Publications for the Church Music Association of America and editor of NewLiturgicalMovement.org**

Standing in front of Monsignor Schuler's portrait in Schuler Hall at the Church of Saint Agnes, Tucker began his lecture by introducing himself as a convert to Roman Catholicism from the Southern Baptist church. He described the experience that attracted him to the Catholic Church: it was attending a Latin chant Mass on a Sunday at the National Shrine in Washington, D.C. He said that he did not understand a word, but was impressed by the chant.

When he became a Catholic two years later, he began looking for a parish church with a Latin sung Mass and was shocked by the music he heard. When he asked where he could hear Gregorian chant, people answered him with "Oh, you mean like Saint Agnes, like what Monsignor Schuler does – a Mass in the Ordinary Form with chant and polyphony." People told him that it was the last vestige of the past. They did not recognize Monsignor's prophetic vision, and Tucker said that Monsignor himself was the subject of much derision.

However, this conference and what is happening in Catholic church music throughout the country currently is a tribute to that very prophetic vision. Tucker then summarized and commented on an article written by Monsignor Schuler titled "Church Music After Vatican II" which was published in *Sacred Music* (Vol. 103, No. 4, Winter 1976). Monsignor Schuler gave five reasons why the enthusiastic dreams of church musicians based on the statements about church music in chapter VI of the *Constitution on the Sacred Liturgy* were dashed.

- A confusion between the sacred and the secular, even a denial of the existence of the sacred;

- Promotion of the vernacular meant the abandoning of the Latin and thus of Gregorian chant;
- A misunderstanding of "active participation," creating a taboo against excluding the voices of the people;
- Lack of training of seminarians;
- Refusal to recognize the need for continuity between the old and the new: every age must stand squarely on the shoulders of the preceding generation.

Tucker concluded by saying that things are changing and that every parish is a future Saint Agnes. He added that we must not forget that there would not be a CMAA today without the work of Monsignor Schuler who literally kept CMAA alive for twenty years by continuing to publish *Sacred Music* magazine.

(Author's note: In an editorial in *Sacred Music,* (Vol. 117, No. 1, Spring 1990), with the title "Is the Church Music Association Dead?" Monsignor Schuler answered the question by saying that for the past two decades the chief activity of the association had been its journal, *Sacred Music*. He concluded, "Hopefully, some day, more vigorous life may be found in the Church Music Association of America. Until that Utopia arrives, our journal, *Sacred Music*, must continue to bear the burden of the association. The journal can be found in libraries on all the continents; it brings a great volume of correspondence to its editors; it will remain an historical record of these troubled times. It is the spark that glows and from which a stronger and more vital society may someday emerge. Surely all blood transfusions, organ transplants, and other life-sustaining procedures are most welcome." Monsignor Schuler served as editor of *Sacred Music* from Vol.102, No. 3, Fall 1975 through Vol. 125, No. 1, Spring 1998, for 88 issues for which he wrote editorials and many articles. See the Bibliography of the work he published in *Sacred Music* in Appendix G.)

"The New Liturgical Movement after the Pontificate of Benedict XVI"
Dom Alcuin Reid, OSB, Monastère St-Benoît,
Diocèse of Fréjus-Toulon, France

(This lecture was published in the Spring 2014 issue of *Sacred Music*, Vol. 141, No.1, p. 10.)

Dom Alcuin Reid introduced his presentation with remarks about his previous visit to Saint Agnes as a guest of Monsignor Schuler (see Commentary following this chapter). The following is an abstract of his remarks at the conference at Saint Agnes.

Abstract

The April 2005 election of Joseph Cardinal Ratzinger to the Throne of Peter gave significant impetus to the "new liturgical movement" for which he had called some years earlier and which he had already done much personally to promote. His example, teaching, and acts of governance as pope gave the movement further momentum.

The unexpected resignation of Benedict XVI in February, 2013, and the election of a new pope with a seemingly different approach to the Sacred Liturgy raised questions, including whether the initiatives of Benedict XVI are now to be set aside and replaced with what are presumed to be the liturgical principles behind the style of the current pope. In some circles anxiety has arisen that genuine progress made in recent years will now be lost. In others these events are regarded as a welcome opportunity to relegate "Benedict XVI-style liturgy" and return to liturgical practices widespread in the 1960s-1990s.

This paper revisits the foundations of the new liturgical movement and reflects on the nature of the liturgical reform of Benedict XVI with reference to the principles of the 20th century liturgical movement and of the Second Vatican Council's *Constitution on the Sacred Liturgy, Sacrosanctum Concilium*. In the light of these considerations, the paper seeks to articulate principles and future pathways for a new liturgical movement that will serve this movement now that its "father," Benedict XVI is no longer the reigning pontiff.

"The Treasury of Sacred Music at Saint Agnes: From Chant to Mozart"
William Mahrt, PhD,
President of the CMAA and Editor of *Sacred Music*

Dr. Mahrt knew the work of Monsignor Schuler well because he came often to Saint Agnes to sing with the *Schola* at Christmas and Easter when it was under the direction of Dr. William Pohl and also traveled with the Chorale in 1974 to the Sixth International Church Music Congress in Salzburg. His reminiscences of his visits to Saint Agnes may be found earlier in this book. He began his lecture by quoting paragraphs 112 and 114 of *Sacrosanctum Concilium* and paragraph 4b of *Musicam Sacram*. He reminded the audience that Monsignor Schuler always emphasized the fact that music for the liturgy must be both sacred and beautiful. "He understood, even before this concept was articulated famously by Popes Saint John Paul II and Benedict XVI, that the *hermeneutic of continuity* was especially important for music; this was placed in contrast with the *hermeneutic of rupture.*" Monsignor Schuler said: "Every age must stand squarely on the shoulders of those who have gone before....Musical styles develop with their roots in the past; eliminate the past and one finds that the wellsprings of musical inspiration and composition dry up too" (Schuler, "Church Music after Vatican II," *Sacred Music,* Vol.103, No. 4, Winter 1976, p.17).

Dr. Mahrt continued by saying that there are four fundamental kinds of sacred music: Gregorian chant, Renaissance polyphony, modern polyphony, and music for the organ. He then explained that Monsignor Schuler set in place all four types of this music at Saint Agnes and that it still exists there. Here is Dr. Mahrt's conclusion:

> We thank Saint Agnes and Monsignor Schuler for holding the course and being a beacon for us. Go ye and do likewise!

William Mahrt, PhD, President of the Church Music Association of America and editor of *Sacred Music,* presenting a keynote address at the CMAA Fall Colloquium. Note the portrait of Monsignor Schuler in the background. Photo by Virginia Schubert.

Two "sons of Saint Agnes," Father Mark Moriarty, current pastor of Saint Agnes, and Father Michael Miller, then pastor of Saint Mary and Saint Michael parishes in Stillwater, Minnesota, were among the speakers at the conference. As a boy, Father Moriarty attended the Latin High Mass at Saint Agnes with his family, who were parishioners even though they lived in a rather distant suburb of Minneapolis. He was ordained in 1999 and celebrated his Mass of Thanksgiving at Saint Agnes. His topic at the colloquium was "Saint Agnes Parish as an Expression of the Will of the Council." Father Miller grew up on a farm in rural Minnesota. In his presentation, *"Cum Angelis Canere: To Sing with the Angels, or A Farm Boy Learns to Sing Mozart,"* Father Miller said that he had never heard of Gregorian chant until he was 22 years old. He had planned to farm with his father, but he was drawn to the priesthood. As a student at the (then) College of Saint Thomas, he met Monsignor Schuler and discovered things such as Latin, the Communion rail, and orchestral Masses. He began singing in the Chorale, and in 1996, he offered his Mass of Thanksgiving after his ordination at which the Chorale sang Beethoven's *Mass in C* with orchestra. His conclusion:

> Nothing speaks more eloquently than beauty and I have seen the effect of the sacred in myself and others.... It is said that an Ecumenical Council takes a hundred years to be realized. Monsignor Schuler did so from the start.

Father Miller still sings with the Chorale often for the Mozart *Requiem* on the feast of All Souls, when his pastoral duties allow.

Many of the participants at the colloquium attended because they knew the work of Monsignor Schuler and wanted to participate in the liturgy at Saint Agnes. Two priests were overheard saying that they would like to take the altar boys home with them, so well-trained were they for the solemn liturgy. The Twin Cities Catholic Chorale sang Mozart's *Vesperae solennes de confessore*, K 339 with orchestra as a concert on Sunday evening, October 13. The Chorale and orchestra also performed Joseph Haydn's *Missa in Tempore Belli* or *Paukenmesse* for an Extraordinary Form Mass on the Feast of Saint Teresa of Avila, October 15, 2013. Dr. Robert L. Peterson directed the Chorale and orchestra. Paul W. LeVoir directed the Gregorian chant sung by the *Schola Cantorum* for the Mass. Mary Elizabeth LeVoir, DMA, was the organist for both events which took place at the Church of Saint Agnes.

The year that began with such intensity continued apace. In addition to its regular schedule, on January 11, 2014, the Chorale sang the Mozart *Requiem* at an Extraordinary Form Mass for the funeral of Permanent Deacon Bernard A. G. Pedersen, who was also a former member of the Chorale. Several distinguished clerics were celebrants at Sunday Latin High Masses for which the Chorale sang. On January 19, 2014,

Father C. Frank Phillips, CR, pastor of Saint John Cantius in Chicago, Illinois, lecturing in Schuler Hall at the Church of Saint Agnes, January 19, 2014. Photo by Joe Oden. Saint Agnes Parish Archives

the Sunday closest to the patronal feast of Saint Agnes, Reverend C. Frank Phillips, CR, pastor of the renowned Saint John Cantius parish in Chicago, was the celebrant. As is the tradition for the feast of Saint Agnes, the Chorale sang the Gounod *Saint Cecilia Mass*. There is a close relationship between these two parishes because it was the advice of Monsignor Schuler to establish a music program at Saint John Cantius that helped bring parishioners to the church when it was in danger of being closed. Father Phillips gave a very inspirational lecture in the afternoon. The Chorale added to its repertoire by singing Haydn's *Nikolaimesse* for the first time on February 9, 2014.

On Sunday, June 1, 2014, The Most Reverend Alexander K. Sample, Archbishop of Portland, Oregon, was the celebrant for the feast of the Ascension. The Chorale sang Johann Nepomuk Hummel's *Mass in B Flat*. Before going to the seminary, Archbishop Sample lived at the Saint Agnes rectory while he studied philosophy at the University of Saint Thomas so it was a true pleasure to welcome a son of Saint Agnes home. Archbishop Sample, as a student at Saint Thomas, was the lector for the taped recordings the Chorale made in 1986. Archbishop Sample has been a strong advocate of the solemn liturgy in Latin, and of Gregorian chant and the great treasury of Catholic church music.[30]

The Chorale year concluded on the Solemnity of Corpus Christi with Schubert's *Mass in G.*

The May/June 2014 issue of *Our Catholic Journey,* the official publication of Catholic United Financial, carried a three page article on the Twin Cities Catholic Chorale, "Our Joyful Noise." It explains the activities of the Chorale and its long term connection with Catholic United Financial (formerly Catholic Aid Association). Monsignor Schuler was spiritual director of Catholic Aid for many years; there is a Schuler Trust for Seminarians held by Catholic United Financial, and the Chorale's endowment is also administered by them.

The fortieth year of the Chorale's residency at Saint Agnes was an exciting celebration of our history. The mission now was to continue in like manner and meet the challenges of the future!

COMMENTARY

Memories of a Visit to the Church of Saint Agnes

During a visit to the USA in the summer of 1992, it was my privilege to be the guest of Deacon and Mrs. Harold Hughesdon. A friend who had stayed with the Hughesdons some years before insisted that I simply could not be in the USA and fail to visit them and the Church of Saint Agnes. The visit was planned to include a weekend, of course, so as to participate in Sunday solemn Mass and Vespers at Saint Agnes.

The imperative to visit Saint Agnes arose from its renown as a centre of liturgical and musical excellence in a period – and it is important that we do not forget this – which was liturgically very turbulent indeed: we seminarians and younger clergy who thought the liturgical rites promulgated by Paul VI should be celebrated according to the norms those books contained were frequently regarded with suspicion and deemed "rigid," "reactionary" or "not open to formation," whilst those who used the modern rites as a basis for visiting their subjective enthusiasms on liturgical celebrations were praised for their "creativity" and "openness" and duly promoted.

Saint Agnes was a prominent liturgical oasis in the English-speaking world – a *refugium liturgicum* in an otherwise arid period – deservedly taking its place alongside the London Oratory and other churches and parishes where (exceptionally) the Sacred Liturgy was celebrated with fidelity to the desires of the Council and to the liturgical norms, as beautifully as possible, and the opportunity to visit was not to be missed.

Sunday morning brought the bustle customary in a large parish; servers, musicians, clergy and other ministers preparing their various tasks. Deacon Harold insisted that I read the epistle (he wanted it read with an English accent!). In due time the activity ceased and its purpose, the liturgical action, began. One could remark on the very many people placing their different talents at the service of the Sacred Liturgy, and rightly. But what was more impressive than the generosity of individuals was the experience of the Church of God assembled in Saint Agnes united in the worship of Christ. Beauty abounded, in music and ritual certainly, but pre-eminently in people of all ages and in entire families caught up thereby in the action of Christ in His Church in the Sacred Liturgy. The silence and awe of all as the priest raised the Sacred Host and Chalice for adoration was tangible. Our full, conscious and actual participation was facilitated through profound respect for the riches and multivalency of the Church's rites. Something sacred was being done. Something sacred was happening within each of us.

Meeting a priest shortly before he is to celebrate Mass is far from ideal. Deacon Harold had presented me to Monsignor Schuler when we arrived. His welcome was warm. After Mass, the Monsignor sought me out, almost apologetic for not having engaged in conversation beforehand. An invitation to remain for luncheon quickly ensued. Deacon Harold, unsurprised by this, left me until Vespers.

I recall little of the specifics of the conversations over the following hours, save that it was clear that all those at Monsignor Schuler's table shared his concern at how the Second Vatican Council's desire for liturgical reform had too often been misinterpreted and erroneously implemented, and his passion for celebrating the liturgy as the Church wished it to be celebrated as worthily as possible. Here was a man of the Church whose priestly heart ached over her troubles, but which beat ever stronger so as to share his zeal for her Sacred Liturgy with others. It was a privilege to lunch with him and to be fed by his wisdom, fidelity and vision.

Monsignor Richard Schuler was a priest "thoroughly imbued with the spirit and power of the liturgy" (*Sacrosanctum Concilium,* 14) who never ceased to work for the formation of others in that spirit. He laid important foundations from which the "new" liturgical movement can build today, particularly through his fatherly care of the many priestly vocations with which Almighty God blessed Saint Agnes.

The work of the new liturgical movement may be somewhat different to the task (almost one of survival) of but a few decades ago. Monsignor Schuler's pastorate preceded the gifts given to the Church by Benedict XVI in *Sacramentum caritatis* and *Summorum pontificum* – gifts at which he would surely have rejoiced – and today we may freely celebrate both forms of the Roman rite and even look toward their mutual enrichment. Nevertheless, in continuing the liturgical apostolate, in seeking in our turn to pass on and form others in that liturgical spirit Monsignor Schuler so fruitfully shared, his heroic fidelity to the Church and to the true celebration of her Sacred Liturgy cannot but give us inspiration and strength.

Dom Alcuin Reid, OSB
Monastère St-Benoît
Diocèse of Fréjus-Toulon, France
Eastertide, 2014

COMMENTARY

"*Cum Angelis Canere* " Recollections of Beauty

The one and only time I had a chance to speak with Monsignor Schuler was as he lay dying in the final months of his substantial and important life. I had only been a priest for a few months, and the rector of the Cathedral, where I was then serving as parochial vicar, took me to visit his dying friend. I of course knew of "The Monsignor," as I had been a student at Saint Agnes High School during the final years of his pastorate, and had therefore been present for many Masses he celebrated on Tuesdays for the school body. As providence would have it, I sang in the school choir, which was fortunate enough to sing some of the great masterworks of the Vienna School within the context of the weekly liturgies. I still remember clearly the conclusion of one such Mass, where the Monsignor, noticeably emotional, thanked the choir for its powerful rendering of one of his favorite pieces. While I do not remember the piece we sang, I certainly remember the effect it had on the visionary shepherd. I also remember quite clearly the effect another piece sung in that world-famous loft had on me, though we will return to that impression in a moment.

Unsurprisingly, it was not only from the choir loft that I knew the long time pastor of Saint Agnes. I also knew of him by reputation. While I had not been fortunate enough to take classes under his tutelage within the "other seminary" that was the Saint Agnes rectory dining room, classes offered for years and whose graduates include present-day bishops, it was impossible to speak his name in the presence of local churchmen and not receive some kind of visceral response. As expected, the vast majority of priests within the local Church viewed the Monsignor as a conservative, someone who held firmly to the traditions and trappings of the past. Whether or not this was a laudable trait was of course determined by the particular leanings of the priest who was responding to the invocation, "Monsignor Richard Schuler." But the reality of the Monsignor's life and work was not so easily defined as to be placed neatly within a political category. Great men are much more complicated than such categories allow. All the same, my own leanings as a young priest were decidedly of a more traditional bent, and hence, it was easy to look to the pastor and parish of Saint Agnes as a kind of paragon. He was a priest, a priest who dressed like a priest and who acted like a priest. The parish too was a place of clearly defined identity, and this is one of the real desires of young Catholics these days, it seems to me – we long for clear identity.

I do not remember the conversation I had with Monsignor as he lay upon what would become his death bed. I am certain that Father Joseph Johnson did most of the talking. I do seem to remember that the Sacrament of the Anointing was administered, though even this recollection is obscured by the distance of 8 years. What I do remember, however, is my feeling of gratitude to God that He had allowed me to pay respects to a man who had played a significant part in my own vocational discernment, though a part certainly unknown to him.

Sometime during the Easter season of my freshman year of high school, I clearly remember singing, perhaps as a recessional piece, the "Hallelujah Chorus." As a devotee at the time of much less refined music, my reaction in the choir loft was wholly unexpected. I was moved to tears, and entered into what I believe to be a moment of authentic joy, a holy reveling in beauty and goodness and truth. Within this powerful piece of Handel was a marriage of the natural and of the divine – a piece of human art, inspired by the saving action of God, and created for the Glory of this same God. "If this is what happens," I thought, "when Faith and Reason work together, then perhaps a life dedicated to the Catholic Faith would not be such a dreary and drab thing after all."

Now I had been raised Catholic, and have always practiced my Faith, if badly most of the time. But the experience within the choir loft of Saint Agnes Church that Tuesday morning close to two decades ago was a defining stage in my own conception of the Faith. Not simply a collection of truths to be recited like an algebraic equation, it had been revealed to me as a thing of beauty and power and romance. Sacred Art is perhaps the best medium to communicate this reality of the Faith, second only to the beautiful, powerful and romantic lives of the Saints. And among the most effective languages of art capable of conveying the beautiful, powerful, and romantic is music.

I wonder if any other Catholic high school in the Archdiocese would have allowed me to experience what I did in the spring of 1995. I doubt it, for few other parochial schools, if any at the time, viewed an education in Sacred Music as worthy of effort. But Monsignor Schuler, who served as superintendent of Saint Agnes, clearly did, and I now consider my exposure to Sacred Music as one of the most important pieces of my formation during my high school years, a piece of formation that opened me up to a consideration of the priesthood as a particularly beautiful way of life.

I now live as a priest in residence within the old campus of the "other seminary." I also serve as the Director of the Office of Worship for the Archdiocese of Saint Paul and Minneapolis, a position I have held for as long as I have lived at Saint Agnes. Within my work for the Archdiocese, particularly within the planning of major Archdiocesan Liturgies, I continue to be inspired by my experience singing in the choir of Saint Agnes high school. Beauty matters, and it particularly matters as it relates to evangelization. Beautiful liturgies, with substantial and powerful music accompanying ceremonies conducted with due reverence and solemnity, can move believer and unbeliever alike, reminding us of our great hunger for Truth and Goodness. For the unbeliever, it can even be the first stirrings of Faith.

I remain ever so grateful to Monsignor Schuler for teaching me this lesson, through his patronage and care of the music department of Saint Agnes High School. May he rest in eternal peace, and may he sing forever with the angels, glorying in the God who calls all men to Himself through the universal language of beauty.

Reverend John Paul Erickson
Director, Office of Worship
Archdiocese of Saint Paul and Minneapolis

Part Five

*"The Council established clearly that music is an integral part (pars integrans) of liturgy; it **is** liturgy. Two requirements were demanded; music for the liturgy must be sacred and it must be art.*

"Saint Agnes, Sunday Morning"
by Monsignor Richard J. Schuler
in *Sacred Music*, (Vol. 114, No. 3)

CHAPTER XIV

Toward the Future – 2014 and Beyond

The CMAA Conference celebrating the Chorale's 40th year of residency at the Church of Saint Agnes inspired the Officers and Board of the Chorale and its Music Director with a renewed dedication to its mission. The three keynote addresses highlighting the extraordinary contributions of Monsignor Schuler after Vatican II and the Chorale's unique mission to the Liturgy of the Holy Sacrifice of the Mass were central to this impetus. In addition, those responsible for the Chorale realized that the spring of 2014 marked the seventh year since the death of Monsignor Schuler and that the Chorale had not fallen victim to the ominous prophecy that his death would mean the end of the Chorale.

In May, 2014, at this author's request, Dr. Robert L. Peterson, Music Director, wrote this reflection on the future of the Chorale.

> The only characteristic I consider to be certain about the Twin Cities Catholic Chorale is our fragility. Our organization is "one of a kind" in religious music organizations in the United States and possibly the world. We do not know of another ensemble that produces a full season of orchestral/choral Masses as a part of the actual celebration of the Mass (as they were intended). Because of the great costs and demanding schedule, and because we are self-financed, we are totally dependent on our fund raising committee and donations from the "Friends of the Chorale," to keep us solvent. Last, but certainly not least, is the required support of the pastor of the Church of Saint Agnes plus a dedicated and talented volunteer group of singers that make up the Twin Cities Catholic Chorale. A number of reasons can help to explain this phenomenon of fragility:

1. Professional orchestra members and soloists are very expensive. These two elements of our program must include top flight professional musicians that do not require weekly rehearsals. They are paid to come on Sunday mornings with music prepared.

2. Western art music (classical music) does not have the mass appeal of contemporary praise band music so common in the mega churches of today.

3. Although the Latin High Mass is enjoying somewhat of a renaissance, it is still not as widely accepted and understood since Vatican II.

4. Our Masses are longer (or are perceived to be longer) since we perform all sections of the Ordinary of the Mass set to music and the Proper of the Mass is sung in Gregorian chant by the *Schola Cantorum*. This may make it more difficult for large families with young children and the more senior members of our congregation to participate. However, this is not universally true because there are those in both categories who are faithful to the Latin High Mass. There are also those who seek the shortest Mass possible. Most Chorale Masses with orchestra last about an hour and thirty minutes.

Many followers of the Twin Cities Catholic Chorale predicted that the Chorale would not survive after the death of our founder, Monsignor Richard J. Schuler. I made a promise to him on his death bed to do what I could to keep this very important liturgical and musical treasure alive and well. It has been seven years (to date) since his death. During the first year or two, it was quite difficult to attempt to maintain funding. However, the past few years have proven to be very successful in reaching our financial goal. I credit an aggressive fund raising committee and numerous activities by our Board of Directors plus several very generous donors for keeping our organization solvent. If, in future years, funding would decrease, the Chorale could possibly dissolve. This is very difficult to consider since it is extremely important to keep this historic and artistic music alive as a part of the liturgy. All of the Masses we sing with orchestra are famous enough to be heard in concert halls throughout the world. But this is not the same as hearing and seeing these great works as *pars integrans* (an integral part) of the liturgy for which they were intended.

I also believe that if a season would be curtailed because of a lack of funding, it would never be revived. We have assembled a group of highly talented singers and instrumentalists. Most would find other sources for their talent in short order. To start over would be nearly impossible.

With the current group of singers and instrumentalists, I believe that the Twin Cities Catholic Chorale has a bright future. We seem to be attracting more interest and visibility for our efforts. We continue to add new repertoire to our schedule each season. We also continue to attract new singers to perform these great works.

I am honored to continue as Music Director of the Chorale. It is a special opportunity to prepare and conduct these masterpieces of great religious literature, and keep them alive as a part of the liturgy at the Church of Saint Agnes.

Dr. Peterson's commentary is very realistic. However, while the fragility he mentions is very real, it should not give cause for undue worry or alarm. It is countered by the energetic commitment and hard work of the Officers and Board of the Chorale, its Music Director and organist, its singers (all volunteers), and its professional musicians and soloists, as well as the *Schola Cantorum* and its director. It is also countered by the strong support of the current pastor of the Church of Saint Agnes and the successful completion of 41 years singing the Latin High Masses at Saint Agnes.

The 2014-2015 season began with Joseph Haydn's *Little Organ Solo Mass* on October 12, 2014, followed by Haydn's *Paukenmesse* on October 19, which corresponded with the Fall Festival at Saint Agnes, always a joyous occasion with many visitors. In 2014, All Souls' Day (November 2) fell on a Sunday so the Mozart *Requiem* was sung at the regular 10:00 a.m. Mass. It was decided to sing the Gounod *Saint Cecilia Mass* twice because it is such a favorite. After the Gounod *Saint Cecilia Mass* was sung on the celebration of the feast of Saint Agnes in January, 2015, the Chorale received the following e-mail which reconfirmed that decision.

> Dear Catholic Chorale and Orchestra:
> Last Sunday...my wife and I invited two of our dearest friends...to attend the 10:00 a.m. Mass for the Patronal Feast of Saint Agnes with Gounod's *Solemn Mass for Saint Cecilia*.
> This was the most beautiful Sacred Music we had ever heard; we all were moved to tears numerous times during this extraordinary Mass. My wife and I have been to others of these Masses at Saint Agnes (we are parishioners) and have a great appreciation for the Sacred Music at these 10:00 a.m. Masses, but this Mass for Saint Cecilia was beyond extraordinary; it was truly Divinely inspired. Our two wonderful friends will never be the same.

On Easter weekend, all associated with the Chorale were delighted to open the *Saint Paul Pioneer Press* to find a picture of the Saint Agnes choir loft and the caption "Classical: The Twin Cities Catholic Chorale" in the category of something not to be missed. The music critic wrote: "Sunday: You might not find better music to match the celebration of Easter than at Saint Agnes." This was completely unsolicited! Our season finished as usual on the Solemnity of Corpus Christi, June 7, 2015, with the Schubert *Mass in G*.

Even as the Chorale enters its 42nd season, spreading the message in the local metropolitan area of the existence of this full program of Latin High Masses with orchestra is always difficult. The mission of the Chorale is spiritual, but the Board understands that we must use marketing techniques to become more widely known. Our budget is not large enough to do generalized advertising in the secular press, so the decision was made to do targeted advertising and to use social media as much as possible. Thus the Board decided to make 2014-2015 the Year of Marketing. Some of the strategies included advertisements in the Catholic print media and on Catholic radio; posts online in various classical music venues, cards with the schedule placed in major local hotels, bookmarks with the schedule printed on the back distributed widely to donors and others. The Board chose to "boost" certain Masses on our Facebook page which increased greatly the numbers who consulted the page.

There was a concerted fund raising effort also. The most successful part was the music sponsorship program. Our music sponsors increased from four in 2012-2013 to ten in 2013-2014 to thirteen in 2014-2015. Music sponsors also were provided with the option of designating the intention of the Mass as a way to honor someone, living or dead, or to celebrate a special event. This is a good place to repeat that the Chorale is financially independent of the parish and the archdiocese, although the parish usually sponsors the music for one Mass each year. (Please see Chapter X on the finances of the Chorale.)

Plans are in place for the 2015-2016 season. The Chorale will sing 28 Masses with orchestra, beginning on October 4, 2015, and finishing on May 29, 2016. The decision has been made to perform the Gounod *Saint Cecilia Mass* twice, once at the traditional date in January to celebrate the feast of Saint Agnes and once in April, on the Sunday closest to the anniversary of the death of Monsignor Schuler. The Mozart *Coronation Mass,* K 317 will also be performed twice; once in October, and once, as usual, at Midnight Mass on Christmas. The Chorale will add Mozart's *Spatzenmesse,* K 220 to its repertoire. Our goal is to find music sponsors for twelve Masses in 2015-2016 and to continue the active marketing campaign that was carried out in 2014-2015.

The Twin Cities Catholic Chorale is alive and well.

CHAPTER XV

Conclusion

In his preface to this volume, Father Robert Skeris links the mission of the Twin Cities Catholic Chorale to the vision and teaching of the role of sacred music in the liturgy as enunciated by Pope Saint Pius X in his *Motu Proprio on Sacred Music* (1903) and to the *Constitution on the Sacred Liturgy* of the Second Vatican Council (1963).

Father Skeris quotes Monsignor Schuler's oft-repeated words about music in the liturgy:

> "The last ecumenical Council declared that two elements are required for music in the liturgy: it must be sacred and it must be art" (See "Saint Agnes, Sunday Morning," *Sacred Music*, Vol. 114, No. 3, Fall 1987, p. 15).

Father Skeris also explains that the Chorale is carrying on the legacy of the rich treasury of liturgical music of the Roman Catholic Church beginning with Gregorian chant and continuing with the music of the great masters who composed for the liturgy. He quotes Monsignor Schuler's words,

> In every way, what is done at Saint Agnes is in perfect accord with the directives of the Holy See and the reforms of the Second Vatican Council. Liturgy at Saint Agnes is not a home-made activity....It remains for the priest and the people to carry it out as the Church prescribes it with as much care, reverence, and solemnity as possible.

When Monsignor Schuler founded the Twin Cities Catholic Chorale, times were very different in the Church. The young Father Schuler set out to continue the work of his teacher and mentor, Father Francis A. Missia, by using the Chorale as a means of instructing choir directors, choirs and organists in the Twin Cities. He did this by introducing them to music from the great treasury of Catholic liturgical music and from modern composers whose works showed the characteristics of being sacred and being true art. The Chorale at that time was composed of many organists and choir directors. It sang concerts and also Masses in churches on invitation. Perhaps Monsignor Schuler should have foreseen the winds of change that would sweep all before them in the wake of Vatican II, but in fact, not even the leaders of the papal church music association who came to Saint Paul to plan the Fifth International Church Music Congress in Chicago and Milwaukee were really prepared for the vehemence of the dissent to that congress.

However, Monsignor Schuler was not only brilliant and well-schooled in sacred music, he was practical, extremely hard-working, stubborn, and fearless when it was a question of principle. An anecdote illustrates his legendary stubbornness and also his ready wit. While he was pastor of Saint Agnes and superintendent of the grade and high schools, he was called down to the diocesan education office because of a controversy he was having with the Sisters teaching in the parish high school and the education office over the materials taught, especially in the religion classes, the responsibility and obligations of the pastor, and ultimately, over orthodoxy. During the meeting, the Sister representing the religious Order said that she had never met anyone as stubborn as Father Schuler. His answer was that evidently she had never met his mother!

He was well placed as pastor of a parish with a solid tradition of being faithfully Catholic, and he was also the music director of the Twin Cities Catholic Chorale. He often used to say that the pastor and the choir director got along perfectly. In addition, he was a scholar with a national and international reputation in the area of Catholic church music, having the best combination of a devotion to the priesthood, the Holy Sacrifice of the Mass and his "flock." His knowledge and talent were complemented by a warm, witty, and yet determined personality. At Saint Agnes Monsignor Schuler set about carrying out a program, that, by example and instruction, implemented the teachings of Vatican II on the liturgy. As this book attempts to demonstrate, it was not easy, and the progress in spreading this message to a wider audience was often slow.

How often did he have to say that the Latin Mass was not forbidden by the Second Vatican Council, but rather, despite the widespread use of the vernacular in the post-conciliar Church, the Latin language is still the venerable tongue of the Latin Rite in the *Novus Ordo* as well as in the *Usus Antiquior?* He repeated constantly that the Mass as it was (and is) celebrated at Saint Agnes was not forbidden, but rather the *Novus Ordo* Mass according to the 1970 *Missale Romanum* and now the 2002 *Missale Romanum*. He affirmed and re-affirmed that Gregorian chant was not outlawed (quite the contrary, it was to be given pride of place), that sacred music was *pars integrans* of the liturgy, that it was perfectly permissible to sing a Mozart or Haydn Mass with orchestra in church as the music for the Mass, that he was not behind the times, but rather forty years ahead of the times. It was very important for Monsignor Schuler to remain always in conformity with Rome, a faithful son of the Church. He used to say that it was possible to get off of a streetcar either to the right or to the left, but in either case, one was off of the streetcar!

The annual program of Latin High Masses with music by composers such as Mozart, Haydn, Beethoven, and Schubert with full orchestral accompaniment remains unique in the United States. With the essential support of the pastors of Saint Agnes who have followed Monsignor Schuler, including the current pastor, Father Mark Moriarty, the Chorale has managed to continue beyond its founder, even though, at the time of his death, many predicted that it would not last. The Twin Cities Catholic Chorale, in the beautiful Saint Agnes choir loft, continues "to sing with the angels," both literally and figuratively. The lovely angels playing stringed instruments, who are depicted in one of the stained glass windows of the choir loft and who grace the cover of this book, continue to accompany us as we sing.

New challenges will confront the Chorale in the future, but they will be met, as they have in the past, with hard work, energy, commitment, and prayer. On the positive side, there is a new appreciation in the Church for Masses in Latin, in both the Ordinary Form (*Missale Romanum* of 2002) and the Extraordinary Form *(Missale Romanum* of 1962). Let us remember the admonition in Latin with which Father Skeris concluded his preface. *Non jam frustra doces, Pater reverende!* (You do not now teach in vain, Reverend Father!) Let us pray that, with the grace of God, the Twin Cities Catholic Chorale may continue its mission to the sacred liturgy. *Ad multos annos.*

NOTES

Chapter 1

1. "Father Francis A. Missia (1884-1955)," by Father Richard J. Schuler, *The Catholic Choirmaster*, Vol. XLVI, no. 4 (Winter 1960).

2. *The Motu Proprio on Sacred Music by Blessed Pius X*, Archdiocese of Saint Paul, 1954, p.34.

3. Review of the concert by Frances Boardman in the *Saint Paul Pioneer Press*, Jan. 20, 1938. This clipping is in the scrapbook of Father Richard J. Schuler, currently in the Schuler Archives. Scrapbooks assembled by Father Schuler serve as a rich source of documentation for this history of the Twin Cities Catholic Chorale.

4. Programs of the concerts of 1938, 1939, 1940, 1941, 1942, 1948, 1949, 1950, 1951, 1952, 1953 are reprinted in *The Motu Proprio on Sacred Music by Blessed Pius X, op.cit.* Original copies of the programs of 1939-1942, 1948-55 are in the Schuler Archives at the Church of Saint Agnes.

5. Letter in Father Schuler's scrapbook.

6. Review by John H. Harvey in the *Saint Paul Pioneer Press*, April 22, 1955.

7. "Monsignor Richard J. Schuler: A Biographical Sketch" by Richard M. Hogan in *Cum Angelis Canere: Essays on Sacred Music and Pastoral Liturgy in Honour of Richard J. Schuler*, edited by Robert A. Skeris, 1990, Catholic Church Music Association of America, Saint Paul, Minnesota, p.11.

8. From an undated letter from Father Sweeney in the Schuler Archives.

9. From an undated review by John H. Harvey in the *Saint Paul Pioneer Press*.

Chapter 2

10. Essay in concert program, Dec. 17, 1956.

11. Review of the concert by John H. Harvey in the *Saint Paul Pioneer Press*, Dec. 18, 1956.

12. Letter from Father Richard J. Schuler dated Sept. 15, 1957 in a scrapbook in the Schuler Archives.

13. Documentation for this history, unless otherwise noted, comes from materials located in the Schuler Archives.

14. This comment on the difficulties of coordination between the Chorale and the orchestra makes note of a problem that existed until 1974, when the Chorale began singing regularly at the Church of Saint Agnes with a core orchestra which ensured some consistency of players. However, even to this date, finances and schedules preclude rehearsal time with the orchestra except when the Chorale introduces a new work to its repertoire.

15. The Most Reverend James P. Shannon was consecrated auxiliary bishop of the Archdiocese of Saint Paul and Minneapolis on March 31, 1965. He resigned on Nov. 22, 1968, stating as the reason his opposition to Pope Paul VI's encyclical, *Humanae vitae*.

Chapter 3

16. "Reactions on the Recent Church Music Congress," *Sacred Music*, Vol. 93, Autumn 1966, p.97-109. Two reviews of the Fifth International Church Music Congress; the first by Virginia A. Schubert; the second by Robert J. Snow.

17. *Sacred Music and Liturgy Reform after Vatican II*, (Proceedings of the Fifth International Church Music Congress), Chicago-Milwaukee, August 21-28, 1966; Rome, *Consociatio Internationalis Musicae Sacrae*, 1969.

Chapter 4

18. Gerhard Track was well-known to Monsignor Schuler because he had taught and directed the choir previously at Saint John's University in Collegeville, Minnesota. They had collaborated when Monsignor Schuler was on the faculty of the College of Saint Thomas in Saint Paul, Minnesota (now the University of Saint Thomas). Track had also been director of the Vienna Boys Choir at one time. He was active in CMAA and served as its president.

Chapter 6

19. Lawrence Barnhart, French horn and tympani; John Miller, bassoon; Francis Thevenin, violin, and Clement Volpe, trumpet, who played in the orchestra in the first season at Saint Agnes (1974-75), are still playing in the orchestra during the 2014-2015 season.

20. "Tonight's Views with P.M. Clepper," *Saint Paul Dispatch*, Dec. 21, 1976.

21. "The Twin Cities Catholic Chorale," by Richard M. Hogan, *Sacred Music*, Vol.104, No. 4, Winter 1977.

22. Mary Elizabeth Gormley and Paul W. LeVoir were married in December, 1980.

23. In a recent novel, *Storm Front*, (Penguin Group, 2013) John Camp writing under the pseudonym of John Sandford mentions Saint Agnes on p. 368 when one of his characters says: "I had a girlfriend, sort of a musical hippie, back a while ago, she'd take me over there for those orchestral Masses....I gotta say that whole Roman Catholic High Mass thing can get a grip on you, with the incense...and the vestments and the big gold crucifix...."

Chapter 7

24. Recordings of Gounod's *Saint Cecilia Mass* (Christmas), Haydn's *Paukenmesse* (Easter), and Beethoven's *Mass in C* (Pentecost), including Gregorian chant Propers, are available from the Leaflet Missal Company, 976 W. Minnehaha Avenue, Saint Paul, Minnesota, 55104 (www.leafletonline.com), (1-800-328-9582). A recording of Christmas music in several languages featuring the Chorale and orchestra is also available from the Leaflet Missal Company.

Chapter 8

25. *View Behind the Painting: Memories of Monsignor Richard J. Schuler,* published by the Twin Cities Catholic Chorale, 2007.

26. "High Mass at The Church of Saint Agnes," by Neil E. Dexter. A Commentary on the Roman Catholic High and Solemn High Masses at the Church of Saint Agnes.

27. *Christmas at Saint Agnes*, CD of Christmas music in Latin, German and English. May be ordered from the Leaflet Missal Company. See footnote 24 for details.

28. See footnote 24 for details of how to order the CDs.

29. *View Behind the Painting*, op. cit.

Chapter 13

30. When he was Bishop of Marquette, Michigan, Archbishop Alexander K. Sample, now Archbishop of Portland, Oregon, issued a pastoral letter, "Rejoice in the Lord Always," on sacred music in divine worship to the priests, deacons, religious, musicians and faithful of the diocese on the Memorial of Saint Agnes, January 21, 2013. Archbishop Sample gave an address, "Celebrating the Spirit of the Liturgy," to the Church Music Association Colloquium in Salt Lake City, Utah on June 19, 2013. In his introduction to that conference, he explained his relationship to "the great Monsignor Richard Schuler," noting that he had lived in the rectory at Saint Agnes for a year when he pursued studies in Philosophy at the then College of Saint Thomas. "I sang in the Gregorian *Schola Cantorum*, and it was there that I experienced my first true formation in the sacred liturgy. I dedicate this talk to Monsignor Schuler with deep gratitude for all he taught me, by word and example. May he forever rejoice with the choirs of angels in the heavenly liturgy."

Appendices

APPENDIX A

Biography of Monsignor Richard J. Schuler
By Charles W. Nelson

Richard Joseph Schuler was born in Minneapolis, Minnesota, on December 30, 1920, the third child of Otto and Wilhelmine Schuler. One of his favorite quips in later life was that all great people were born in December – including God! Following the deaths of his elder brother and sister, however, he was raised as the eldest son to his younger sisters, Catherine and Jeanne.

A part of his early years was spent working in the family business, the Schuler Shoe Store, where he learned two insights from his father which were to affect his pastoral approach in later years: you cannot serve customers if the store isn't open and you shouldn't change the familiar hours of operation.

He began his schooling in the Ascension Grade School under the tutelage of the Sisters of Saint Joseph of Carondelet who nourished and developed his Catholic faith. Father Schuler particularly remembered the time he spent in the classroom of Sister Anne Patricia Doyle who awakened his interests in literature and music. While at Ascension, he began his musical education taking lessons in the piano and flute which he played in the school orchestra. Richard also became an altar boy in the fifth grade and had many memories of his pastor, Monsignor Dunphy. At funerals, the good prelate delivered the eulogy standing next to the coffin and often laying his hand on the casket when he referred to the deceased. He also liked to bang on the bier while trying to make a point. Father Schuler and his fellow servers often wondered if someday the deceased might sit up and demand to know who was knocking on the coffin!

In 1934, Richard entered De La Salle High School, a Christian Brothers institution. While pursuing his secondary school education, Father Schuler began organ lessons at the MacPhail School of Music where he did so well that he was hired as the substitute organist at the Basilica of Saint Mary in downtown Minneapolis. He often recalled the peculiarities of its Rector, Monsignor Reardon, who always insisted that services began on time – even if the hearse had not yet arrived. Father remembered beginning the Requiem Mass several times a full ten minutes before the appearance of the mourners and the body!

Richard graduated from De La Salle in 1938 and enrolled at the College of Saint Thomas, where he majored in English. Because he had taken summer courses at the University of Minnesota, he had a surplus of credits and, in 1940, with the encouragement of his pastor and priestly professors, he entered the Saint Paul Seminary. After his third year, he had finished the requirements for a Bachelor of Arts and was awarded an English degree from Saint Thomas. Because of World War II and the need for chaplains and more parish priests to take their places, classes continued all year at the seminary so that Father Schuler was ordained earlier than scheduled on August 18, 1945, and celebrated his First Solemn Mass the next day at the Ascension Church.

During his years at the seminary, his abilities as an organist had attracted the attention of Father Francis A. Missia, the Professor of Music, who appointed him the accompanist of the Seminary Choir. Father Schuler recalled Father Missia as an exceptionally talented, but demanding musician who had a formidable temper. One year, having arrived at the Cathedral to play for the Ordination Ceremony, Father Schuler realized that he had left the score for the *Ecce Sacerdos Magnus* (which happened to be the processional) back at the seminary. Father Missia had begun warm-ups for the choir while Father Schuler was desperately trying to find transportation back to his rooms. He finally appealed to the father of one of the other seminarians who raced back to the seminary and returned with the score in the nick of time, thus avoiding a liturgical catastrophe as the choir was not prepared to sing *a capella* or endure a tirade from its director!

Following his ordination, Father Schuler was assigned to Nazareth Hall, the preparatory seminary in the Fall of 1945, where he taught Music and History. He was also sent as weekend assistant to Holy Childhood Parish where its pastor, Father John Buchanan, was starting his choir school. The Archbishop felt that Father Schuler's musical talents could be put to good use in this endeavor, but Father Schuler was not favorably disposed towards boy sopranos as he preferred the real thing, and so devoted his time to training the altar boys, so that Holy Childhood became known not only for its music, but also for its flawless liturgy.

With the encouragement of Father Missia, Father Schuler began graduate studies at the Eastman School of Music in Rochester, New York, in the summers, earning his Masters in 1950. That same year, he was assigned as weekend assistant and Choir Director at the Church of the Nativity in Saint Paul whose pastor, Bishop James J. Byrne, wanted a choir to rival the Cathedral's. Following a year's study in Rome on a Fulbright Scholarship, Father Schuler returned to Nativity, but not to Nazareth Hall as Archbishop Murray appointed him to the faculty of the College of Saint Thomas, where, in addition to directing the Liturgical Choir, he also taught Music and Theology.

While he was in Europe, Father Schuler's friend and mentor, Father Missia, died and with him the Saint Paul Catholic Choral Society. Not wanting to lose such a valuable musical asset to the Archdiocese, Father Schuler drew on its former members and added new ones from his own choirs, to found the Twin Cities Catholic Chorale in 1955, which is the subject of this book. He likewise became involved in the Guild of Catholic Choirmasters and Organists, an organization of parish choirs from throughout the Archdiocese. As a choir director with several ensembles at his command, Father Schuler introduced innovation and change in the choir loft including the extensive use of Gregorian chant and orchestral accompaniment for the sung Masses. In 1967, he completed work on his Doctorate in Music History at the University of Minnesota.

Because of his extensive work with parish and diocesan choirs, Father Schuler became more widely known in national and international Catholic church music circles. He wrote articles, gave invited lectures, composed, and participated in choral workshops and seminars such as those at Boys' Town and Christendom College. The fame of the Nativity Choir grew as Bishop Byrne got his wish. Father continued to expand its repertoire and embellish it performances. He was a demanding taskmaster and a stickler for excellence, but remained popular with his singers and the parishioners. On one of the interminable Sundays after Pentecost in 1960, a careless celebrant began the Collect when an authoritative voice proclaimed from the choir loft for all to hear: "There IS a *Gloria* today!" leaving the choir too much in hysterics to sing. On one Fall Tuesday evening, a prospective new singer came puffing up to the loft and gasped to Father Schuler that he would like to audition for the choir. After a brief pause, the choirmaster looked at the man and said that if he could still sing after making it up all those stairs, he was in! One of the director's favorite remarks during rehearsals was to look quizzically at the choir after going through a musical selection and say, "That was very interesting, but now let's try and sing it the way Schubert wrote it!"

In 1961, Father Schuler attended the Fourth International Church Music Congress in Cologne, Germany, where he met Monsignor Johannes Overath and became involved with the international church music establishment which led to his holding national and international offices and helping to organize two international church music congresses.

In the aftermath of the Second Vatican Council, many erroneous interpretations of its documents and wrongheaded applications of its directives took place which did irreparable damage to many aspects of the Church – especially to its treasury of sacred music. Due to a complete misunderstanding of the *Constitution on the Liturgy,* Monsignor Steiner, then Pastor of Nativity Church, was persuaded by one of his assistants that choirs were no longer needed as the congregation would be doing all the singing. As a result, the Nativity Choir was disbanded in May, 1966 and Father Schuler was assigned elsewhere. There were tears, tantrums, recriminations, and a rift in the parish, but the damage was done and the work of sixteen years undone. The rancor persisted for years.

Father Schuler was sent to the College of Saint Catherine as Chaplain to the community of Sisters who were already making dramatic changes in their Order. He tried unsuccessfully to caution them against the drastic actions they were initiating and warned of the havoc which would (and did) result. During this same time, Father Schuler got to know Monsignor Rudolph Bandas, Pastor of Saint Agnes Parish, who had been a *peritus* at all four sessions of the Second Vatican Council and had a clear and orthodox understanding of the intent of the Council fathers. Because of his influence, his parish had implemented the changes recommended by the Council, but without the turmoil and controversy. With worsening relations with the Sisters of Saint Joseph, Father Schuler was happy to be assigned as weekend assistant at Saint Agnes, and, in 1969, following the death of Monsignor Bandas, he became its eighth pastor.

When he assumed the office of pastor of Saint Agnes, Father Schuler informed his congregation that he saw his responsibilities as threefold:

- to carry out the reforms of the Second Vatican Council carefully and correctly in keeping with the intentions of the framers of the documents;
- to encourage vocations to the priesthood and religious life; and
- to embellish the sacred liturgies with the treasures of the Church's rich history of sacred music.

Because his predecessor had maintained the traditional ceremonies and liturgies of the Church, Father Schuler found a solid basis already in place, and he immediately began to build on it through a vigorous recruitment and training program for the altar boys, instilling in them a true sense of the solemnity of the rites they were performing. He likewise focused his attention on the growth and improvement of the parish schools as the best incubators of vocations.

He began visiting, and even teaching, some high school classes to encourage and foster interest in the religious life, as well as initiating the practice of dialogue homilies with the elementary school students at school Masses. Finally, he gave funding and encouragement to the parish choir and its director, Sister Hermana Mauer, SSND. He also brought his own Twin Cities Catholic Chorale to Saint Agnes on occasion to sing the High Mass.

In 1970, Father Schuler celebrated the 25th anniversary of his ordination with a special Mass at Saint Agnes sung by the Twin Cities Catholic Chorale and the Dallas Catholic Choir under the direction of Father Ralph March, O. Cist., accompanied by organist Paul Manz. At that Mass, it was announced that the jubilarian had been named an honorary prelate (Monsignor) of the Church by Pope Paul VI. In spite of this honor, the pastor preferred the title of "Father" to "Monsignor." The first, he explained was conferred by a sacrament, while the second was bestowed by a piece of paper.

But all was not peaceful at Saint Agnes as the misunderstandings of Vatican II infected the Notre Dame Order as well as the diocesan Board of Education who demanded drastic changes in the teaching of the essentials of the Catholic Faith. Supported by a majority of the parents of the parish and many of the teaching Sisters, Monsignor Schuler held out for continued orthodoxy. They eventually were successful but, as a result, a rift developed in the parish and the School Sisters of Notre Dame began to withdraw from the Saint Agnes Schools. With the help of local educators, Monsignor Schuler began the hiring of lay faculty to teach with the few Sisters who remained so that the parish school continued uninterrupted in its mission of educating the Catholics of the future.

In 1974, Monsignor Schuler and Father March rehearsed their choirs separately in order that they could sing together at the Sixth International Church Music Congress in Salzburg, Austria. On their way to the conference, the two choirs sang a daily High Mass in many abbeys, cathedrals and parish churches. On August 15, the Feast of the Assumption, they sang Joseph Haydn's *Paukenmesse* in the Alte Peterskirche in Munich, accompanied by members of the Munich Symphony Orchestra. It was this extraordinary experience which led Monsignor Schuler to make Saint Agnes the permanent home of the Chorale accompanied by professional musicians aided by professional soloists which has made the parish famous around the world for the beauty of its music and the perfection of its liturgies. Three popes were familiar with Monsignor Schuler's accomplishments and one of them (Benedict XVI) sent condolences to his parish after his death.

When he first took over as pastor of Saint Agnes, Monsignor Schuler began the practice of praying for vocations every Sunday as the congregation asked God for "many priests, deacons, brothers and sisters for the Church." The prayer, augmented by the concentrated efforts and encouragement of the pastor, has yielded a rich harvest – as a result of his thirty-two years at Saint Agnes, thirty-eight priests were ordained, five permanent deacons were anointed, and two bishops and one archbishop were consecrated. All seminarians were welcomed to Saint Agnes to participate in the liturgies, to sing in the Chorale, and to benefit from the spiritual direction and canonical instruction of Monsignor Schuler.

In spite of his devotion to the Magisterium of the Church and his insistence on orthodoxy in all aspects of parish life, or perhaps because of these, Monsignor was often reviled, criticized, mocked, and insulted. Yet, through it all, he never lost his confidence and faith that all would eventually work out for the best. Father Eric Olson, a priest of the Diocese of Marquette, Michigan, who first met Monsignor at one of the summer workshops he conducted at Christendom College and knew him for the rest of his life, said of him: "He never grew bitter or angry as some of the clergy did. In spite of all the hardships and disappointments, he always remained a perfect gentleman and the ideal of a what a Catholic priest should be. He was an inspiration to all of us."

He also managed to keep his sense of humor and perspective which made him such a joy to work with. On several Tuesday nights, as he arrived in the Saint Agnes choir loft, he would complain that they had added steps to the staircase. Dr. Thaddeus Chao, a physician and long-time member of the Chorale, used to marvel at Monsignor's good health and strong constitution. He was sure it was due to his German genes! But even German genes eventually begin to age, and, in the new millennium, Monsignor's strenuous lifestyle began to catch up with him. As a result of his sixty years of arduous labor and busy schedules, Monsignor started to slow down, and in June, 2001, he stepped aside as pastor of Saint Agnes, but remained in the parish and continued as Director of the Chorale, although he did appoint Dr. Robert L. Peterson as Associate Director.

Monsignor continued to attend the Sunday High Masses, but Dr. Peterson now directed the Chorale. He likewise still worked with and advised seminarians so that the First Masses of newly ordained priests continued, and on May 28, 2006, Father Sean Magnuson celebrated his Mass of Thanksgiving at Saint Agnes in the presence of the Pastor Emeritus. The next day, Monsignor suffered a stroke from which he never fully recovered. He spent the rest of his days in assisted living facilities and nursing homes, where he continued to celebrate daily Mass and receive visitors.

In 2007, his health continued to decline, and on April 20, he died while listening to a Chorale recording of Beethoven's *Mass in C* – surely a preview of the angelic music he would soon be hearing in the Courts of Heaven.

Well done, good and faithful servant.

APPENDIX B
Father Francis A. Missia (1884-1955)
By Reverend Richard J. Schuler

(Originally published in *The Catholic Choirmaster*, Vol. XLVI, No. 4, Winter 1960. Reprinted with permission of *Sacred Music* magazine, the continuation of *The Catholic Choirmaster.*)

August 4, 1903, found the cardinals of the Holy Roman Church in conclave to elect the successor to Pope Leo XIII. Their choice fell on Giuseppe Sarto, who on that day became Pius X. The news *"Habemus papam"* was heard around the world. By courier from another ship it reached a steamer in mid-Atlantic bound for North America. On board was a young man whose whole life would be closely bound up with the new Pope and his efforts to restore the music of the liturgy.

Francis A. Missia was born January 26, 1884, in the town of Mota in the province of Styria, then a part of the Austro-Hungarian Empire, today in Yugoslavia. His early education was fostered by his parents and his parish priest, of whom he often spoke very fondly in later years. He learned German in addition to his native Slovenian, and at the invitation of his uncle, Monsignor [Bishop] Jakob Missia, the young student matriculated at the Jesuit gymnasium at Kalkburg, near Vienna, for his classical and musical studies.

Monsignor Missia was one of two great heroes in the life of the young student. Born at Luttenburg on June 30, 1838, he studied at the Gregorian University in Rome while he lived at the Germanicum, residence for German-speaking ecclesiastical students. In 1884, Pope Leo XIII named him Bishop of Ljubljana or Laibach, as it was called in German. He held the position of chaplain to the Austrian empress.

Later he was appointed Archbishop of Gorizia (Görz in German), and in June of 1899, he was elevated to the Sacred College of Cardinals. He died in 1900. One of Father Missia's treasured souvenirs of his uncle was a program for the presentation of one of Perosi's oratorios at which the Archbishop of Gorizia and the Patriarch of Venice, Giuseppe Sarto (soon to be Pius X) presided. (A portrait of this famous alumnus is still among the possessions of the Collegio Germanico in Rome, hanging in the convent attached to the ancient church of Santo Stefano Rotondo on the Celian Hill.)

Among the guests who stopped at the residence of the Slovenian prelate was Archbishop John Ireland of Saint Paul, Minnesota, who was making one of his frequent tours through Europe in search of young priests and students who would volunteer for service in his fast-growing, young archdiocese in Minnesota. Perhaps without knowing it, Ireland became the other great hero in the life of Francis Missia, and this admiration never dimmed throughout his life. Archbishop Ireland knew well that his recruiting efforts would be fruitful, since many of the clergy working in the regions around the headwaters of the Mississippi and in the Great Lakes area had come from Carniola and Slovenia. Among them were Frederick Baraga, first Bishop of Marquette, the seasoned Indian missionary; Franz X. Pierz, father of Catholicism in the Diocese of Saint Cloud; and a host of others whose names that harked back to their Slovenian fatherland became familiar in Minnesota; Trobec, Seliskar, Buh, Savs, Gruden, Bajec.

Invitation Answered

When his uncle, the cardinal, died quite unexpectedly in 1900, young Missia recalled the invitation of the American prelate, and bidding good-bye to his parents and the familiar surroundings of the Austrian capital, he followed the footsteps of his countrymen to carry the work of Christ to the American Midwest. He arrived on this continent on August 15, 1903.

Archbishop Ireland welcomed the young Slovenian student to Minnesota and enrolled him in his newly founded Saint Paul Seminary, where in addition to the courses in philosophy and theology he undertook the study of the English language, a task at which he was not alone in the seminaries of those days. His musical ability and in particular his strong, rich voice soon came to the notice of the seminary professors, and after ordination on June 8, 1908, Archbishop Ireland assigned him to the faculty of the seminary as professor of sacred music and choirmaster, a position he had in fact filled during his last year as a student, and one he would hold for forty-seven years to come. The seminary was his only assignment in the diocese; it became his whole life; and his near half-century of service there became identified very closely with the first half-century of the seminary's history.

Like so many immigrant priests, Father Missia was anxious to learn about his newly adopted country. He travelled widely through the United States, especially during the summer vacations and when he served as a Knights of Columbus military chaplain during World War I. On several occasions he returned to Europe for extensive travel. He was one of the first to acquire an automobile, and the students at the Saint Paul Seminary long remember his nervous antics behind the wheel. His driving seemed to usher in the jet age long before the discovery of jet propulsion.

Summer vacations at the seminary also found the young priest doing parish work among the Slovenians in the dioceses of Duluth and Saint Cloud or teaching summer courses in liturgical music at the College of Saint Thomas in Saint Paul, or in Concordia, Kansas, where he was invited by the Sisters of Saint Joseph, or in Detroit, Michigan, or Winona, Minnesota. In his later years, his summers were spent more and more at his "villa" among the pine trees along the Willow River in western Wisconsin, only twenty-five miles from the seminary. Here he re-created a European atmosphere of hospitality and culture, he himself filling magnanimously the roles of both host and chef for his chosen friends.

Eucharistic Congress

Perhaps the greatest triumph in the life of the Maestro, as many fondly called him, was the Ninth National Eucharistic Congress, held in Saint Paul and Minneapolis in June, 1941. It was also his most burdensome assignment, a herculean task. He planned, rehearsed, and directed all the music for the congress. More than a year of almost endless regional rehearsals went into the preparation of the massed choir made up of sixteen thousand school children who sang one of the pontifical Masses of the Congress. He worked likewise with the combined choirs of the parishes of the archdiocese who sang the *Missa Eucharistica,* written especially for the congress by Father Missia's close friend Pietro Yon. But his most loving work went to his Saint Paul Catholic Choral Society, an organization he founded in 1936 to exemplify the finest music in the vast repertory of the Church. Its accomplishments, particularly in singing the polyphonic music of the Renaissance composers, were widely acclaimed. Further, he prepared the seminarians for their role of singing the proper sections of the Masses in Gregorian chant; he edited and published a special Eucharistic hymnal for the use of the pilgrims to the congress; he appointed the personnel for the various musical positions at the many holy hours and Masses during the congress; and he himself directed the congregational singing of the thousands who walked in procession or who worshiped from the grandstand during the final Eucharistic function. All this labor and activity left its mark on the health of the maestro. During the days of the congress he was confined to the hospital with a severe case of pneumonia. Against the orders of his doctors he left his bed to continue his work of direction in order to coordinate the massed choirs, his choral society, the members of the Minneapolis Symphony Orchestra, and his seminarians in the vast plan for praising his Eucharistic Lord through music. This tremendous expenditure of effort and energy left him with bronchial ailments and a strained heart that stayed with him until his death.

Cathedral Ceremonies

Hardly an event of importance took place in the archdiocese that did not see Father Missia in charge of the music, whether it was the laying of the cornerstones or dedication ceremonies for the great Cathedral of Saint Paul or the Basilica of Saint Mary in Minneapolis; the famous consecration of six bishops in one ceremony in the chapel of the Saint Paul Seminary in 1910; various national conventions that came to the Twin Cities; the consecration of bishops or the ordination of priests. All this put him in the public eye, but his chief work remained the preparation of his seminarians. He firmly believed that every student must be taught to sing his part of the liturgy with dignity, beauty and ease. He instilled into his students a great respect for and devotion to the liturgical services. That the liturgical apostolate had its American beginnings in Minnesota is due in no small way to the work of Father Missia with the seminarians at the Saint Paul Seminary. The event of the week was the Solemn Mass and Vespers of Sunday. Any number of alumni of the Saint Paul Seminary will testify to the beauty of the sacred liturgy as carried out in Saint Mary's Chapel, particularly during the days of Holy Week. They likewise will attest that after ordination, which brought the young levite into the world, the part of seminary life most often remembered was the richness of the liturgy and its music as he had known it for the six years under Father Missia. Even the texts of the breviary as they were read in silence seemed to recreate for him the musical settings in which they were first learned and sung in the seminary. *Zelus domus tuae comedit me: tenebrae factae sunt; locus iste a Deo factus est; requiem aeternum dona eis domine.* The Maestro had taught well; music was the means of projecting the sacred texts and implanting their meaning in the young theologian.

Father Missia trained the seminarians to love the liturgy and to carry out their musical roles as ministers of the Mass to the best of their ability. But he well knew that the task of providing for the music of the High Mass in the parishes fell on the layman. Thus in 1935, and for two years following, he conducted summer sessions for organists and choirmasters at the College of Saint Thomas in Saint Paul. All of the musicians functioning in the parishes and institutions of the archdiocese were obliged by the Archbishop to attend and pass an examination qualifying them for a certificate of fitness without which they could not direct or play in church. In order to continue this educational project, Father Missia organized the Guild of Catholic Choirmasters and Organists, which today is still functioning very actively, twenty-five years after its foundation, attempting to carry out the purposes outlined by its founder.

In the forty-seven years that Father Missia was a member of the seminary faculty, hundreds of students, coming from most of the dioceses of the Midwest, sat in his classes of Latin and music. After ordination, many of them returned to their homes and became active as diocesan directors of music or teachers of church music in various colleges and seminaries. Among his students, Father Missia was particularly proud of Monsignor Francis Schmitt, director of music at Boys' Town and editor of *Caecilia.* (Monsignor Schmitt had the pleasure in 1953 to present Father Missia with the Boys' Town Caecilia medal, one of the few public honors given him in his lifetime. Others include Father Frederick Reece of Des Moines, Father Donald

Krebs of Crookston, Father John Sweeney of Saint Paul, Father Frank Melovasich of Duluth, Father Harold Pavelis of St. Cloud, Father Leander Ketter of Lincoln, Father Otto Sartorelli of Marquette, and this writer.

His Character

It is always difficult to sum up a man's character in a few words, especially when he is a man whose personality is itself as overpowering as Father Missia's was. Father Walter H. Peters, in a sermon on the first anniversary of Father Missia's death, compared him to Saint Jerome, and it is an apt comparison. They were both natives of Dalmatia; they were both self-made men; they were both masters of the art of pedagogy. But if one were to name only three traits that most clearly characterized Father Missia, they would be these: 1) his deep love of the Eucharist; 2) his indefatigable energy for work; and 3) his sincere loyalty to his friends.

1. The Eucharist is, of course, the center of every priestly life, but it was especially so of Father Missia, and this was apparent so often. His musical talents were aimed solely at adoring his Eucharistic Lord. His efforts at training the seminarians, often a task of great drudgery when he would have to drill with his famous "B" chant class, were founded only in the belief that these men would be glorifying the Eucharistic Christ someday, and that demanded his complete efforts to make them worthy of the task. His words in class constantly underlined this thought that the Eucharist must be the center of the priest's life. He loved a holy hour; he never missed the Solemn Masses, Vespers or holy hours in the Seminary schedule.

2. One never found Father Missia idle. He never rested. The accomplishments of his life testify to that, but only those who knew him well were aware of the phenomenal number of tasks he undertook, from editing a hymnal for the diocese to binding the music to be studied by his choral society. He was a person of great order, whether he was assigning a seating arrangement in the seminary chapel or preparing a dinner for his friends at his summer cottage. When one called on him at his room, one always found him at his desk or his work table or his piano.

His work was exceptionally neat; he wrote a beautiful musical script. The various musical libraries that he built up were his pride and he kept them in first-rate order, he himself repairing all the music with meticulous care. With all that he undertook and accomplished, he could not afford to be idle.

3. Father Missia had an extraordinary number of acquaintances. He was widely known by people of several generations, both Catholic and Protestant. The school children for forty years knew him; the clergy from all parts of the Midwest constantly quoted him to their choirs. He was recognized by sight; but very often just because of his voice, one knew that Father Missia was in the church. His funeral from the Cathedral of Saint Paul was one of the largest ever witnessed there. The vast edifice could not contain the throng that came. Over five hundred priests and nearly five thousand people attested to the magnetic personality of this priest-musician. Those whom he accepted as close friends were fewer in number, of course, but the sincerity of his friendship equaled the breadth of his acquaintanceship. People either loved Father Missia much or they disliked him intensely. There was no middle ground. But those who disliked him really did not know him. When he seemed to be unduly severe, it was only to bring out the best in a person, to form him for future responsibility, or to help him throw off some unfortunate defect. Once a man had gained his friendship it was forever, and it entailed a loyalty on the part of both. He never failed in that responsibility. When a friend needed him, Father Missia was ready. He spoke the truth to one's face; he expected the truth to be spoken to him; he tolerated no sham and he saw through pretention, deceit, and ambition. He had an uncanny sense of character judgment.

No one who had met Father Missia ever forgot him. He was about six feet in height and in middle age he became quite corpulent. However, daily work on the extensive property about his "villa" during the summer months gave him a glow of health so that his excess weight in no way slowed his activity. It was only in the last few years of his life that his hair turned grey. His complexion was somewhat swarthy, attesting to his Adriatic origin. His eyes were remarkably large and seemed to have an inextinguishable fire in them. When he seemed unmerciful in scolding a student whom he liked, those eyes continued to show a merriment and kindness. He might be directing a thousand high school students in a huge arena, but he never had a problem of discipline. When he detected a lack of attention in an area of the auditorium, those piercing eyes found the tittering offender, and decorum was restored seconds before the terrifying and vociferous verbal blast followed. His speaking voice was strong and sonorous. In a group he was witty and jovial, dominating the conversation with his mock truculence which was always expected of him. His erect carriage, his smooth, unwrinkled skin, his full head of greying hair, his lightsome eye, his commanding voice, all conspired to belie his seventy years.

Death came to Father Missia suddenly on May 21, 1955, as he returned to Saint Paul from his summer cabin in Wisconsin. It was a Saturday evening, and he was returning to his Sunday obligations of parish Masses and sermons, the Seminary High Mass and Vespers. He probably had a heart attack while driving, because he struck a truck from behind in circumstances which would not have existed if Father Missia had been in control of his car. His ability to maneuver his car was almost legendary; he could easily have moved into another lane had he been well. He died on the highway, fortified by the sacraments of the Church. He lies buried in Resurrection Cemetery near Saint Paul. - RIP.

APPENDIX C

Guild of Catholic Choirmasters and Organists
By Monsignor Richard J. Schuler and Virginia A. Schubert

(A brief history of the Guild of Catholic Choirmasters and Organists was published in a booklet, *The Motu Proprio on Sacred Music by Blessed Pius X* (The Archdiocese of Saint Paul, Saint Paul, Minn., 1954). No author is given, but it was most probably written by Father Richard J. Schuler. It is reproduced here.)

The Guild of Catholic Choirmasters and Organists was established by Reverend Francis Missia in the year 1939, following a three years' course of summer school devoted to the study of the *Motu proprio* by Blessed Pius X. The Guild's objective was and continues to be the unification of aims and methods in developing Catholic Church Music along lines laid down by authoritative pronouncements and in providing opportunity for the discussion of problems arising from the proper application of the prescribed regulations.

On account of the inconvenience of assembling the members of the Guild of Catholic Choirmasters and Organists who reside within the Twin Cities in one place of meeting, it was decided by His Excellency, The Most Reverend Archbishop John Gregory Murray, S.T.D., on September 15, 1946, that the organization shall be divided into two chapters, one within the City of Saint Paul to be called the Saint Paul Chapter, and one in the City of Minneapolis to be called the Minneapolis chapter, the territory of the former embracing all of Ramsey County and the territory of the latter including all of Hennepin County, under the direction and supervision of the Archdiocesan Chairman, Father Missia. A Liturgical Advisor, appointed by the Archbishop from among the clergy of the Archdiocese, was placed in charge of each chapter in order to be responsible for the program in keeping with liturgical legislation as it may be promulgated from time to time by ecclesiastical authority.

For the past eight years and the current season the Liturgical Advisor for the Saint Paul Chapter was and remains the Reverend Richard J. Schuler, M.A., Professor of the Preparatory Seminary, Nazareth Hall, and the one for the Minneapolis Chapter is the newly appointed Liturgical Advisor, the Reverend Joseph L. Baglio, director of the Minneapolis Catholic Youth Centre.

The Saint Paul Chapter, last season, devoted its study entirely to the *Motu Proprio* from various points of view.

This is the end of the essay published in 1954. Documents in the Schuler Archives indicate that the Saint Paul Chapter of the Guild, under the direction of Father Schuler met monthly and that members also received a monthly mimeographed newsletter announcing upcoming meetings, informing members of other concerts and activities, and explaining any directive from the hierarchy. This aspect took a more prominent place after the Second Vatican Council and the publication of the *Constitution on the Sacred Liturgy*.

In the fall of 1956, Father Schuler announced that he would teach a course in Catholic church music on Tuesday evenings at Saint Thomas College. The cost for the course would be $5. A roster of members in 1960-61 indicates that the two chapters had combined and that Father Schuler, now teaching at the College of Saint Thomas, was the ecclesiastical moderator for the combined association. There was a chairman for each former chapter. Meetings were now on Mondays; dues were $2.

The history of the Twin Cities Catholic Chorale gives details of the annual Masses sponsored by the Guild. The most ambitious of these took place in the Saint Paul Cathedral in 1965, when Monsignor Johannes Overath, president of the papal church music society, the *Consociatio Internationalis Musicae Sacrae*, was the celebrant and the massed choirs from the Twin Cities parishes sang Jean Langlais's *Missa Salve Regina*.

The monthly newsletters sent after the publication of the *Constitution on the Sacred Liturgy* of the Second Vatican Council and after the Fifth

International Church Music Congress, held in Chicago and Milwaukee in 1966, begin to reflect the dissension in the ranks of Catholic liturgists and church musicians. In the October 1966 newsletter, Father Schuler suggested that the group study the *Mass in Honor of Saint Cecilia* by Hermann Schroeder which was commissioned for the Congress in Milwaukee.

Father Schuler says: "...this work is (in my estimation) the first truly significant piece of music written in the vernacular and in the spirit of the reforms of the Vatican Council."

However, in the April newsletter it is announced that there is not sufficient interest in singing the Schroeder Mass so the annual festival Mass was cancelled for 1967. Father Schuler comments thus:

> Therefore, since the number of choirs has dwindled and the interest in church music has fallen off, we shall NOT have the annual festival Mass that the GUILD has sponsored for the past ten years. I cannot help adding that in my estimation this is only another indication that the "renewal" intended by the Fathers of the Vatican Council has been misled and even sabotaged by those who are the self-appointed interpreters of the Council in this country.

Father Schuler would persevere with the Schroeder Mass which would be sung by the Twin Cities Catholic Chorale at a final Mass of Thanksgiving for the Guild. The Mass was celebrated in English and the congregation was invited to sing the people's part. This Mass was instead of the annual festival Mass.

The last year for which there are newsletters in the Schuler Archives is 1967-68. In the February newsletter, Father Schuler suggests a contemporary Mass in English for the annual festival Mass. It was *A Community Mass* by Sister Mary Magdalen Mageau, OSB, of the College of Saint Scholastica in Duluth, Minnesota. Father Schuler described its style as modal, based on Gregorian themes. However, in the March, 1968 newsletter, it was announced that at the February meeting it was decided unanimously not to use the English Mass suggested by Father Schuler. It was stated that the choir directors and choir members preferred to sing a Mass composed in a more traditional idiom. The decision was thus made to revive the *Krippenmesse* by Joseph

Kronsteiner which was sung at the festival Mass in 1962. A statement is made that Latin remains the official language of the Catholic Church and the Roman Liturgy. The use of Latin is completely in accord with the *Constitution on the Sacred Liturgy.*

The final paragraph in the May 1968, newsletter written by Father Schuler makes a statement on musical instruments in church. He reaffirms that the pipe organ is the most fitting instrument for worship. He continues:

> The problem in my mind is not the instrument itself, but rather what is the repertory being played on it. And here the imagination cannot keep up with the aberrations and abuses that exist in our parishes and institutions! How much has been lost in this diocese by those who make up a "rebellious minority" as Archbishop Dwyer [Archbishop of Portland, Oregon] calls them.

Does this newsletter mark the end of the activities of the Guild of Catholic Choirmasters and Organists? Since there are no more newsletters in the Schuler Archives, it seems a valid conclusion which has been corroborated by consultation with an organist who has also retained documents from the Guild.

APPENDIX D

Choir of the Church of the Nativity of Our Lord: 1950-1966
By Charles W. Nelson

The Church of the Nativity of Our Lord was founded in 1922 by Archbishop Austin Dowling in the new neighborhood of Macalester-Groveland, Saint Paul, Minnesota. Sacred music has always been a major component of the character of the parish. One of the earliest documents in its archives is an article describing the first Christmas Mass in the auditorium-church of the newly built school and it mentions specifically that the parish choir was very well prepared and that the Mass from beginning to end was especially beautiful as the singing and services were inspiring.[1]

Father Terrence Moore, the founding pastor of Nativity, died in 1948, and Auxiliary Bishop James J. Byrne was appointed to succeed him by Archbishop John Gregory Murray. Bishop Byrne had a great interest in church music and was anxious to continue the choral tradition established by his predecessor. One of his first actions after being installed in his new parish was the purchase of a Wicks Pipe Organ which he had installed in the still new permanent church building.

In 1950, Father Richard Schuler received his Master's Degree from the Eastman School of Music in Rochester, New York, and returned to teach music at Nazareth Hall Preparatory Seminary in Saint Paul. Using all his influence and connections in the diocesan Chancery, Bishop Byrne had Father Schuler assigned as weekend assistant and choir director at Nativity Parish.

At their first interview, the Bishop gave Father Schuler a generous budget, his enthusiastic encouragement, and the charge to develop a choir which would rival that of the Cathedral.

After hiring Mrs. Myron Angeletti as organist, Father Schuler began recruiting singers and building his sections. Actually, because of the Bishop's wishes, he ended up with four choirs: a Men's Choir, a Boys' Choir (which he disliked), a Women's Choir, and a Girls' Choir. Early on, he established a Men's *Schola* and trained them in the rudiments of Gregorian Chant. This careful attention to the oldest musical tradition in the Church was to be a hallmark of Monsignor Schuler's entire career. After a few months of rehearsal, the Men's and Boys' Choir began singing the 11:00 a.m. High Mass every Sunday and soon developed a varied repertoire. This tradition continued for the next fifteen years, although the make-up of the performing choir changed.

In 1954, an interruption occurred as Father Schuler was awarded a Fulbright Scholarship for a year's study in Rome. Upon his return, Father Schuler was reassigned to the College of Saint Thomas where he taught Religion and Music. He also resumed his position at Nativity, having brought back much music from his year of research in Rome. So popular had his Christmas programs become that for many years, there were two Midnight Masses – one in the Main Church sung by the Men's and Boys' Choirs and another in the Lower Church sung by the Women's and Girls' Choirs, and both overflowing with congregants. During this time, Father Schuler introduced the use of orchestral accompaniment, hiring musicians from the Colleges of Saint Catherine and Saint Thomas, and on Christmas Eve, 1956, the patronal feast of the parish, the first orchestral Mass was sung at Nativity. Bishop Byrne had gotten his wish, as his parish choir more than rivaled that of the Cathedral.

Unfortunately, at this point, Bishop Byrne was transferred to Boise, Idaho, but his successor, Father Clarence Steiner continued to support and encourage the musical program. Some major changes occurred, however, with the Bishop's departure as the Boys' Choir was disbanded and the remaining ensembles reduced to two: the Senior Mixed Choir and the School Choir which sang the High Masses on Holy Days and All Souls' Day when the Senior Mixed Choir was unavailable. With only two groups left to work with, Father Schuler concentrated his time on improving and expanding the repertoire of his main choir and introduced more demanding music which attracted larger and larger congregations. In addition to works by Palestrina, Vittoria, Benevoli, Tartini, and Soriano, the Choir also performed Schubert, Franck, Haydn, Mozart, Bach, Fassler, Pietro Yon, Langlais, and Tittel.

During the late '50s and early '60s, Father Schuler recruited new voices from the Colleges of Saint Thomas and Saint Catherine, and also performed some more contemporary music such as the *Mass in Honor of Saint Thérèse* by Saint Paul organist and choirmaster, Leopold Bruenner. At about this same time, Father Schuler became Liturgical Advisor of the Guild of Catholic Choirmasters and Organists, which was made up of choir directors and organists from most parishes in the Twin Cities. Every year, the massed choirs of these parishes rehearsed and sang a Mass, and the Nativity Choir was an important part of the ensemble. (See article on the Guild in the Appendix).

As with any group which was together as long as the Nativity Choir, there are many stories of amusing incidents – usually involving the Director. This was not unusual as Father Schuler always tried to provide a harmonious atmosphere in which his choir could sing. Although the choir performed from September until June, the highlight of the year was always the Midnight Mass on the patronal feast of the parish, which after 1956, was always an orchestral Mass. The musicians were paid by the hour and so the length of the liturgy was always a concern. Father Steiner, the pastor, had a tendency to preach at length on major feasts. As he continued to speak, Father Schuler would grow increasingly restless at the length of the sermon and would pace back and forth in the limited space of the choir loft. One Christmas Eve, after going to the balustrade and leaning over it, he 'accidentally' sat on the organ keyboards producing a blast of sound which stopped the preaching pastor in mid-sentence. In later years, Father Schuler insisted that it had been an accident, but most choir members had a hard time believing him.

On another Christmas Eve with the same scenario, the Director suddenly started waving his arms wildly and caught the eye of Father Frederick Fleming who was serving as Deacon of the Mass. Father Schuler made a parallel motion with his hand across his throat, i.e. 'cutting it off.' Father Fleming got the message and went over to the pulpit and tugged on the pastor's chasuble so he immediately returned to the altar and intoned the *Credo*. Unfortunately most of the choir was laughing so hard that they almost couldn't sing.

There was another occasion when he was directing quite vigorously and sent the *Saint Gregory Hymnal* in his hand sailing out into the congregation. After a startled reaction, he saw that the book had landed safely in the aisle and not on a parishioner's head. Once on Easter Sunday, Mrs. Angeletti (who was famous for the size and complexity of her hats) was playing the prelude with such vigor that her Easter bonnet fell off her head and flew into the pews. Once more, the choir needed some time to compose itself.

Father Schuler himself said that the early sixties were the Golden Age of the choir as its repertoire had expanded and its numbers had grown. Several of its members had developed into talented soloists and the *Schola* had matured into an excellent ensemble. Father Fleming, who was an expert on the liturgy, worked closely with Father Schuler, so that the actions at both ends of the church were of the highest quality. An incident illustrates this quite clearly. The Sullivans were one of the premier families of the parish and Tom 'Sully' Sullivan was the patriarch of the clan and the head usher. His daughter was married on the Feast of the Assumption one year at a special noon Mass sung by the choir accompanied by orchestra. As Father Schuler came down the stairs from the choir loft, 'Sully' met him and greeted him with the joyous exclamation: "Now THAT was music!"

By the middle '60s, unfortunately, there were others who felt that the music performed by the Nativity Choir was not appropriate for the 'New Liturgy' supposedly mandated by the Second Vatican Council. Following the many misunderstandings of the Council documents, one of the new assistants at Nativity somehow persuaded Father Steiner that a parish choir was no longer necessary since congregational singing would now be the norm. On Pentecost Sunday, 1966, Father Schuler announced to an appalled choir that he had resigned as director and the group would be disbanded.

While in such shock that they could barely sing, the choir performed the *Mass in Honor of Saint Cecilia* by Josef von Wöss as their swan song. After Mass, there were both tears and anger which spread through the parish and caused a rift which lasted for many years. But that was not the end of the Nativity Choir as other directors, such as John Vanella (one of Father Schuler's protégés), took over and built on the foundation that Father Schuler had so firmly established.

In 1997, at the 75th Anniversary Mass celebrating the founding of Nativity Parish (and at which then Monsignor Schuler was present), Father Patrick Lannan (then pastor) gave a glowing tribute to Monsignor Schuler and all that he had accomplished. Pointing to the choir loft,

Father Lannan declared that the fine choir which was singing at that Mass was the direct result of the years of effort and dedication put in by the then Father Richard J. Schuler. A standing ovation followed.[2]

Endnotes

1. As quoted in The Nativity Parish Golden Anniversary *Program.* September 10, 1972, p.11.

2. Quoted from the Homily given by the Reverend Patrick Lannan at the 75th Anniversary Mass of the Founding of Nativity Parish, September 7, 1997.

APPENDIX E

Repertoire of the Twin Cities Catholic Chorale

Masses and Major Works in the Repertoire before 1974

Ludwig van Beethoven, *Mass in C*

Orazio Benevoli, *Messa La Cristiniana*

Anton Bruckner, *Choralmesse*

Anton Bruckner, *Mass in C*

Anton Bruckner, *Mass in E Minor*

Leopold G. Bruenner, *Mass in Honor of the Little Flower*

Guido Fassler, *Messe zu Ehren der HL.Dreifaltigkeit*

Noel Goemanne, *Missa Internationalis* (commissioned for the Sixth International Church Music Congress, Salzburg, 1974)

Joseph Haydn, *Little Organ Solo Mass (Kleine Orgelsolomesse)*

Joseph Haydn, *Paukenmesse*

Michael Haydn, *Requiem in C Minor*

Joseph Kronsteiner, *Krippenmesse*

Jean Langlais, *Missa Salve Regina*

Marius Monnikendam, *Missa Festiva*

G.P. da Palestrina, *Missa Dies Sanctificatus*

G.P. da Palestrina, *Missa Ut, Re, Mi, Fa, Sol, La (Hexachord Mass)*

Daniel Pinkham, *Missa Internationalis* (commissioned for the Fifth International Church Music Congress, Milwaukee, 1965)

Hermann Schroeder, *Missa Coloniensis*

Franz Schubert, *Mass in G*

Ludwig Senfl, *Missa super "Per Signum Crucis"*

Ernst Tittel, *Missa Magnus et Potens*

Ernst Tittel, *Muttergottesmesse*

Josef von Wöss, *Mass in Honor of Saint Cecilia*

Other Major Works:

Antonin Dvořák, *Stabat Mater*
Hermann Schroeder, *Magnificat*
Hermann Schroeder, *Te Deum Laudamus*
Guiseppi Verdi, *Quattro Pezzi Sacri (Four Sacred Pieces)*

Works added to the Chorale repertoire beginning in 1974

Masses added in 1974-75 (First season)

Joseph Haydn, *Heiligmesse*
Joseph Haydn, *Mariazellermesse*
W. A. Mozart, *Coronation Mass*, K 317
The Chorale sang 18 Masses with orchestra and 4 Masses in Renaissance polyphony.

Mass added in 1975-76

Franz Schubert, *Mass in B Flat*
The Chorale sang 22 Masses with orchestra and 2 Masses in Renaissance polyphony.

Mass added in 1976-77

W.A. Mozart, *Requiem*, K 626

The Chorale sang 20 Masses with orchestra and 2 Masses in Renaissance polyphony.

In September 1977, the Chorale sang with orchestra the American premiere of the *Mass in Honor of St. Oranna* by Father Jean-Pierre Schmit of Luxembourg.

Masses added in 1977-78

Joseph Haydn, *Theresienmesse*
Joseph Haydn, *Schöpfungsmesse*
The Chorale sang 27 Masses with orchestra and 2 Masses in Renaissance polyphony.

Masses added in 1978-79

Franz Schubert, *Mass in C*
Joseph Haydn, *Nelsonmesse*

The Chorale sang 30 Masses with orchestra. In addition, the Chorale sang the Mozart *Requiem* twice, in memory of His Holiness, Pope Paul VI and His Holiness, Pope John Paul I.

Mass added in 1979-80
W.A. Mozart, *Mass in C*, K 337
The Chorale sang 29 Masses with orchestra.

Mass added in 1980-81
Joseph Haydn, *Harmoniemesse*
The Chorale sang 29 Masses with orchestra.

Masses added in 1981-82
Charles Gounod, *Mass of Saint Cecilia*
W.A. Mozart, *Piccolomini Mass*, K 258
The Chorale sang 32 Masses with orchestra.

Mass added in 1982-83
W.A. Mozart, *Waisenhaus Mass*, K 139
The Chorale sang 30 Masses with orchestra.

Mass added in 1983-84
None
The Chorale sang 31 Masses with orchestra.

Mass added in 1984-85
Luigi Cherubini, *Fourth Mass in C*
The Chorale sang 30 Masses with orchestra.
On October 14, 1984, the Mass from Saint Agnes was recorded by WFMT as a part of their series, Lincoln's "Music in America." The Chorale sang Beethoven's *Mass in C*. The program, which was broadcast nationally, included an interview with Monsignor Schuler.

Mass added in 1985-86
None
The Chorale sang 29 Masses with orchestra.
On June 5 and 6, 1986 the Chorale made professional recordings of the Masses of Christmas, Easter and Pentecost under the title: *Saint Agnes, Sunday Morning*. The Christmas Mass is Gounod's *Mass of Saint Cecilia*; Easter is Haydn's *Paukenmesse*, and Pentecost is Beethoven's *Mass in C*.

The recordings included the full Mass with chants and readings. The recordings were sponsored by The Leaflet Missal Co. and were later re-issued in CDs omitting the homilies, etc.

Mass added in 1986-87
W.A. Mozart, *Trinitatismesse*, K 167
The Chorale sang 31 Masses with orchestra.

Mass added in 1987-88
None
The Chorale sang 31 Masses with orchestra.

Mass added in 1988-89
Antonin Dvořák, *Mass in D*
The Chorale sang 27 Masses with orchestra.

Mass added in 1989-90
W.A. Mozart, *Missa Longa*, K 262
The Chorale sang 32 Masses with orchestra.

Mass added in 1990-91
Carl M. von Weber, *Mass No. 1 in G*
The Chorale sang 29 Masses with orchestra.

Mass added in 1991-92
None
The Chorale sang 32 Masses with orchestra.

Mass added in 1992-93
Carl M. von Weber, *Mass No. 2 in E Flat*
The Chorale sang 31 Masses with orchestra.

Mass added in 1993-94
None
The Chorale sang 30 Masses with orchestra.

Mass added in 1994-95
None
The Chorale sang 30 Masses with orchestra.

Mass added in 1995-96
None
The Chorale sang 30 Masses with orchestra.

Mass added in 1996-97
Josef Rheinberger, *Mass in C,* Opus 169
The Chorale sang 29 Masses with orchestra.

Mass added in 1997-98
None
The Chorale sang 30 Masses with orchestra.

Mass added in 1998-99
None
The Chorale sang 29 Masses with orchestra.

Works added in 1999-2000
Franz Schubert, *Mass in A Flat*
W.A. Mozart, *Vesperae solennes de confessore,* K 339
Sung for the dedication of the statues of Saints Peter and Paul which were subsequently installed in the sanctuary and the inauguration of the tower lighting on May 9, 2000. The Chorale sang 31 Masses with orchestra plus the Vespers.

Mass added in 2000-2001
None
The Chorale sang 31 Masses with orchestra.

Mass added in 2001-2002
None
The Chorale sang 29 Masses with orchestra.

Mass added in 2002-2003
Heinrich von Herzogenberg, *Messe,* Opus 87 (North American premiere)
The Chorale sang 31 Masses with orchestra.

Mass added in 2003-2004
None
The Chorale sang 30 Masses with orchestra.

Mass added in 2004-2005
None
The Chorale sang 28 Masses with orchestra in its regular program. In addition, the Chorale sang the Mozart *Requiem* with orchestra on April 12, 2005, at a 7:30 p.m. Latin High Mass in memory of His Holiness, Pope John Paul II, who had died on April 2, 2005.

Mass added in 2005-2006
None
The Chorale sang 28 Masses with orchestra in its regular program.

Mass added in 2006-2007
None
The Chorale sang 28 Masses with orchestra in its regular program. In addition, it sang the Mozart *Requiem* on April 24, 2007, for the funeral Mass of Monsignor Richard J. Schuler, its founding director.

Mass added in 2007-2008
W. A. Mozart, *Missa Brevis in D*, K 194
The Chorale sang 27 Masses with orchestra, including the Mozart *Requiem* at a special Mass in memory of Monsignor Richard J. Schuler on the first anniversary of his death. The season was dedicated to Monsignor Schuler.

Mass added in 2008-2009
Gabriel Fauré, *Requiem in D Minor*
The Chorale sang 27 Masses with orchestra.

Mass added in 2009-2010
W. A. Mozart, *Missa Brevis in F,* K 192
The Chorale sang 27 times with orchestra.

Mass added in 2010-2011
None
The Chorale sang 27 times with orchestra.

Masses added in 2011-2012
Johann Nepomuk Hummel, *Mass in B Flat*
Maurice Duruflé, *Messe Cum Jubilo* for male choir and organ, sung by men from the *Schola Cantorum* and the Chorale.
The Chorale sang 27 times with orchestra.

Mass added in 2012-2013
None
The Chorale sang 27 times with orchestra.

In addition, the *Schola* and the men from the Chorale sang Duruflé's *Messe Cum Jubilo* with organ.

2013-2014 – The Chorale's 40th Season
Mass added in 2013-2014
Joseph Haydn, *Nikolaimesse*
The Chorale sang 30 times with orchestra.

In addition, the Chorale sang twice with orchestra for the Church Music Association of America conference at Saint Agnes and the Cathedral, October 13-15, 2013.

The Chorale sang Mozart's *Vesperae solennes de confessore,* K 339 as a concert and Joseph Haydn's *Missa in Tempore Belli* or *Paukenmesse* at an Extraordinary Form Mass.

The Chorale also sang the Mozart *Requiem*, K 626 for the Extraordinary Form Funeral Mass of Deacon Bernard A. G. Pedersen.

Mass added in 2014-2015
None
The Chorale sang 27 times with orchestra.

APPENDIX F

Recordings Made by the Twin Cities Catholic Chorale

The Mass In Honor of the Little Flower **by Leopold G. Bruenner** (33-1/3)
Recorded by the Catholic Choirmasters Chorale in 1956
Reverend Richard Schuler, Director; Mrs. M. Angeletti, Organist
SIDE 1 – *Kyrie, Gloria, Credo*
SIDE 2 – *Sanctus, Benedictus, Agnus Dei*; *Jesu Dulcis Memoria, Our Father, Ave Maris Stella* (all by Bruenner)

Twin Cities Catholic Chorale with Brass Ensemble (33-1/3)
Recorded in 1959
Reverend Richard J. Schuler, Conductor;
Mrs. Myron J. Angeletti, Organist
SIDE 1 - *Missa Magnus et Potens* by Ernst Tittel (Opus 15); *Kyrie, Gloria, Credo, Sanctus, Benedictus*
SIDE 2 – *Missa Magnus et Potens, Agnus Dei; Ecce Sacerdos Magnus* by Strategier; *Messa La Cristiniana* by Orazio Benevoli; *Kyrie, Sanctus, Agnus Dei*; *Sicut Cervus Desiderat* by Palestrina; *Diffusa Est Gratia* by Nanini; *Ave Regina Coelorum* by Soriano; *Magnificat* by Hermann Schroeder

Viennese Church Music (33-1/3)
Recorded in 1964
Richard J. Schuler, Conductor; John F. Vanella, Organist
Soloists: Nell Renwald Connor, soprano; Lawrence Bauer, tenor; Cyril DeMars, baritone;
String Orchestra
SIDE 1 – *Mass in G,* (Opus 141) by Franz Schubert; *Ave Verum Corpus,* K 618 by W. A. Mozart
SIDE 2 – *Mass in Honor of Saint Cecilia* by J.V. von Wöss, (Opus 32, no. 3); *Ave Maria* by Anton Bruckner

***Mass in E Minor* by Anton Bruckner**   (33-1/3)
Recorded live in Saint Agnes Church, Saint Paul, Minnesota in 1970, by the Twin Cities Catholic Chorale, (Monsignor Richard J. Schuler, Conductor), and the Dallas Catholic Choir, (Reverend Ralph S. March, O. Cist., Conductor). Mass to celebrate the 25th anniversary of Monsignor Schuler's ordination to the priesthood.
Reverend Ralph March was the conductor of this live performance; Dr. Paul Manz, Concordia College, Organist.
SIDE 1 – *Ecce Sacerdos* by Tappert; *Kyrie, Gloria, Credo* of the *Mass in E Minor*
SIDE 2 – *Credo* (continued), *Sanctus, Benedictus, Agnus Dei*

Every Year at Christmas Comes the Holy Child (33-1/3)
Recorded by the Twin Cities Catholic Chorale at the Church of St. Agnes in 1971
Monsignor Richard J. Schuler, Music Director
Brass Ensemble of the College of Saint Thomas; Tim Carson, Organist; Soloists: Carl Fox, tenor; Christina Colson, zither

Saint Agnes Sunday Morning: Masses of Christmas, Easter and Pentecost
(cassette tapes)
Recorded by the Twin Cities Catholic Chorale and members of the Minnesota Orchestra in the Church of Saint Agnes, Saint Paul, Minnesota in June, 1986.
Three 100-minute cassette tapes with Masses of Christmas, Easter and Pentecost. The tapes include the complete Masses: the chant Propers of the Mass, the liturgical singing of the priest, the Readings, homilies and organ compositions. The Chorale and orchestra performed Joseph Haydn's *Paukenmesse,* Beethoven's *Mass in C* and Charles Gounod's *Mass of Saint Cecilia.* The three cassette tapes were sold in a sturdy case for $29.95 by the Leaflet Missal Co. in St. Paul, Minnesota.

Gounod at Saint Agnes, Haydn at Saint Agnes, Beethoven at Saint Agnes
Three CDs made from the cassette recordings and advertised in 1996-97 for the first time.
Available from The Leaflet Missal Co., 976 W. Minnehaha Avenue, Saint Paul, Minnesota, 55104. (1-800-328-9582) (www.leafletonline.com), 1997.

Gounod at Saint Agnes (CD)
Messe solennelle à Sainte Cécile by Charles Gounod. Proper of the Mass. Gregorian chant for Christmas Day.

Haydn at Saint Agnes (CD)
Missa in Tempore Belli (Pauken Mass) by Joseph Haydn. Proper of the Mass. Gregorian chant for Easter Sunday. *Victimae Paschali Laudes* by Pietro Yon.

Beethoven at Saint Agnes (CD)
Mass in C by Ludwig van Beethoven. Proper of the Mass. Gregorian chant for Pentecost.

Christmas at Saint Agnes (CD)
Christmas music in Latin, German and English. 1991.
Twin Cities Catholic Chorale and Orchestra.
Available from The Leaflet Missal Co., 976 W. Minnehaha Avenue, Saint Paul, Minnesota, 55104. (1-800-328-9582) (www.leafletonline.com).

APPENDIX G

Bibliography of Major Articles and Editorials
By Monsignor Richard J. Schuler

(Published in *Sacred Music* Volume 102, No. 3, Fall 1975 through Volume 129, No. 3, Fall 2002. These articles may be accessed on the website of the Church Music Association of America at musicasacra.com)

"What We Profess"(editorial), Vol. 102, No. 3, Fall 1975, p.3.

"How Can You Have A Latin Mass?" Vol. 103, No. 1, Spring 1976, p.26.

"Wedding Music," Vol. 103, No. 2, Summer 1976, p.32.

"Church Music After Vatican II," Vol. 103, No. 4, Winter 1976, p.15.

"1967 Instruction - Ten Years Later," Vol. 104, No. 3, Fall 1977, p.3.

"*Motu Proprio* (1903-1978)," Vol. 105, No. 4, Winter 1978, p.21.

"Sacred Music and Contemplation," Vol. 106, No. 1, Spring 1979, p.23.

"Gregorian Chant and Latin in the Seminaries" (editorial), Vol. 107, No. 1, Spring 1980, p.3.

"The Sacred," Vol. 107, No. 3, Fall 1980, p.17.

"An Impoverishment" (editorial), Vol. 108, No. 1, Spring 1981, p.3.

"The Funeral Liturgy," Vol. 108, No. 4, Winter 1981, p.11.

"A Chronicle of the Reform, Part I, *Tra le sollicitudini,*" Vol. 109, No. 1, Spring 1982, p.7.

"A Chronicle of the Reform, Part II, *Musicae sacrae disciplina,*" Vol. 109, No. 2, Summer 1982, p.7.

"A Chronicle of the Reform, Part III, *Sacrosanctum concilium,*" Vol. 109, No. 3, Fall 1982, p.7.

"A Chronicle of the Reform, Part IV, *Musicam sacram,*" Vol. 109, No. 4, Winter 1982, p.15.

"A Chronicle of the Reform, Part V, *The Place of Music in Eucharistic Celebrations,*" Vol. 110, No. 1, Spring 1983, p.5.

"A Chronicle of the Reform, Part VI, *Music in Catholic Worship,*" Vol. 110, No.2, Summer 1983, p.11.

"A Chronicle of the Reform, Part VII, *Documents on the Liturgy,*" Vol. 110, No. 3, Fall 1983, p.7.

"The Purpose of Sacred Music" (editorial), Vol. 109, No. 3, Fall 1982, p.3.

"Gregorian Chant since the Second Vatican Council," Vol. 109, No. 3, Fall 1982, p.17.

"What Did the Council Want?" (editorial), Vol. 111, No. 3, Fall 1984, p.3.

"Liturgy in the Seminaries," (editorial), Vol. 111, No 4, Winter 1984, p.5.

"The Tridentine Mass," Vol. 111, No. 4, Winter 1984, p.7.

"What Makes Music Sacred?" Vol. 112, No. 2, Summer 1985, p.7.

"Ecclesiology and Church Music," (editorial), Vol. 113, No. 2, Summer 1986, p.3.

"Saint Agnes, Sunday Morning," Vol. 114, No. 3, Fall 1987, p.15.

"Participation," Vol. 114, No. 4, Winter 1987, p.7.

"Gregorian Chant in Today's Parish," Vol. 115, No. 2, Summer 1988, p.13.

"The Training of the Clergy," (editorial), Vol. 115, No. 3, Fall 1988, p.4.

"'Concert' Masses," (editorial), Vol. 115, No. 4, Winter 1988, p.3.

"The Tridentine Mass," (editorial), Vol. 116, No. 2, Summer 1989, p.3.

"We Need the Sacred," (editorial), Vol. 116, No. 3, Fall 1989, p.3.

"Church Bells," Vol. 116, No. 3, Fall 1989, p.25.

"Has the Liturgical Reform Been Successful?" (editorial), Vol. 116, No. 4, Winter 1989, p.3.

"Is the Church Music Association Dead?" (editorial), Vol. 117, No. 1, Spring 1990, p.5.

"Our English Translations" (editorial), Vol. 117, No. 2, Summer 1990, p.3.

"The Training of a Church Musician," Vol.117, No. 3, Fall 1990, p.18.

"Liturgical and Musical Reforms: An Honest Assessment," Vol. 117, No. 4, Winter 1990, p.3.

"Sacred Space," (editorial), Vol. 118, No. 1, Spring 1991, p.3.

"Inclusive Language" (editorial), Vol. 118, No. 1, Spring 1991, p.4.

"Style" (editorial), Vol. 118, No. 2, Summer 1991, p.4.

"What is Sacred Music?" (editorial), Vol. 118, No. 3, Fall 1991, p.3.

"Growth or Revolution?" (editorial), Vol. 118, No. 4, Winter 1991, p.3.

"The Attack on the Church Musician" (editorial), Vol. 119, No. 4, Winter 1992, p.3.

"They're Wrong!" (editorial), Vol. 120, No. 1, Spring 1993, p.3.

"'Turned-Around' Altars" (editorial), Vol. 120, No. 2, Summer 1993, p.4.

"Vespers," (editorial), Vol. 120, No. 3, Fall 1993, p.3.

"*Lex Orandi, Lex Credendi*: The Outrage of Inclusive Language," Vol. 121, No. 2, Summer 1994, p.6.

"Sacrilege" (editorial), Vol. 121, No. 4, Winter 1994, p.3.

"An Interview with Monsignor Schuler," first published in German in *Sinfonia Sacra,* Vol. 122, No. 2, Summer 1995, p.27.

"A Suggestion for the 'Reform of the Reform'" (editorial), Vol. 123, No. 1, Spring 1996, p.3.

"An Organic Development" (editorial), Vol. 123, No. 4, Winter 1996, p.3.

"Three Encyclicals of Pope Pius XII" (editorial), Vol. 124, No. 2, Summer 1997, p.3.

"The Sacred," Vol. 124, No. 2, Summer 1997, p.12.

"Beauty in the Liturgy: A Culture Problem" (editorial), Vol. 124, No. 3, Fall 1997, p.3.

"*Mediator Dei* and *Participatio Actuosa Populi,*" Vol. 124, No. 3, Fall 1997, p.7.

"The Covenant" (editorial), Vol. 124, No. 4, Winter 1997, p.3.

"The Reform: A Selected Bibliography," Vol. 125, No. 1, Spring 1998, p.12.

"Reverence," Vol. 126, No. 2, Summer 1999, p.20.

"Fifth International Church Music Congress" (Guest editorial), Vol. 129, No. 3, Fall 2002, p.3.

CONTRIBUTORS

Mary Eilen

Mary Eilen is the oldest of six children, with five younger brothers. She grew up in Saint Paul, Minnesota, and attended Saint Agnes School, for both grade school and high school. She is a proud thirteen-year Aggie. Mary graduated with a BA from the University of Saint Thomas in Saint Paul in 2013. At Saint Thomas, she studied Elementary Education and Catholic Studies. Mary returned to Saint Agnes to teach third grade after graduation and is currently in her third year there. She sings in two choirs at the Church of Saint Agnes, the Twin Cities Catholic Chorale and the Chamber Choir. Her hobbies include reading, singing, playing the piano, watching movies, and enjoying time with friends and family.

Michael A. Eilen

Michael Eilen joined the tenor section of the Twin Cities Catholic Chorale in 1993. He had sung previously with the Saint Paul Cathedral choir, directed by his father-in-law, Dr. Richard Byrne. When Dr. Byrne retired from his position at the Cathedral, he suggested to Michael that he join the Chorale directed by Monsignor Richard J. Schuler at the Church of Saint Agnes. Dr. Byrne and Monsignor Schuler were close colleagues and good friends. Mr. Eilen is from Delano, Minnesota. He graduated from Saint Thomas College in 1978 with a BA in Philosophy. During his sophomore year, while continuing his education at Saint Thomas, he entered Saint John Vianney College Seminary to begin studies for the priesthood. Following graduation from Saint Thomas, he worked at Midway Hospital for a time, and then enrolled in the Respiratory

Therapy Program at Saint Paul College. He currently works in that field. Mr. Eilen is a leader in the tenor section of the Chorale, and sings solos from time to time. His wife Kathleen and daughter Mary also sing in the Chorale.

Reverend John Paul Erickson

Father Erickson, ordained in 2006 for the Archdiocese of Saint Paul and Minneapolis, has been the Director of the Office of Worship for the Archdiocese since 2008. Father Erickson graduated in 2002 from Thomas Aquinas College in California with a Bachelor's degree in Liberal Studies. He is currently pursuing a Master's degree at the Liturgical Institute at Mundelein. Besides his work in the chancery, Father Erickson is parochial administrator of Blessed Sacrament parish in Saint Paul, Minnesota.

The Most Reverend John M. LeVoir
Bishop of New Ulm, Minnesota

His Excellency Bishop John M. LeVoir was appointed the fourth bishop of New Ulm, Minnesota, on July 14, 2008 by Pope Benedict XVI and was consecrated on September 14, 2008. His episcopal motto is *Nolite Timere* (Do Not Be Afraid). Previous to his appointment as bishop, he had served as pastor of both the Church of Saint Michael  and the Church of Saint Mary in Stillwater, Minnesota, and before that, pastor of both Holy Trinity Church and Saint Augustine Church in South Saint Paul, Minnesota. He received a Bachelor of Science degree in chemistry in 1968 from the University of Saint Thomas and a Bachelor of Science degree from the University of Minnesota in accounting in 1971. Prior to entering the Saint Paul Seminary he worked as an accountant. He was ordained to the priesthood in 1981. In a statement Bishop LeVoir made at the time of his appointment as bishop of New Ulm, he especially thanked Monsignor Richard J.

Schuler for his support during his years at the seminary. Bishop LeVoir co-authored *Covenant of Love: John Paul II on Sexuality, Marriage and Family in the Modern World* and *Faith for Today*. He is also a consultant for the Image of God grade school religion series and author of the eighth grade text for that series.

William Mahrt

William Mahrt received his PhD at Stanford University in 1969. After having taught at Case Western Reserve University and Eastman School of Music, he returned to Stanford, where he teaches Medieval and Renaissance music. Since 1972 he has directed the Stanford Early Music Singers; he was a founding member of the Saint Ann Choir and has been its director since 1964, singing Mass and Vespers in Gregorian chant and classical polyphony on Sundays and holydays. Dr. Mahrt is president of the Church Music Association of America and editor of its journal, *Sacred Music*, the oldest continuously published music journal in the United States. A collection of his essays, *The Musical Shape of the Liturgy* was published in 2012. Dr. Mahrt traveled to Germany, Italy, and Austria in 1974 with the Twin Cities Catholic Chorale.

Charles W. Nelson

Charles W. Nelson was a member of the Boys' Choir, the School Choir, and the Senior Mixed Choir at the Church of the Nativity of Our Lord in Saint Paul, Minnesota, when the young Father Schuler was the director of those choirs and weekend assistant at Nativity. He  is currently a lector at the Church of Saint Agnes and a member of the Board of the Twin Cities Catholic Chorale, where he serves as chairman of the Schuler Archives Committee. Dr. Nelson graduated with a BA from the College of Saint Thomas. He earned the MA and PhD degrees at the University of Nebraska in English Literature with specialties in Medieval and Renaissance Literature. He is Professor

Emeritus from Michigan Technological University and is currently a Visiting Professor at the University of Saint Thomas in Saint Paul.

Robert L. Peterson, Music Director

Robert L. Peterson received his BA, MA, and PhD degrees from the University of Minnesota in Minneapolis. His main areas of concentration were Music Education and choral conducting. Before his PhD, he spent eight years teaching at U.S. Military Bases in Japan and Europe. In 1976, he returned to his home in Minnesota and began his 22-year career as Director of Choral Activities at Edina Senior High School. After retirement in 1998, he was appointed Director of Choral Activities and Chair of the Music Department at Macalester College in Saint Paul, Minnesota, until 2008. In 2001, Monsignor Richard J. Schuler appointed Dr. Peterson as Associate Director of the Twin Cities Catholic Chorale, and Director in 2006. Dr. Peterson also teaches at Chesterton Academy in Edina. In 2013, he received the F. Melius Christiansen Lifetime Achievement Award in Choral Conducting from the American Choral Directors Association (ACDA) of Minnesota.

Reverend C. Frank Phillips, CR

Father Phillips received a Master of Divinity degree from Saint Louis University. A member of the Congregation of the Resurrection, he was ordained a priest in January of 1977. He taught music history and theory, choir, and religion for 11 years. In 1988, he was assigned as pastor of Saint John Cantius parish. Father Phillips has done much to restore this landmark Polish-American parish in Chicago. Mass is offered in both the Ordinary and Extraordinary Forms, in Latin and in English. Saint John Cantius is renowned for its commitment to classical church music. In 1998, Father Phillips founded the Canons Regular of Saint John Cantius, a Roman Catholic religious community of men dedicated to the restoration of the sacred in the context of parish ministry. Its mission is to help Catholics rediscover a profound sense of the sacred through worship, art, and an appreciation of the Church's heritage. Its mission is reflected in the community's motto: *Instaurare Sacra* (Restoration of the Sacred).

Dom Alcuin Reid, OSB

Dom Alcuin Reid is a monk of the Monastère Saint-Benoît in the Diocèse of Fréjus-Toulon, France. After studies in Theology and in Education in Melbourne, Australia, he was awarded a PhD from King's College, University of London, for a thesis on twentieth century liturgical reform (2002), which was subsequently published as *The Organic Development of the Liturgy* with a preface by Joseph Cardinal Ratzinger (Ignatius Press, 2005). He has lectured extensively on the sacred liturgy. On behalf of his Bishop, Dom Alcuin was the principal organizer of *Sacra Liturgia 2013*, and is the editor of its proceedings, *Sacred Liturgy, The Source and Summit of the Life and Mission of the Church* (Ignatius Press 2014).

Reverend William E. Sanderson

Father Sanderson was ordained in 1983 for the Archdiocese of Omaha, Nebraska, where he is currently pastor of two parishes: Saint Mary and Holy Ghost. He is also the chaplain for the Catholic Home School Association in Omaha. Father Sanderson is originally from Sioux Falls, South Dakota, where he completed his baccalaureate degree at the University of Sioux Falls in 1974. He studied for the priesthood at the Saint Paul Seminary and during that period began his association with the Church of Saint Agnes in Saint Paul and Monsignor Schuler, who became an important mentor and a good friend. His First Mass was celebrated at the Church of Saint Margaret Mary in Omaha, but his First Mass in Latin was at Saint Agnes where he celebrated Mass on November 2 that year, the feast of All Souls, for which the Twin Cities Catholic Chorale sang the Mozart *Requiem*. In 1986 when the Chorale recorded the Masses of Haydn, Gounod and Beethoven in a format which included the full Mass, Monsignor Schuler asked Father Sanderson to be the celebrant for those recordings. He recounts that experience in chapter seven of this book. Father Sanderson was invited to be the celebrant and preach on the first anniversary of Monsignor Schuler's death when the Chorale sang the Mozart *Requiem* in his memory.

Reverend Robert A. Skeris

Father Skeris was ordained in 1961 for the Archdiocese of Milwaukee. He has a doctorate in Theology from the Rhenish Friedrich-Willhelms University in Bonn, Germany. He is currently Director of the Centre for Ward Method Studies in the Benjamin T. Rome School of Music and Chairman of the Administration Committee of the Dom Mocquereau Fund at the Catholic University of America. He was previously Director of the Hymnology Section in the international Institute for Hymnological and Ethnomusicological Studies at the Abbey of Maria Laach in Germany and then Prefect of the Pontifical Institute of Sacred Music in Rome. Father Skeris has published widely on the theology of worship and its music, hymnology, and Gregorian chant. A founding member of the Church Music Association of America, Father Skeris was president of the association from 1996-2004 and edits the continuing series, *Musicae Sacrae Meletemata*. He has been invited to teach master classes and summer courses in Portugal, Hungary, and Lithuania. He was one of the chairmen of the Fifth International Church Music Congress in Chicago and Milwaukee (1966) and the Sixth International Church Music Congress in Salzburg, Austria (1974), both under the sponsorship of the *Consociatio Internationalis Musicae Sacrae*.

Acknowledgments

It is difficult to know where to begin to thank all the people who helped me with this book, either by their concrete contributions or by their encouragement and wise counsel.

First of all, my gratitude to Monsignor Schuler for his faithful commitment to the treasury of sacred music composed for the Roman Catholic liturgy and for giving us the Twin Cities Catholic Chorale. In addition, I would like to acknowledge all the volunteer singers and those who have supported the organization with their time and treasure over these sixty years of its existence as well as the Church of Saint Agnes and its current and former pastors. Saint Agnes has given the Chorale its spiritual home since 1974. Without all of the above mentioned, the Chorale as it is today would not exist.

On a more practical level, my thanks to those who have contributed specifically to the creation of this book: to Cindy Paslawski, my faithful copy editor; to Christopher Foote for designing the very attractive cover for the book and the dedication page as well as for preparing the section of pictures in color; to Tricia York for encouraging me, for responding to all of my calls for help, and for working with the printer; to Robert L. Peterson, the Chorale's Music Director; to Mary Elizabeth and Paul W. LeVoir; to Mary Sherman Hill, Richard Ellsworth, and John DeJak, for their helpful advice and encouragement.

I thank all who have given me advice on parts of the book including the aforementioned Paul and Mary LeVoir, as well as John DeJak, Linda Ann Long, M.D., Father Mark Moriarty, the pastor of Saint Agnes, Father John Paul Erickson, Father James McConville, and Father Timothy Cloutier. My gratitude also to Charles Nelson for his advice and faithful help over many hours spent proofreading the book.

I would like to thank most sincerely all who were contributors to the book. They were brave enough to link their names to this enterprise, sight unseen. They include The Most Reverend John M. LeVoir, Bishop of New Ulm; Reverend Robert A. Skeris, Director of the Centre for Ward Method Studies at Catholic University of America; William Mahrt, President of CMAA and Editor of *Sacred Music* magazine; Reverend C. Frank Phillips, CR, Pastor of Saint John Cantius in Chicago; Michael Eilen and Mary Eilen, members of the Chorale; Dom Alcuin Reid, OSB, Monastère St-Benoît, France; Reverend William E. Sanderson, the pastor of the parishes of Saint Mary and Holy Ghost in Omaha, Nebraska; Reverend John Paul Erickson, Director of the Office of Worship of the Archdiocese of Saint Paul and Minneapolis; Charles W. Nelson, PhD, Professor Emeritus of Michigan Technological University and Visiting Professor at the University of Saint Thomas in Saint Paul, Minnesota; and Dr. Robert L. Peterson, Music Director of the Twin Cities Catholic Chorale. I want to especially thank Father Skeris who agreed to write the preface, thus setting the book on a good course, and who wrote an important interpretive essay on the role the Chorale played in both the Fifth and Sixth International Church Music Congresses organized by CIMS.

I am very grateful also to those who provided very specific material contributions: photographers Joe Oden, Richard Graner and Chorale member Caecilia Lee, who allowed me to use some of their beautiful photographs; John Ernster, the Saint Agnes parish archivist, for lending me photos from the parish archives; the Saint Agnes Advancement Office; and Jeffrey Tucker, former Managing Editor of *Sacred Music* and currently CMAA Director of Publications, for the permissions he gave so willingly to reprint from that journal and its forerunners, *Caecilia* and the *Catholic Choirmaster*. I am grateful as well to journalists over the years who have told our story, among them Gareth Hiebert, Katherine Kersten, and James Klobuchar. His words are still true today: the Chorale's music can "ignite the blood."

I realize that in trying to express my gratitude, I might have forgotten someone. If so, please forgive me. So many have helped me tell this story by remembering an anecdote or encouraging me or asking with a warm smile, "How is the book coming?" I am especially grateful for all the prayers. Thank you all.

Finally, I am very grateful to my family, especially my brother Bob and his wife Patty and my nieces and their husbands, who were always interested and encouraging; and to my dear friends who helped me along the way with their wise advice and support.

VAS

Index

A
Angeletti, Agnes (Mrs. Myron J.), 25, 26, 29, 54, 209, 212, 223
Articles of Incorporation and by-laws, 142, 152

B
Bandas, Monsignor Rudolph G., 15, 31, 47, 51, 192, 193
Bevan, David, 87, 88, 91
Board of Directors of the Chorale, 148, 150, 152, 153, 174, 175, 176
Buchanan, Reverend John, 26, 33, 34, 37, 50, 190

C
Catholic Aid Association (see also Catholic United Financial), 49, 83, 90, 141, 162
Catholic Bulletin (see also *Catholic Spirit*), 28, 92
Catholic Spirit (see also *Catholic Bulletin*), 149
Catholic Choirmaster magazine, 33, 54, 197, 238
Catholic Choirmasters' Chorale, 25–29, 223
Catholic United Financial (see also Catholic Aid Association), 90, 141, 162
Caecilia magazine, 53, 201, 238
Church Music Association of America (CMAA), 39, 52, 54, 55, 62, 75, 85, 87, 90, 94, 95, 124, 155–158, 173, 183, 221, 227, 238
CMAA Conference at Saint Agnes in 2013, 155–158
Consociatio Internationalis Musicae Sacrae (CIMS), 10, 34, 39, 40, 42, 45, 48, 50, 53, 55, 56, 62, 63, 124, 206, 236
    Fifth International Church Music Congress (1966), 35, 39, 45, 46, 48, 54, 69, 236
    Sixth International Church Music Congress (1974), 54, 55, 61, 71, 159, 194, 236
Constitution on the Sacred Liturgy, 35, 39, 44, 48, 75, 87, 124, 156, 158, 179, 206, 208
Cowley, The Most Reverend Leonard P., 27, 37
Creagan, Reverend Michael, 118, 139

D
Dexter, Neil, 109, 110
Donelson, Jennifer, 155

E

Eagle, David and Elaine, 120
Eilen family, 125, 133–136
Erickson, Rev. John Paul, 167–169, 232
Ettel, Michael, 83

F

Finances, 131, 132, 177
Fund raising, 84, 92, 103, 131, 153, 155, 173, 174, 177
Fortieth anniversary in Residence, 9, 75, 155-162

G

Gregorian chant (see also *Schola Cantorum*), 11, 12, 14, 26, 35, 41, 45, 47, 52, 68, 76, 77, 79, 88, 91, 94, 114, 128, 156, 157, 159, 160, 161, 174, 179, 181, 191, 200, 210
Guild of Catholic Choirmasters and Organists, 25, 27, 28, 30-35, 191, 205–208, 211

H

Herzogenberg, Heinrich von, 139, 140, 148
Hiebert, Gareth, 83, 86, 87, 92, 94, 103, 238
Hogan, Reverend Richard M., 22, 25, 90, 141, 146
Holy Childhood Church (see also Reverend John Buchanan), 26, 28, 30, 31, 33, 34, 35, 37, 50, 190, 191
Hugheson, Deacon Harold, 88, 91, 99, 110, 123, 163

I

Influence of the Chorale/orchestra Masses, 92, 102, 103, 106, 126, 135, 136, 168, 176, 184
Internal Revenue Service nonprofit status, 142

K

Kersten, Katherine, 152, 238
Klobuchar, Jim, 102, 152, 238
KSJN, 88, 98

L

Latin High Mass at Saint Agnes, 33, 52, 53, 76, 79, 83, 84, 88, 91,–94, 97, 102, 109, 110, 116, 119,123, 124, 128, 132, 135, 145, 149, 150, 152, 153, 160, 161, 174, 175, 176, 181, 184, 193, 195

INDEX

Leaflet Missal Company, 97, 100, 101, 116, 218, 224, 225

LeVoir, The Most Reverend John M., 12, 126, 232, 233, 237

LeVoir, Mary Elizabeth, 91, 99, 117, 118, 120, 127, 161, 184, 237

LeVoir, Paul W., 91, 99, 128, 161, 184, 237

M

Magnuson, Reverend Sean, 142, 195

Mahrt, William, 64, 79, 158, 159, 233

March, Reverend Ralph S.,O. Cist., 46, 51, 52, 54, 77, 193, 194, 224

Marketing, 147, 150, 152, 153, 176, 177

Masses in Ordinary and Extraordinary Form, 123, 149, 156, 160, 161, 181, 221, 234

Miller, Reverend Michael, 160

Minnesota Monthly, 152

Minnesota Orchestra, 11, 37, 84, 86, 87, 98, 114, 127, 128, 132, 133, 150, 224

Minnesota Public Radio, 88, 98, 150, 152

Mirageas, Evans, 97–100

Missia, Reverend Francis A., see Appendix B, 9, 13–15, 19, 21–23, 26, 29, 30, 32, 33, 36, 37, 67, 75, 114, 179, 190, 191, 205

Moriarty, Reverend Mark, 153, 160, 181, 237

Mozart Society of America, 152

Music sponsorships, 103, 155, 177

N

Nativity, Church of the Nativity of Our Lord, see Appendix D, 9, 15, 28, 29, 31, 33, 47, 51, 120, 191, 192

National Wanderer Forum, 36, 50, 53, 85, 86, 90

P

Pedersen, Deacon Bernard, 125, 126, 161, 221

Peterson, Robert L., PhD, 125, 139, 140, 141, 145, 146, 148, 150, 152, 160, 173, 175, 195, 234, 237

Phillips, Reverend C. Frank, C.R., 105, 106, 161, 234, 238

Pioneer Press/Dispatch (Saint Paul newspapers), 14, 19, 20, 22–24, 26, 32, 33, 47, 51, 83, 84, 86, 87, 91, 92, 94, 103, 176, 183

Pohl, William, PhD, 55, 64, 76, 77, 158

R

Recording project of Masses, See Appendix F for listing; 97-103

Reid, Dom Alcuin, O.S.B., 157, 158, 163–165, 235

Repertoire of the Chorale, see Appendix E

S

Saint Paul Catholic Choral Society, 9, 14, 15, 19, 20, 21, 22, 24, 26, 32, 114, 191, 200

Saint Paul Seminary, 11, 14, 19, 21, 22, 24, 97, 139, 148, 190, 198–201, 232, 235

Sacred Music magazine, (see Appendix G), 10, 25, 42, 48, 52–55, 86–88, 90, 95, 107, 114, 115, 117, 118, 124, 142, 155–159, 179, 197, 233, 238

Sacrosanctum Concilium (See *Constitution on the Sacred Liturgy*), 39, 47, 69, 105, 123, 158, 159, 164

Sample, The Most Reverend Alexander K., 75, 126, 161, 185

Sanderson, Reverend William E., 97-100, 148, 235, 236, 238

Schmit, Reverend Jean-Pierre of Luxembourg, 62, 89, 216

Schola Cantorum (See also Paul W. LeVoir), 56, 88, 91, 117, 118, 128, 152, 153, 158, 161, 174, 175, 185, 220, 221

Schuler, Monsignor Richard J., 1920–2007 (see Appendix A),
    Education and background, 14, 15, 75, 124
    Teaching career, 11, 22, 25, 206
    St. Paul Catholic Choral Society, 15, 21
    Choirmasters' Chorale, 25-29
    Nativity Church (see Appendix D), 9, 28, 33, 47
    St. Agnes 15, 51 onward; residency, 83
    Twin Cities Catholic Chorale, 9, 10, 15, 29, onward
    Writings (see Appendix G), 86, 87

Shannon, The Most Reverend James P., 36, 184

Sirba, The Most Reverend Paul D., 126

Skeris, Reverend Robert A., 9, 16, 39, 40, 62, 67–73, 179, 181, 183, 236, 237

Soloists, 28, 34, 50, 84, 91, 98, 121, 125, 127, 128, 139, 174, 175, 194, 212, 223, 224

Star Tribune articles (Minneapolis newspaper), 102, 152

T

Thevenin, Francis, 120, 184

Track, Gerhard, 53, 85, 90, 184

Tucker, Jeffrey, 51, 52, 95, 156, 157, 238

Twin Cities Metro magazine, 150

U

Ubel, The Very Reverend John L., 145, 146, 148, 149, 150, 152, 153

V

View Behind the Painting, 120, 126, 148, 185

Vocations from the Chorale, 11, 12, 75, 106, 119, 126, 142, 160, 164, 168, 169, 185, 193, 194

W

Welzbacher, Reverend George, 140

WFMT public radio, 97–99, 102, 217

Z

Zuhlsdorf, Reverend John, 142